My Dear Nellie

The Civil War Letters
of William L. Nugent to Eleanor Smith Nugent

EDITED BY

William M. Cash

AND

Lucy Somerville Howorth

UNIVERSITY PRESS OF MISSISSIPPI

JACKSON

1977

Copyright © 1977 by the
University Press of Mississippi
Manufactured in the United States of America
Designed by Barney McKee

This volume is authorized and sponsored by
DELTA STATE UNIVERSITY
Cleveland, Mississippi

Library of Congress Cataloging in Publication Data

Nugent, William Lewis, 1832–1897.
  My dear Nellie.

  Includes index.
  1. United States—History—Civil War, 1861–1865—
Personal narratives—Confederate side. 2. Nugent,
William Lewis, 1832–1897. 3. Confederate States
of America. Army—Biography. 4. Soldiers—Con-
federate States of America—Biography. I. Nugent,
Eleanor Smith. II. Title.
E605.N83 1977 973.7'82 77-24597
ISBN 0-87805-036-1

My Dear Nellie

Contents

List of Illustrations

Maps

Preface and Acknowledgments

One of the editors was introduced to the Civil War letters of William Lewis Nugent in 1906, when the letters were presented to her mother, the daughter of Colonel Nugent. The editor-to-be was but eleven years of age, yet was significantly impressed by the letters and was given permission to attempt decipherment. The initial interest culminated in her dedication to preserve, to deposit in archival repositories, and hopefully to publish these historically significant letters.

The co-editor first learned of the letters some sixty-eight years later through an invitation "to sample a few letters." However, the cursory examination was transformed into a perusal and subsequently an endorsement that the letters merited publication.

The letters are in remarkably good physical condition. Fortunately, the letters had been tied with plain cotton thread and then placed flat in a box, thus avoiding the destructive folding. The archival nemesis of acid has taken its toll as evidenced in the fading ink and discoloration of the paper. However, only limited segments, which the editors have indicated, have been destroyed or rendered illegible.

In general, the editors adopted the maxim of presenting the letters with minimum interpolation. Notwithstanding the fine penmanship of Nugent, letters written under such self-described adverse conditions as poor lighting, cold hands, and roughing it in the field expectedly produced some obstacles to deciphering. Too, expressions, spelling, and punctuation common to the period of 1860–65 created minor difficulties. In the view of the editors, the employment of [*sic*] to indicate that Nugent's spelling is now archaic encumbers rather than enlightens. Likewise, efforts by the editors to apply modern punctuation appear presumptuous for letters that are clearly readable and eloquent in style. Even his abbreviations are deemed within acceptable bounds of clarity and remain unedited.

Nugent, however, did have a few writing inconsistencies. Especially notable was his careful placement of periods and commas in the designation of locale and date of a letter and his omission of such punctuation in a following letter. In addition, he usually included the apostrophe in his contractions yet on occasion failed to include same. For clarity, the editors assumed license to add this limited punctuation. A further inconsistency appeared in Nugent's capitalization. Indeed, he might write "our Army defeated the Yankee army," or "the troops moved to the Railroad." Candidly, the editors could not at times determine Nugent's intention, whether a letter was enlarged by a looping style or perhaps capitalized for emphasis. The editors thus elected to present his capitalization as best ascertained, and they acknowledge his inconsistency as well as probable errors in transcribing. Nevertheless, the editors contend that such minor flaws do not detract from his highly literate and beautiful prose.

Nugent was an eyewitness and his letters reflected his candid opinions and observations. An attempt to critique or to evaluate his remarks with respect to extant literature would expand the manuscript beyond workable limits and would in part destroy the true historical value of the letters. In brief, it was his account, and the editors view without reservation his letters as worthy to present his 1860–65 story. Consequently, footnotes have been limited to identification, clarification, and brief commentary.

The editors are profoundly grateful to the Mississippi Department of Archives and History and the Schlesinger Library on the History of Women in America of Radcliffe College. Directors Elbert Hilliard and Patricia King of the repositories of the Nugent letters granted permission for publication and graciously provided assistance to the editors. We are deeply appreciative to President Kent Wyatt and the Delta State University Press Committee for encouraging and financially supporting the publication. We are sincerely indebted to our friend Dean William F. La Forge for his valuable suggestions and for writing the Foreword. Director Barney McKee and the staff of the University Press of Mississippi deserve our gratitude for their technical expertise. Numerous individuals assisted our research, and we sincerely acknowledge the contributions of Nugent's granddaughters, Mrs. Audley Shands of Cleveland, Mississippi, and Mrs. John H. Walsh of Jackson, Mississippi, and Nugent's great granddaughter,

Mrs. John M. Martin of Alexandria, Virginia. Delta State University Professors Sammy Cranford, Allen Dennis, and Curt Lamar made valuable suggestions, and Professor U. S. Walker assisted with the illustrations. We thank Mrs. William Kennedy and Mrs. Danny Underwood for their tape transcriptions and typing the manuscript. A special vote of thanks goes to Joseph M. Howorth, who served as our general assistant for the entire production. Our final gratitude is expressed for the courtesies and services rendered by the staffs of the National Archives, Washington, D.C.; Millsaps College Library, Jackson, Mississippi; Robinson-Carpenter Library, Cleveland, Mississippi; and W. B. Roberts Library, Delta State University. We generously credit all who encouraged and assisted the project and invite each to share in the merits of the work. Yet, the editors alone accept responsibility for the shortcomings.

Foreword

Considering the existing volume of Civil War correspondence already published, both scholars and the general reading public can legitimately question the value of yet another collection of letters from "the front." But the letters of William Lewis Nugent to his wife are in several ways unique, and they do make some important contributions to an understanding of the critical 1860–65 period of American and Southern history.

They are unique in that, unlike much of the published correspondence, these letters were written by an intelligent and educated man in a style both articulate and grammatical. Behind this correspondence is seen a logical mind combined with a sensitivity to the crises, both major and minor, of the times. The collection is also unusual in that it embraces nearly the whole 1860–65 period, thus enjoying an important thread of continuity. Finally, Nugent included in his letters surprisingly candid, if not always correct, evaluations and judgments concerning military strategy and tactics, an aspect not often found in such correspondence.

Nugent's letters make a direct and obvious contribution in expanding both knowledge and understanding of the history of the time as it relates to Mississippi and, especially, to the Delta region of the state. They also account for an important segment in the life of an influential and respected man who was prominent in the leadership of post-Civil War Mississippi. Beyond this state and local relevance, this collection has application to the broader spectrum of the United States history. The allusions to wartime conditions on the home front, to his reading habits, and to the interfamily relations which characterized the society of the time provide useful insights into the cultural and social history of the period. Nugent's prose style and the moral values which he unabashedly expressed serve as models for understanding the point of view and mode of expression of the educated class of the age. Finally, a reading of these intimate letters of a man to his young wife sheds a great deal of light on broader questions concerning the nature of man which, after all, are the ultimate questions which the historian seeks to answer.

That this collection of William L. Nugent's letters has been preserved is owed to a set of those fortuitous "accidents" which are so intriguing to historians. The letters were first stored in the attic of Locust, the home of Nugent's second wife, Mary Catherine Montgomery, who died in 1868. In the spring of 1906 they were found and turned over to Nugent's daughter, Nellie Nugent Somerville, who ensured their preservation. Had the letters remained undiscovered at Locust they would have been lost in the fire which destroyed the Montgomery house in the 1960s. Further, had William L. Nugent taken these letters with him to Jackson in 1871, they would have been destroyed with the rest of his personal papers in a fire shortly after his death.

The intrinsic value of the collection has been enhanced by the editors by setting it in context in the introduction and the epilogue and by clarifying and explicating any obscurities in the letters. The result of this excellent editorial work is a valuable contribution to the literature of the period.

W. F. La Forge
Delta State University

My Dear Nellie

CHAPTER I

Introduction

William Lewis Nugent was descended from illustrious forebears. His father, John Pratt Nugent, a member of a distinguished Irish family, immigrated to Philadelphia, Pennsylvania, in 1809. His employer sent him initially to New Orleans and subsequently to Washington, Mississippi, where he married Amelia Forman, who died within a year. William's mother, Anne Lavinia (Lewis) Nugent, was likewise of prominent ancestry: her father, Seth Lewis, served as Chief Justice of the Mississippi Territory. Anne rode horseback from Opelousas, Louisiana, to attend Elizabeth Female Academy in Washington. While there, reportedly because of a common interest in horseback riding, she developed a relationship with John. They were married in 1827, following her graduation, and shortly thereafter moved to Louisiana.

William, born in 1832 in East Baton Rouge Parish, was the third of nine children of the union. His early years were especially marked by his demonstrated love of learning and by his affiliation with the Methodist Church from age eleven. These early influences had a pronounced impact on young Nugent's life. At sixteen he accepted employment in a New Orleans business house, but his yearning for additional schooling prompted his resignation and subsequent enrollment at the Methodist-sponsored Centenary College. Graduating with honors in 1852, he wrote the graduation hymn, displaying a taste and talent for versification which he exercised throughout life.[1]

In 1852, William took a steamboat to the developing Mississippi Delta community, Greenville. The Greenville at which he arrived has been described as a frontier settlement in a heavily wooded wilderness. With muddy streets and plank sidewalks, it had a population of fewer than 500.

---

[1]Mrs. James E. Edmonds (Anne Marie Nugent), comp., The Lewis, Hardeman, and Nugent Family Records and Papers. Manuscript (typewritten) in possession of Lucy Somerville Howorth, Cleveland, Mississippi. Hereinafter cited as Edmonds, Nugent Family Papers.

John Pratt Nugent, born in 1792, died 1873. Father of
William L. Nugent. Silhouette made in 1830.

Mrs. John Pratt Nugent (Anne Lavinia Lewis), born 1807, died 1873. Mother of William L. Nugent. Silhouette made in 1830.

Among Greenville's unpretentious buildings were two multiple-storied structures—the homes of Dr. and Mrs. John Finlay and Abram F. Smith and his benevolent wife, S. Myra.[2] Nugent's personal possessions were in harmony with the pioneer village, since he brought but a satchel containing a change of clothing, a few books, and his beloved violin.[3]

In Greenville, Nugent became a member of the Smith household. Smith was a native Kentuckian who had practiced law in Vicksburg. While attending court in Princeton, he had met and soon thereafter married S. Myra Cox.[4] The Smiths settled in Washington County where he acquired a plantation, practiced law, and represented the county in the Mississippi legislature in 1846 and again in 1857–58.[5]

Nugent's initial role in the household was tutor for the Smith children of educable age, Alfred, Eleanor, and Evelina.[6] However, in 1854 Nugent combined his tutorship with a readership of law under A. F. Smith, and in 1856 he was admitted to the practice of law in partnership with Smith.

In June 1860, the Smiths departed for the "Grand Tour," ultimately to visit Blue Lick Springs, Kentucky, Illinois, and New York.[7] Early in 1860 Nugent became engaged to Eleanor, the Smith's eldest daughter, and during the "Grand Tour" began a series of letters to his betrothed.

[2]William D. McCain and Charlotte Capers (eds.), *Papers of the Washington County Historical Society, 1910–1915* (Jackson: Mississippi Department of Archives and History and Mississippi Historical Society, 1954), 12. Hereinafter cited as PWCHS. The *Papers* in unabridged form appeared originally in the Greenville *Times* and Greenville *Democrat*.

[3]The scanty belongings of Nugent were recollected by S. Myra Smith in conversation with Nellie Nugent Somerville, who subsequently related the description to Lucy Somerville Howorth. Conversations of Lucy Somerville Howorth with Nellie Nugent Somerville, Mrs. W. R. Trigg, Catherine McCauley, Mrs. W. P. Kretschmar, Sr., Henry T. Ireys, and George M. Helms are hereinafter cited as Recollections of LSH.

[4]S. Myra Cox was residing in Washington County with her brother, Alfred Cox, who served in the Mississippi legislature between 1836 and 1840. Cox (Cocks) Family Bible, in possession of Lucy Somerville Howorth.

[5]Smith Family Bible, in possession of Lucy Somerville Howorth.

[6]The addition of students to the school led some to state that Nugent inaugurated the first public school in Greenville. See for example, PWCHS, 327. In reality, the school was never more than a tutorial program taught in the Smith home for the Smith children and a few neighboring children. One member of the class was Catherine McCauley, the granddaughter of an Irish washerwoman hired by Mrs. Smith. The washerwoman departed for New Orleans with the child, but Catherine had so impressed Mrs. Smith that she requested her husband to locate the child and rescue her from a projected life of hardship. Smith did locate Catherine, and she became a member of the Smith household. Recollections of LSH.

[7]The Smith children included: Alfred Cox (Alf), born 1841; Eleanor Fulkerson (Ellen, Nell, or Nellie), born 1844; Evelina H. (Evy or Evie), born 1848; and Abram F. Jr. (Aby, Abe, Abie, or Abey), born 1856. Smith Family Bible. See also, S. Myra Smith Diary, a copy of which is in possession of Lucy Somerville Howorth.

CHAPTER II

To Labor and to Wait

June 22, 1860–November 26, 1860

> At Home [Greenville, Miss.]
> Friday evening
> June 22, 1860

Dearest Nellie,[1]

Mr. McAllister leaves this evening for Blue Lick Springs, and I seize the opportunity thus afforded, to send you a memento, cold and formal as ink and pen always make such things, of my unabashed affection.[2] And you may well conjecture that the pleasure of communicating with you even thru' a letter is esteemed by me, as not the least among the privileges entailed upon me by my present position. In fact the anticipation of meeting your thin face blooming in health and bouyant in spirit, has almost reconciled me to the idea of wearily dragging my existence thru' the months of July and August. Strange that the human heart can so readily adapt itself to so great a change; but hope, ever welling up from the great deeps of the soul, points with my finger to joys that slumber in the future. And so we jog along; rising in the morning, going thru' the labors of the day as we were wont, & wrapping the mantle of our couch about us at night. The recurrence of the same scenes make time slip glibly away—and the "twilight dews" delight us with their phantom footfalls before we are aware that the peaceful old sun has gone to take his daily bath in the western ocean.

I make Clarence come home every night, and drum up some one every day to eat dinner with me.[3] Indeed I think if you stay away long I shall

---

[1]Unless otherwise noted, the originals of all letters are deposited in the Mississippi Department of Archives and History, Jackson, Mississippi.

[2]Augustus W. McAllister owned Wildwood Plantation located on Rattlesnake Bayou. His plantation adjoined Locust Plantation where Nugent's letters were discovered. PWCHS, 281. Blue Lick Springs was a community in northern Kentucky at which many Delta residents visited during the summer. The 1860 Manuscript Census Returns indicate a number of Kentucky natives were residents of Washington and Bolivar counties.

[3]Clarence Jewell Nugent was William's younger brother, born in 1843, who was visiting. He is a frequent subject in the letters and Epilogue. Edmonds, Nugent Family Papers.

become proverbial for my hospitality. Already have two or three of "our" clients dined with me, and I flatter myself that I did the honors of the table with becoming dignity. At least I have heard no complaints on that score. Dr. Penny, who by the way, is going all the time, came to see me the other evening, and we *"serenaded"* one another with a song & two or three airs on the violin & flute—"Home Sweet Home," "Last Rose of Summer" and divers and sundry other songs of that ilk.[4] I stood the Drs. suggestions of loneliness very bravely. Indeed I feel, dear Nellie, that while reposing in the consciousness that I possess your heart's best affection, I am strong enough to withstand the world in arms; deprive me of them, & I am weak indeed.

The servants have been conducting themselves remarkably well. Ike is now "on his good behaviour," and hasn't so I have learned been up town since you left. I had to straighten "Bally" up however.[5] I regret, though, to inform that the little Blackman Rose, I believe she was called, is *dead.* Her demise was entirely unattended by any paroxysms of great pain—so Casius says.

Housekeeping gives me something to think about, and the attention necessary to be bestowed upon the sick negroes prevents me from nursing my disposition to be lonesome. I do not, I assure you, feel entirely reconciled to the idea of being away from you; for despite all my philosophy, I can't help feeling desperately blue at times. I have hastily written thus far in a light pleasant strain more for the purpose of relieving your mind from any unpleasant reflections upon my situation, than to indicate the existence of stoicism on my part. My heart, I hope, goes with you;—my only comfort, in your absence, is the anticipation of seeing you shortly, & renewing after the trying absence of a summer, the plighted vows I have so freely & heartily & unreservedly given. In the calm still hour of twilight do your thoughts ever wander hither, Nell? But I must not sadden you. May God bless & protect you is the daily prayer of

Yours devotedly
Wm. L. Nugent

---

[4] B. F. Penny was a doctor before and after the war in Greenville. PWCHS, 274.

[5] Nugent and Mrs. Smith employed the term "servants" rather than slaves. Nugent never owned slaves, but he appeared to utilize the Smith servants as needed. Ike served as body servant to Alfred Cox Smith and Nugent. Bally went with Nugent throughout the war as a body servant.

Greenville, Miss.
July 2, 1860

My own dear Nellie,

As the grateful sunshine after a storm, or the cool, balmy summer breeze after the noon-day sun, was the affectionate missive this day received from you. I had started for Issaquena County, but deferred the trip when the little mail boat rounded to at our landing in anticipation of receiving a letter from you. The lately improvised Post Office is in Penrice & McMulkins' warehouse, & consists of a little box partitioned into pigeon holes, elegantly illustrated with the different letters of the alphabet.[6] A parcel of us were sitting lazily, yet impatiently, as is the wont of men waiting the opening of the mail, aroused, when the clerk called out Mr. Nugent and politely handed me your letter. So much was I engaged in my own mind with the anticipation conjured up by the occasion, of receiving the identical letter, that I involuntarily exclaimed: "That's it." Fortunately no one present could from the isolated remark gather the happy train of my reflections, & they were all too polite, I presume to hazard the inquiry as to who the letter was from. You need scarcely, therefore, in future profer the request that I should look with a lenient eye upon the imperfections of your letters. Each pen-traced line from you is dear to me, not only as an evidence of your continued affection & kind recollections of one whose greatest happiness it is, to love you, but in carrying me back to years ago & making my heart, as the poet has it, "play old times" over again. The old house where I first loved you, the quiet rambles on the River bank, & the days when yet a girl, young in years and the discretion incident to youth, you bound me to you by a simple act of justice against all the proclivities of your nature under the circumstances. I love to think of the old Library & the time I first had the audacity to kiss you; you didn't then quite understand the nature of that kiss; it was a mixture of gratitude & affection; I was passing through an ordeal then, and longed to have a sympathizing bosom into which I could pour my troubles.[7] Like "as a dream when one awaketh" are these old memories; the best of them have left a hallowed influence over

---

[6]J. S. Penrice came to Princeton, and in 1852 opened a quality merchandise store and tavern in Greenville. PWCHS, 65.

[7]The Old Library refers to the "Old House" on Oakwood Plantation that the Smiths built prior to 1850.

my life-experience; the worst, I trust, have only the chastening they at the time afforded to recommend them. Through all, our lives have glided peacefully, though for the nonce, tortuously, as those gently flowing rivulets you so felicitously described as gurgling their quiet way between the rocky cliffs that guard the rolling Ohio.—The hand of a Kind Providence was, unknown to us, leading us along a path, the roses of which were not discovered until their thorns had wounded us. I can, while taking a grateful retrospect of these by-gone experiences find abundant cause for praising the Giver of all good. We would not know how to appreciate the favors we receive, did not we know that the happiness of life is sometimes dearly purchased. We have many things, dear Nellie, to bind our hearts together by the indissoluble chords of unceasing affection; and I hope each recurring year will greatly multiply them.

You are not exactly just to your own capabilities when you think you fail in descriptive powers. The few periods in your letter summing up the scenery on the Ohio show that you have caught the salient points of all that it is beautiful. It only needed a little filling up; & had you less diffidence of your own ability, you would have given me an essay that might have found its way *incognito* to some journal. The comprehensive painting of that little village suggests a world of thought. How easy and how natural for the *imagination* to visit the little vine trellised cottage snugly hiding under the "shadow of a great rock" & have a quiet chat with the neatly capped matron, with her specs & sewing:—to pause beside the church whose airy steeple vainly attempts to reach up high toward Heaven; to flash along the busy marts of commercial life; & to wander among the marbled monuments of the dead. And the little brook bubbling along its way over a rocky bed, the tiny fish frolicking in its cooling waters, & the lowing herds gathering hard by the brink to slake their thirst. The very fact that you gathered up at one view the most important & impressive, as well as practical features of the scenery is a strong indication of your ability to do yourself justice, if you were not so diffident & distrustful. The truth is, I know you can appreciate, notice & describe the "haps & hazards" of a summer's town, & I hope to be able to convince you that I am correct in my judgement.

I wrote to you by Mr. McAllister who left two or three days—upon reflection I think it was a week—after you, & I presume the letter has reached you before now.

I have, to a certain extent, accommodated myself to my present solitary life—rendered bearable alone by the reflection that it is not long to continue. The duties that are devolved upon me—the housekeeping, gardening, law business &c—require time & thought; & leave very few moments for the "blues." Indeed I would not suffer myself the selfish gratification of taking from your enjoyment by the recital of all my "bluish" feelings. They at rare intervals surge over me; but I am now entirely reconciled to the necessity of your absence for a time. It will restore your health & give you some experience in the manners & customs of the world.

I am happy to be assured by you that it is *impossible* for me to be forgotten by you; and that home is the dearest place when those you love best are there. My vanity induces me to convert the pronoun "those" into "he"—& thus I have it, that home is dearer to you, since I am there. "'Tis home where'er the heart is"; and I frequently ask the question with the old song: "And lingers one gloomy shadow round them, Which only my presence can light?"

I went up to the plantation today, rode all through the crop, trimmed the peach trees in the yard, shook hands with most all the negroes, talked sometime with Isabelle & old Ned, & returned home this evening to write this letter, while the old clock ticks incessantly on the mantle.[8] The negroes are all well, & send their love to you. Isabelle sends "her best love to you all"—as does Caroline and Catherine.[9]

I suppose you will have heard before this reaches you that Mr. Byrnes had the great misfortune to lose his store with almost the entire stock of goods. The books & mail were saved. I worked like a Trojan to save the "Drug Store," perspiring profusely for half an hour with the fire warming me heartily, & took a glass of champagne at the conclusion to keep off a cold—by the advice of Dr. Penny, who was a good assistant. Talbott, Penny, Bassett & myself—with a little help from Haycraft—were detailed of our own accord to save the drugs & chemicals.[10] At the winding up we left Bassett perched up on the roof with no way of escape for a season. He

---

[8]The plantation was Smith's Oakwood, located then on Black Bayou in Washington County, but presently in southern Bolivar County.

[9]Catherine McCauley. See Introduction.

[10]Erskine P. Byrne was co-owner of Byrne and Wallis Drugstore, and he later was an incorporator of the Greenville, Deer Creek, and Rolling Fork Railroad. PWCHS, 319. Charles P. Talbott was a doctor before and after the war in Greenville. He is frequently mentioned in the letters. PWCHS, 278. W. A. Haycraft served as Washington County clerk of the probate court in 1860 and signed Nugent's marriage certificate. Haycraft is mentioned in several of the letters. PWCHS, 274.

was somewhat alarmed and with reason—for the side of the house was too hot at one time to be comfortable to the touch. I hope you may find time to write me more frequently than you anticipate; it will lend a charm even to my absence; and believe me when I say that those I love are far above any criticism if that could be at all used. Their very weaknesses if they have any, do but go to make up the ideal around which my clustering affections fondly linger. So bravely write. I have already perused your letter four times & with increasing interest each time. And further I expect to read it over daily until I receive another burdened with the same or greater expressions of your love. Think you I could pause to notice a t uncrossed, or a word mispelled, when my heart was brimful all the while & my mind all aglow taking in the *thoughts*? If you do, dear Nellie, you do me a great crying injustice. To know you love me; to know my image goes with you in your wanderings; and to be assured of the fact by your affectionate letters is *all* I ask. The studied phraseology of a carefully written letter would, I assure you, be a poor tribute to both. When the heart is swelling with feeling, & the tear of tender recollection is glistening in the eye the pen cannot always discharge its obligations without blurring the virgin page. I feel that writing is a poor way of talking with you; but poor as it is, I am loth to cease. The question obtrudes itself "lovest thou me more than" all the giddy throng in whose amusements you participate?—As often in our quiet evening talks I have told you, so now do I repeat it—you have my heart's deepest, most constant affection—It is eleven o'clock & I *must* quit—Please kiss Abe for me; Evy has long since ceased to permit me this pleasure and tell him "William" wants to see him "mighty bad" too—Love to your Mother, Mr. Smith & Alf & Evy—May God bless you & keep you from being led away by trying exigencies thru' which you are called to pass, is the constant prayer of him who breathes no hope of happiness in life disconnected from you,—Good night

Yours devotedly
Wm. L. Nugent

Portrait of Eleanor and Evelina Smith (Nellie and Evie), 1859.

Greenville, Miss.
July 6, 1860

My own dear Nellie,

    I expected to get a letter from some one of you on Friday morning,
failing which I went home & determined to repay evil with good by writing
to you anyhow. I partly carried out the intention by inditing a doleful
serio-comic piece of doggerel, which I include herein, more for the reason
that it was produced from a good motive than from any inherent excellence
of its own.—

In the Library, Dear Nell, where often we have met,
In pleasant conversation which I'm sure you'll ne'er forget;
The Vesper Lamp upon the stand gives out a mellow light
Whose glowing fervid flame dispels the sombre shades of night;
The old six-sided marine clock upon the mantle ticks,
While Abey's Kitten near my chair is playing winsome tricks;
The Bible, Commentary, Law, school & other books,—
Each with its wonted custom .wears its own familiar looks
The lounge too in the corner, in its old position stands,
Invites me to a quiet nap, yet doesn't *extend its hands.*
The chairs at stated intervals around the spacious room,
Are placed for sympathizing friends who wander in the gloom,
Of loneliness & blues—
In utter desperation leave my one-armed rocking chair,
And all intent on killing time to the better scenes repair.
With steady, measured, lengthened steps I stride into the Hall
Where now the lamp suspended casts its light upon the wall,
On either side the wooden center all, the hatstand by the door,
The little table, lately mended, et cetera on the floor.
Umbrellas, Irish patent, writing desk & chinese hats,
To cap the climax Clarence's fiddle, hard at work a-grinding "flats".
The entrance to the scene costs nothing, yet no patronizing friend,
To all its excellences is found his countenance to lend.
Up & down & down & up I go with sober lessening pace,—
Musing Melancholy softly sleeps upon my lengthened face.
My fitful dreamlike, restless thoughts involuntary stray,
In unsuccessful quest of those who wander far away—
In the soft & still & airy flight they're floating to the throng,
Whose minds are dissipated by the dance or by the lively song.
Are those around whose hearts they cling in gladness gathered there?

Or do they, in the quiet moonlight, my lucubrations share?
Or say you; shall we find them where least we think they'd be,
In *rare enjoyment* of the dance & full of merry glee?
When loud the *saintly* promptor screeches out "swing corners, all".
And then while sadness twangs the heart, begins the "Blue Lick ball."
"The Lancers" is the cry of every one; & yet I know full well
Some in that merry dance against their better thoughts rebel—
Thus while they go I sadly feel, if coffined dead can feel,—
Like one when in his narrow bed, the undertakers steel,
Is driving home the screws.
But why prolong the saddening strain,
The giddy world can only well enjoy, the empty one refrain,
I'm on the steps; am seated now, my elbows on my knees—
Am listening to the gladsome wind careening thru' the trees.
My bearded chin is idly resting in my two well-sunburned hands
I'm dreaming while my pensive heart with glowing thoughts expands
Hope whispers consolation to the humbled, anxious mind—
And ghostly, grim forebodings, tripping pleasures, lag behind.
Disquieted & restless still, like ocean's bounding wave,
That heaves against the welcome stone, or murmurs in the cave.
Inclination drives me to the bedroom door, & then I breathe a sigh,
For when I knock & turn the bolt, no answering voice is nigh.
The empty echo of my knocking vain alone repeats the call,
And from the door retreating my weary footsteps fall.
Into my room I musing go; & quick blow out the light—
I'm really dreaming now; its past eleven o'clock, Goodnight—

Thus I had written when the Vesper Lamp burned dim, & the oil oosing out at a little crevice added an offensive odor to the air oppressive with the "steam" so to speak arising from the earth lately drenched by a copious shower. This drove me to the alternate broached in the tiresome doggerel; which I hope may amuse you. To one or two of its excellencies allow me to call your attention. The idea of "sympathizing friends wandering in the gloom of loneliness & blues" is suggestive of a tall friend of mine who with his left hand delights to curl & twist about a heavy beard; and the thought that I would feel under a certain contingency like one "when in his narrow bed, the undertaker's *steel* is driving home the screws," defies successful competition.—It would puzzle a Philadelphia lawyer to describe the feelings of a corpse when the screws to the lid of the coffin are being tightened. The suggestions in connection with the dance are thrown into the *inter-*

15

rogative form, because I do not allow myself to think that you could, without doing violence to your feelings participate in the dissipations of the "Blue Lick Springs" to any considerable extent. I do not wish or desire to be a bugbear to your utmost freedom of action. As to what you will do—I have no suggestions to make. You know my nature, you do not altogether agree; And while I regret that there should be any points of divergence between us, I do not think it would be generous in me to insist upon your adapting your course to suit my fancies. It will be time enough for you to surrender the fashionable amusements of life when you become the wife of a sober-sided Methodist.

I leave for Bolivar County this evening & will remain there for several days; how long circumstances must alone determine. On my return, I shall leave for Jackson to prepare some cases for the High Court, & may not in consequence be able to write to you again for sometime. If you leave the "Blue Lick" on the first August, I shall be at a loss where to direct my letters, & I fear I shall have reluctantly to give up the pleasure of talking with you thru' "Uncle Sam's Mail," unless you will designate some point at which I can address you.—When Clarence leaves, I shall feel very, very lonesome & much think I shall get me a buggy & visit thru' the neighborhood, to the *infinite delight* doubtless of my friends.

Dr. Penny comes to see me frequently although very much engaged, & in his quiet way affords me rare enjoyment; I have taken to the violin again, & play "Home Sweet Home," "The old play ground," "Annie Laurie"—& airs of that "ilk" to my heart's content. Providence has up to the present writing favored me with good health, & my time has been too much occupied to let in many stray bluish thoughts. I miss you all, tho', very, very much; & long for the termination of your summer's tour. Mr. and Mrs. Penrice go up this evening by the *Mo. Ranie*, & I shall accompany them as far as Prentiss[11]— Give my love to all—and accept for yourself what no words can adequately express, the ardent and ever increasing devotion of yours most truly

Wm. L. Nugent

---

[11]Prentiss was the first county seat of Bolivar County, and Nugent went there regularly to serve clients.

N.B. I open this letter to say that the letter which you wrote for *Nania* to *Ike* has come to hand.[12] I am glad you have enjoyed even that many "Spare moments," at Blue Lick Springs.

Greenville, Miss.
July 11, 1860

My own Dear Nellie,

I wrote you a letter a few days since on the eve of a trip to Bolivar County, & contemplated at that time going to Jackson on my return home. As good luck would have it, however, I am at home again & will have to defer my trip Jackson-ward for sometime. This will afford me another opportunity of talking with you, of which I gladly avail myself, despite the fact that I haven't heard from you all for about two weeks or more. Indeed, I could hardly help writing to you were I to make the attempt. The ever abiding sense of your absence, surrounded by the amusements of a water-ing place, and the pleasant associations of friends; and the constantly recurring desire for your presence to relieve the dull tedium of these long, warm summer days, creates a necessity, which impels me *nolens volens* to bear my thoughts winged with affection, through the medium of a letter, far away over hill & dale, to greet you in your privacy & drop the weight of their lonesomeness swiftly & silently into your heart for sympathy. I find that despite the business which in a measure engrosses the greatest portion of the day; despite the "cares" of housekeeping, and the responsibility devolved upon me of looking after the health of so many servants & providing for their daily wants; despite the excitement of the presidential campaign & the engrossing character of the conflicts upon which we have now entered, despite the routine of daily conversations on the streets and the epistolary duties of my profession in the office, when the twilight dews are falling & distilling their gentle health-giving properties upon the green mantle of the earth, I feel that, then is somewhat wanting—some paramount pleasure of which my heart does not fail to acquaint me.

---

[12]Nania was the nurse who accompanied the Smiths to care for Aby.

Here am I now sitting up, while the minute hand of the clock is traveling fast its round to one o'clock, waiting to give Bally the last dose of medicine prescribed by Dr. Penny, which I am to administer at half past one o'clock. Bally was taken sick while I was in Bolivar County, this disease indicates strong tendency towards congestion. He is now apparently relieved, is sleeping soundly, & the Dr. says is out of danger. He ate a good deal of watermelon & was, I presume, imprudent in eating too close to the rind. He has had no appetite for two days except for a little chicken soup—which is all, doubtless for the best. I only speak of this now because it is a matter of some concern to your Mother & Father, & may not be uninteresting to you.

The Miss Smiths are up here, & I went up to the Hotel this evening hoping to meet them, Dr. Penny having informed me they would come down to take a boat tonight, & to renew to them, in the Diplomatic phraseology of the day, the assurances of my distinguished consideration, but failed to see them though I waited until eleven o'clock.[13] Mrs. Theobald and Miss Mag leave next Tuesday for the "Bailey Springs" Alabama, I think.[14] This will break in upon our "small" society here to a great extent. And when they leave I fear our social religious meetings will be sadly broken up. Mrs. Halsey leaves tonight for Cooper's Wells, I think.[15] Brother Fox is looking exceedingly amiable, and dame Rumor says is addressing Mrs. Brooks—Mr. Montgomery says with some prospects of success. I don't know what to think about it. Brother Fox bears bantering bravely, but is ominously silent on the subject. Who knows? Widows, they say, take fancies sometimes, & have a wonderful degree of pertinancity— particularly when they are independent. It may be that our fair and worthy client will entertain the proposition to connect her hopes & fortune with a poor itinerant, & ignore the pomp of wealth & the pride of a great name.[16]

---

[13]The Miss Smiths are the daughters of Ben Smith of Longwood Plantation. The Smith families were not related but were close friends. PWCHS, 345.

[14]Harriet McAllister married Dr. W. W. Blanton who operated a large plantation named Blantonia. After Blanton's death she married Dr. Sam Theobald. Margaret Newman was the niece of Mrs. Theobald and an only child who inherited property located near Catfish Point, which later caved into the river. PWCHS, 51; Recollections of LSH. See also Epilogue.

[15]Cooper's Well was located 4 miles south of Raymond, Mississippi, and before the war was widely known for the medicinal qualities of its water and its splendid social life. Nugent repeatedly urged members of the family to visit the Well. Clipping in possession of LSH.

[16]Brother Fox appears to be an itinerant minister. Records indicate Mrs. Brooks married Felix Boyce. William Pinckney Montgomery developed Locust Plantation on Rattlesnake Bayou. PWCHS, 282.

To the great & mysterious future we must leave the development of this, as of all other earthly projects.

I received a letter from Father yesterday in which he desires to be remembered to my *"sweet little Ellen"*—thus you see the old gentleman has an appreciative opinion of you. Tom also wishes to be remembered to you, & says that when I shall have *foreclosed my mortgages* he doubts not but his affection will be equally divided between you and the home folks—He is now at home.[17] The "Small-pox" so the Dr. said had broken out in Jackson & the boys all scattered like frightened sheep. The report was a false one. The College exercises were, however, suspended in consequence of it. By the way, I forgot to say Father consoled me by saying "he would be glad, were he in my place, that you had gone, & would wish you to remain away until within a few days of the appointed time." In reply, I told him I was both glad & sorry; didn't tell him though, why I was glad & why I was sorry. A mixture of feelings, under the circumstances, is not at all astonishing. I would hardly be selfish enough to wish you to injure your health & debar yourself the pleasure & profit of a summer's tour to gratify me. I esteem it a source of happiness if I may minister to your pleasure & profit even at the considerable expense of being deprived of your society for a season. It may never again be your good luck married as you will be soon to a poor young lawyer. I almost think sometimes I am asking anyhow too great a sacrifice at your hands; but if you are brave enough to share my lot in life, I hope I shall never prove recreant to the important trust you have so confidingly submitted to my keeping—well I must quit—My pen's unwilling—I look upon the lamp & its bright & sparkling flame is surrounded by a beautiful rainbow tinted circle of light—and I think shall our lives thus ever be lit up with rainbows of happiness—shall no shadows darken these radiant consecrations. Love to all: Kiss Aby for me. And may He who tempers the wind to the shorn lamb bless & protect you

Fondly & devotedly yours
Wm. L. Nugent

---

[17]John Pratt Nugent in 1860 was living on a sugar plantation in Atchafalaya, Louisiana. Tom was a brother of William, born 1841, who was attending Centenary College in Jackson, Louisiana. He subsequently went to Texas, fought in the Confederate Army, and became a lawyer and judge in Texas. Edmonds, Nugent Family Papers.

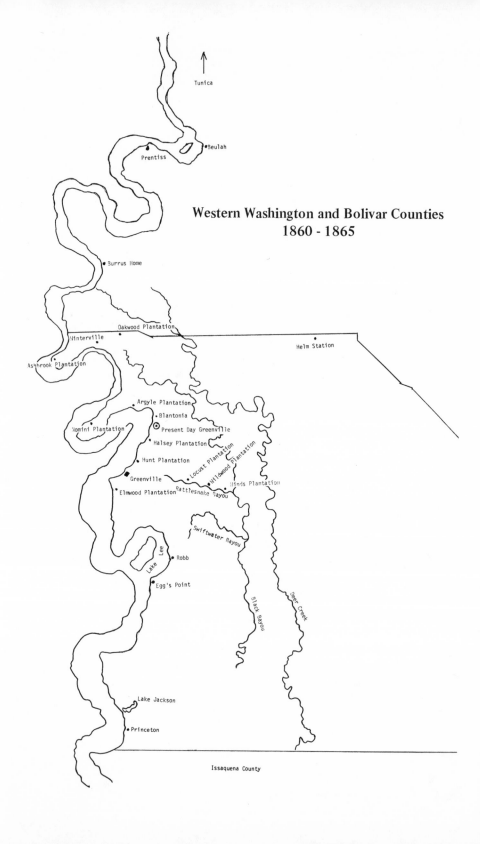

Western Washington and Bolivar Counties
1860 - 1865

Greenville, Miss.
July 16, 1860

My own dear Nellie,

Alas! alas! it is, that joys are but fleeting & that pleasures of the rarest
kind are often but shortlived at the best. Like the poor little butterfly,
whirling his dangerous flight around the lamp beside me, we often riot in
the enjoyment of the passing moment & often lose ourselves in the excessive gratification it affords,—forgetful that when the dreary realities of life
are rudely brought to bear upon us we are poorly prepared for the trial.
Thus thought I, & how I felt it you alone can judge, when having perused
your letter of the 6th instant this morning received, I took my pen to reply.
How many hills & mountains rear their heads between us, how many rivers
roll their turbid waters, how many plains spread out their verdant
bosoms—& how many, many miles measure their ever increasing length.
Thoughts may burst from their secret resting places in the shadowy arcana
of the brain, and wing their subtle flight regardless of time or distance,
while the pointed pen, obedient to the mandate of the will, may check
their flowings & transfer them to this perishable piece of paper—but who
may tell with quill or pen of steel, the warm sympathies and ardent,
gushing affection which the sparkling eye, & tender look alone can certainly portray. Tears are indications of weakness at times; but then too, as
they glisten in the eye and fall upon the cheek they reflect the most
cherished feelings of the soul as surely as they do the glorious sunlight.
They are silent & speechless, yet persuasive messengers from the well-
springs of affections. They do not appear when the will suggests, but only
when some precious sympathy in fondness plays over the chords of the
heart. Who, who, would check their pure outflowings, when the purest
emotions kindle in their every silvery drop? And was my poor absent Nellie
sad? Did something unknown, some undefined foreboding all of ill play
such havoc with her peace of mind? Or did the quiet stillness of the night
give rise to the feeling & mellow the pulsations of her heart to the softened
beating of my own? Ah! how little, my Nellie, do you know the wealth of
love & affection which I lay daily as an humble tribute at your feet! Nor will
you fully realize it, until years hence, when a constant association, in the
unrestrained enjoyment of each other's society shall fully demonstrate it.

'Till then, I count the rolling minutes & to me the slowly revolving hours—Did I think your sadness anything but the momentary depression of the time, I should feel greatly tempted to "hie away" after you. I keep up my spirits bravely though, knowing that a few weeks will soon pass away, & I shall soon be privileged to claim you as my own. 'Till then I shall teach myself to "labor & to wait".—

I have been busy all day writing briefs in some cases, & had my mind harassed by the effort to demonstrate a proposition of law, that would gain a case which we have been compelled to carry to the High Court of Errors & Appeals. It was an uphill business and my brain has been considerably racked: and then too, the case is one in which we are trying to recover Mantia from Dr. Finlay, and I know you don't want success to crown our efforts.[18] I finished it tonight about ten o'clock, & find it a great relief to throw the papers on the stand, & thus relieve the tedium of a lonely hour or two by communing with you. Law books are all around me; newspapers invite my perusal; reviews are anxious for some attention; and the voracious mosquitoes buzzing about my ears & hands present their *bills* for *liquidation*—excuse that *pun*.

The other morning Brother Mullins & wife & Mr. Trigg & Miss Bettie came up & took breakfast with me.[19] I have felt highly honored by the attention, & have been crowing about it ever since. Miss Bettie looks amazingly well, and I thought looked at Trigg very much as if she loved him. My imagination may have misled me; her looks were *knowing* & peculiar. She thinks, doubtless, well old fellow! I've got you secure, and will have my own fun before I'll marry you. A dangerous project is this: the "fellow" may take a notion to leave: and then if the girl *loves* him much— how sad the change. It is a great folly for women to sport with their affections; they are very poorly qualified to bear disappointment in a matter where the heart is concerned. I judged from the way my guests ate that they appreciated the breakfast. As a sort of *arriere pense we had watermelon* (!) & cantaloupes. I have often heard of cantaloupes for break-

---

[18]John L. Finlay was a doctor in Greenville who at times ministered to the Smith family. PWCHS, 65. The Finlay and Smith homes were the largest in Greenville before the war. The Finlay home was one of two homes left standing after the Federal troops burned Greenville. Clipping in possession of LSH.

[19]Wyndham R. Trigg came to Greenville in 1850. He was a neighbor of the Smiths and served in the 28th Mississippi Cavalry. After the war he was a member of the state legislature and chancery judge. Bettie was his wife. PWCHS, 274.

fast, but never of watermelons: but then why not inaugurate the fashion?

I am glad to learn that you are *very* well; hope you may continue to improve in health and *flesh* as long as you remain away. I don't know why it is, but I have an admiration for "fat", plump girls. They seem to have more of geniality of feeling; more ardor; more affection, I never could associate warmth or depth of feeling with a lamp post—never, I have no doubt, however, that a great many lean & tall girls love very much.—It is a great comfort to me to know you miss me; to feel that your thoughts abstract themselves from surrounding pleasures & attractions to pay me a visit in the morning, at the twilight hour, & in the "stilly night"; to believe that you look forward to our marriage as the crowning happiness of your life—as it will be of mine.

I think you had better "fix the day" at the 18th of October—which comes, I believe, on Thursday. On the 8th Mr. Smith will be in Coahoma & will be there until about the 15th; the 18th will, therefore, suit him & myself too—with me, you know, the sooner, 'tis the better. I shall continue to look forward to the time with a great deal of fond anticipation. For the life of me though, some stray thoughts of "bad luck" will come across my mind at intervals, and dash my joy with suggestions of distrust—My hopeful spirit soon rebounds and I am glad again for how could my Nellie now change in her feelings towards me? It *surely* is impossible. I miss you all the time—and expect I shall give you a good "squeeze" when you return—hope we will meet when I shall be at liberty to do so. And now may the Good Spirit watch over, bless direct and protect you from every danger, and bring you safely back again is the prayer of—Yours devotedly

Wm. L. Nugent.

Greenville, Miss.
July 21, 1860

My own dear Nellie,

Your letter of the 12th instant, accompanied by one from Mrs. Smith, was received by me this morning, and was read with a great deal of avidity: yours *twice*. It is a source of no small degree of pleasure to know that you are all enjoying good health, and that your cheeks are beginning to put on a delicate livery of red. If the absence of some few weeks can have the effect to restore you to health, the *effects* of that absence upon me can well be borne. I regret, however, to learn that Mr. Smith still suffers from that oppression upon the chest; and am inclined to think he is afflicted with asthma.[20] If this is the case, he will be, in all probability, spared to us for many years to come, though he will necessarily "wade through deep waters of affliction." How happy would I not feel if in his affliction he could be comforted and sustained by an unfaltering trust in the Giver of all good things. The chastening may be providential; the beginning of a train of dispensations calculated and designed to make him look beyond the con-fines of earth, to the brighter glory-land, where the cruel waves of sorrow never lash the sun-lit shore, and where the billows of suffering never flood the soul.

I am really sorry you didn't send me the letter you wrote after reading mine to your Mother, if in it you "completely opened your heart." I could have borne the lecture, and gladly would I have done so, to have *fully* known you. Your retiring disposition and timidity or *secretiveness* have always hitherto prevented you from making me your confidant to the extent I could have wished. No one is better entitled to it than I. The letter to your Mother was written when I was in a strangely sad and disponding humor. She had advised me of the fact that you had a *beau* a pleasant fellow, open frank face, etc., and told me I mustn't be jealous. I hadn't then heard from you although as I imagined a sufficient time had elapsed. I am aware of the influence of *association* with those antagonistic in opinion or disposition to one upon the minds of individuals. I know I am a sober-sided Methodist reared to believe that all under the sun is change-able, and that there is nothing sure but heaven; and I know that you are opposed in prejudice and principle to the peculiar religious opinions which I hold. I know, or had reason to believe, that engaging in the fashionable amusements of a watering place, would possess unusual attractions to one who had never experienced them, and might superinduce a changed state of feeling: while I had not the vanity to think myself better than all other men. This added to what has already transpired induced me to say I was not "too Hopeful." That the momentary depression of feeling when you left should have made me feel that all was lost, is not wonderful at all. I am not

---

[20]Smith did have asthma according to family recollections and a subsequent statement of Nugent.

a prey to jealousy, and had you, as I have often wished and *besought,* *"completely opened your heart"* to me, doubtfulness, anxiety and forebodings of evil would have been strangers to me. The stake, so to speak, which I have set upon a consummation of our engagement by a speedy marriage is a very considerable one to me. I have wholly and without any reservation whatever entrusted my happiness to your keeping: and were I less anxious about the final result, it would be rather an *unpleasant augury,* somewhat suggestive of a change of feeling. Through evil report and good report, under circumstances when it was scarcely possible for me to do so, I have loved you devotedly, ardently and with singleness of purpose: and this should in some measure atone for any momentary expression of fear, anxiety or distrust. It is like balm to my soul when you say you have confidence in me; and that you were certain when you returned you would find me unchanged and unaltered. But ask yourself the honest question did I ever give you, by act or thought, any reasonable ground to doubt me? Nay, have I not always clung to you with unabashed love? And then, if I were away from home surrounded by a host of pretty girls, most of whom were on the lookout for husbands, wouldn't some random thoughts of an unpleasant kind sometimes stray through your mind? Again, I say, I am sorry you didn't send that letter; for I would like to be the entire confidant of *all* your thoughts and feelings. Your letters reassure me; have removed all, or any uneasy sensations from my mind, and I hope you may not again have reason to feel hurt at anything I may write. But a truce to melancholy, blues, *et id omne genus!* everything of that sort. "Let the dead *past,* bury its dead."

You do not speak of the manner in which you spend your time, as fully as I could wish. How do you enjoy the dances in which you engage? You haven't even told me you dance; *Kind* friends have done that for you. But then I should like to know whether it is *really a pleasure* to you, the fiancee of a poor, sober-sided, Methodist lawyer. If this be the case, I presume you have soberly determined to surrender your connection with the Church, to desert her consolatory offices, and tread no longer her sacred aisles to commune a suppliant at her altars. As on the flashing mount of God, the Saviour of a dying world shall stand, and gather his hosts of weary followers from the chilly North, the sunny South, the East, the West, other far off Ocean isles, do you propose not to be among the throng? Is this your solemn, settled purpose? Or do you not rather wish in this, as other things,

25

to share my joys, my hopes, my sorrows? I would like to see you, yes now long to see you, but to stand idly by the door and see you whirling thru' the mazes of the dance with the devotee of fashion, would be the source of excruciating pain. You may have sometimes felt the well-springs of your heart gradually receding, their gushing fountains repressed, and their exuberant flowings checked. "Hope springs eternal in the human breast;" and that you will gradually learn to assimilate your opinions to mine, I firmly and *persistently* believe. It is this alone, which bears me up. To believe that while I was endeavoring to lead the life of a Christian, you were in *your heart* opposing me, and wishing to frustrate this purpose of my life, would be a sad reflection. But I have unthoughtedly assumed that most ungracious office of the advisor: For what I have said, I ask your kind indulgence; I do not wish, tho', for you not to know my every thought in connection with you. And I could hardly require you to act otherwise than you do, had I the privilege of so doing. You would lead a very prosy life indeed, if you didn't participate in the dances. You occupy a sacred position in my affection; Almost that of an idol—if it is broken and destroyed, who will be the iconoclast? I cannot, cannot think that while you dance *your heart is in it?*

Clarence will leave me next week for home; and then how lonely will the house appear? Fortunately for me I shall have to go to Jackson, whence I shall I think go to Cooper's Well and spend a week or two. This will enable me to somewhat kill time until your return, which I hope may not be delayed further than the middle of September.

I sometimes almost feel weary of life itself! long to lay me down un- noticed and unhonored to die;—to give back my soul to Him who called it into being;—and hurry away to a place where the ways of life are lighted up by the Glory of God's presence continually and disappointments are un- known. But soon the responsibility of life here is presented to my mind; and I feel that I do not live for *myself alone.* I was sitting in the gallery the other evening with my chair against the solitary column musing of the future. I thought of you in years to come, the quiet matron by my side, a sympathetic comforter, and a strong support amidst a host of imaginary trials: and I felt that my experiences would be considerably mixed up with joy and sorrow; and as the unbid sigh welled up and floated idly on the evening air, what relief to depressed thoughts was borne upon its airy wings? But I bear up bravely; "am doing", as Mr. Valliant says, "as well as could be expected."[21]

I haven't heard a word from Will Scott since he left except indirectly thru' Dr. Blackburn who told he was doing well.[22] Miss Lou went up the River the other day and *Bill Starke* went along with her.

I hope you will not feel sad on account of anything I have written. I could not bear to have a single feeling in which you were concerned, a secret from you. In matters of love I think, we should be *excessively honest and candid.* Your letters assure me beyond a doubt of your affection; with this I am content; and I even feel that I might not look so much to the future and yet do better. I am persuaded that after marriage our lives will move on pleasantly and happily in a *single current*—unaffected by the little eddies which difference of opinion may at times occasion. This much I am *fully justified* in hoping. I might have subscribed the usual "your affectionately" and quit, but the ardent invocation for God's blessing upon you demands utterance; and with that, to say Good-bye, impresses me with the fact that now as ever I am devotedly

Your
Will

Greenville, Miss.
July 23rd, 1860

My own dear Nellie,

You have often stood no doubt at evening and watched the glorious God of day dying slowly in the west; and as the golden beams, waning with the hurrying moments, suffused with their mellow tints the dappled clouds that nearest lay and they in turn transferred their beauty to the rest, until the gorgeous red faded away into the softest pink, have felt a musing melancholy steal over you, not unpleasant indeed but soul subduing and enrapturing. And then you may have stood, watching and enjoying the scene, until the joyous stars twinkling in the far off Heavens were marshalled out,

---

[21]Frank Valliant was a lawyer and judge from Greenville. PWCHS, 245.

[22]William Scott resided at Lake Jackson. He was the son of former governor Abram Scott, and he married Martha Cox, the sister of S. Myra Smith. Dr. Blackburn was a physician who resided in the Lake Lee-Princeton area. PWCHS, 115.

and the pale moon rising from her slumbers to the zenith greeted the last flicker of sunlight, How pleasant, too, at such time is music, as it steals upon the ears,—lively and gay, yet plaintive, still, at times as the gentlest murmur of your every sigh, my Nellie. Such thoughts and emotions came over me when I read your letter of the 17th instant. I could have felt in very joy that to let the feeling vent itself in the tribute of a silent tear or two, would have been grateful to me. Never before have you written to me so confidingly and so completely agreeable to my wishes. Never before have you addressed me as one who was fully entitled to demand and have my *entire respect* as well as ardent affection. Hitherto you have written somewhat constrainedly, somewhat after the manner of a person who feels she is addressing a being of a superior nature. I hoped and knew you would overcome this and let your genuine woman's nature assert its privilege. It was a source of some trouble to me to think you regarded yourself as illy qualified to make me happy: to interest and fascinate me by your conversation, as well as personal attractions. In this letter I have the *woman*, not the diffident and retiring girl which you have hitherto persisted in being: and it makes me feel very *light-hearted* I assure you, more especially in view of the time when we shall be one, I fondly hope, in thought and feeling, in affection and interest. This will fully compensate me for your "leaving me": and I am constrained to believe that it is for our mutual good. How mysterious are the ways of Providence! and his wonders past finding out!

Don't think you worry me by long letters. I read them all over three or four times; sometimes oftener—while certain portions of them are even deeply imbedded in my memory—"learned and conned"—to supply in some measure your temporary absence. If I am spared and all things work well, I intend taking with you next summer an extended trip—maybe to the "olden world". How I would delight to read lessons of information and improvement mentally and morally, with you leaning on my arms, in the wonders of the old world. To visit the green shores of Ireland, sail over the dimpled surface of its romantic lakes and scramble among its mountains: to explore the places of Scotland rendered familiar by the novels of Scott and steam up the Rhine by the light of "Bayard Taylor's Travels." Nor will the scenes be less interesting because you are "settled down", if then every pulsation of *my* heart finds a responsive echo in your own.

I wrote a letter to your brother on yesterday which goes up tomorrow;

and one to you which was forwarded on Sunday. In the last letter I wrote you I spoke of your dancing at Blue Lick Springs in a manner thoughtless, which I have no doubt you will fully and readily understand. I have been afraid since, it may occasion some pain; had I thought so at the time I would not have written; I have not said or written a word calculated intentionally to wound you; and would not do so, for *any* consideration. I have formed a resolution never to say an unkind word to you, or to think an unkind thought; so far I have accomplished it. Every momentary feeling of an unpleasant kind has been openly and honestly divulged; but they all were the result of an anxiety on my part or to probable misfortune, of which I now have *no apprehension whatever.* You have no idea of the strength of a feeling that has been assiduously cultivated for years. Discon-nected from you, I have entertained no thoughts of substantial happiness in life. Its lights and shadows, joys and sorrows, all revolved about an orbit in which you occupied the central position alone. The numbers of ladies whom I have seen since the time I just began the attempt to make you love me, have had no influence over me; and that, too, at times when my discernment perceived, what my vanity never would have suggested, that some of them would like to take me as a husband. I can scarcely under-stand how it is that the timid, modest and retiring little girl who used to sit near my side possessed an influence over my man-nature, that no one else did. I can only think and wonder: but how much do I congratulate myself upon the result! The little girl has developed into a lovely and attractive woman—with some faults it is true—but with a substratum in her composi-tion of gentleness, affection, patience, unselfishness and confidence upon which I may reasonably build my largest hopes. Don't think me a flatterer—it were folly for me to make the attempt. I know you well enough to know you will beyond question make a "good wife." I know also very nearly all the points of difference in opinion and prejudices, which I promise myself it will be our delightsome task hereafter to assimilate if need be by a mutual concession.

I am heartily glad you like my doggerel. I didn't think much of it; wrote it off when I was in somewhat of a rhyming humor. I reckon it was to a certain extent applicable to those who mingled in the merry dance. Doubt-less they *called* for the "Lancers"—and the promptor *called* for "swing corners all"—excuse the pun for both *calls* may be harmonized. If I really felt that you would feel complimented by an occasional rhyming epistle, I would give you "a little more of the same sort." It is easy to let the nimble pen stretch out a good humored sentence over half-a-dozen lines and the temptation to *prose* prevails. Another pun, as I live.

If you all go to Mammoth Cave, give me *timely* notice, I will certainly come up to see you unless the servants are sick. "Go where (duty) calls thee"—Moore has it "glory" but I interpolate a word that makes much better *commonsense*. If I go to the Mammoth Cave, the temptation will be almost irresistible to go *farther*. And can I refrain from annoying you upon the subject of marriage? Even now since you have somewhat shortened the probation I think it a long look ahead. By the way Miss *Mag* said she would like to go with me to the Cave. Mrs. Theobald told her you might be jealous; and upon Miss Mag's replying that she didn't think you would have any reason for so being, the old lady shrewdly turned her head and said she didn't know—that you might have some reason to be. Richardson took dinner with me today, and said that when ladies went into the Cave they dressed in a *Bloomer Costume of red flannel*.[23] How would you like it? The gentlemen always lift the ladies over the little pools of water that abound in the cave. I have never tried Miss Mag, and rather suppose she would be a very good load, sufficient to tax all my muscular powers. How would you like to see me undergoing the task of thus handing a fair friend over the water? It would be very primitive to say the least of it. I would much prefer escorting you.

I would like to keep Clarence with me very much. My dear old Mother, however, wants him to come home, and I willingly submit to the deprivation of his society. Clarence has faithfully preserved all of the numbers of Godey's Lady's Book for Evie's special gratification; I believe she requested him to do it. Miss Mary Dunn laughingly sent me her love, and I forgot in my letter to your Mother to reciprocate her kind message; will you supply the omission for me?[24] Probate Court sat today; very little business on hand. Tomorrow I go out to see Judge Yerger in reference to a new suit of unusual occurrence, that will *pay* pretty well.[25] We have a new candidate for Sheriff in the person of *George Shall*. Kate Montgomery is developing

---

[23]Edward P. Richardson purchased Swiftwater Plantation from Alex B. Montgomery. PWCHS, 283.

[24]Mary Dunn resided on the Glenbar Plantation. PWCHS, 327.

[25]Jacob Shall Yerger owned Ararat Plantation and served as judge of the court of probate. He was the father of William G. Yerger, Nugent's law partner for several years after the war. PWCHS, 386.

very fast.[26] The folks at Argyle are going away soon.[27] Miss Bettie is getting along swimmingly with Trigg—I believe. All the talk here now is about a *mule race* to come off next Saturday; Breckinridge and Lane don't create half the excitement. I think I will become a tolerably good quack before the season is over—unless I become a *runaway*—another pun!!!! The leaf is nearly out—Pleasant slumbers to you, don't let the roses leave your cheeks—May God bless you.

Yours devotedly
Will

Greenville, Miss.
August 3rd, 1860

Dearest Nellie,

I received your last letter on *Monday* and only deferred writing up to the present because I was informed you all intended leaving the Springs on the 29th ult. for Niagara Falls, and didn't know when a letter might find you. I am however, today in receipt of a letter from Alf in which he says I must direct a reply to Saratoga, N. Y. To Saratoga then I send my "talk" and Uncle Sam may make the most of it, should it *die* an *untimely* death. If my letter partake at all of my present feelings it will be excessively dull. I have just returned from the Plantation, where I hunted bear, but "alas! poor Yorick" without success, for a whole day; have ridden about twenty miles and despite the regenerating and vivifying influences of a cold bath and a change of linen, am somewhat fagged. How would you like to see me a perfect Nimrod? Hunting in the swamps, taking O'Malley leaps over logs, whooping like an Indian, and "discoorsing" in the idiomatic language of a connoisseur in field sports? How soon one learns the formulas of the craft! A little practice perfects aim, and then the little neighborhood is all astir with the prowess of the valiant slayer of a timid deer, or a rollicking bear. In these latter-day hunters we do not see that indomitable energy, preserving sagacity and "patience" of hunger and thirst which forces us to admire

---

[26]Mary Catherine Montgomery (Kate) of Locust Plantation was the daughter of William P. Montgomery. See also the Epilogue. PWCHS, 201.

[27]Argyle Plantation was located two miles north of present Greenville. The William R. Campbell family owned the property which was burned during the war. Nellie and Evelina attended classes there in their earliest years, and Nugent later taught the Campbell children. Clipping in possession of LSH.

the brave old Trapper and skilful hunter of revolutionary memory. The scene is now a ridge or two of cane, flanked by open sloughs, a pack of dogs arouse the intended victim from his lair, force him through the "stands", and the *eager* hunter, perhaps at a distance of twenty feet, brings him down with a load of *buckshot*. Let this tribute tho' be given to them. They do the best their circumstances allow, angels can do nothing better. To this extent they do well; act wisely. There is some excitement about the chase. It is a manly art, develops the muscles, and associates us with scenes of danger and bloodshed. Bob Coleman is enthusiastic upon the subject of *bear* killing, and told me this morning he would *kill three* dogs tomorrow. That is to say, he would have an exciting day's sport! Mirable dictu! "How long, O Ceasar, wilt thou abuse our patience?" It is not enough to slay the sooty ranger of the wood; but there must be some dog-killing to lend an additional charm to the sport: without this, the sport would be tame. A homily on hunting to you—who would have thought it?

Time is flitting on its endless way and the dull days of August have been ushered in upon us. A few days more, and then—

I had promised myself the pleasure of a temporary jaunt to Blue Lick Springs to see you, when the news came that you all intended leaving. I assure you I felt the disappointment very keenly, and were it not for my well-grounded belief that all things work together for good, I might be disposed to grumble somewhat. As it is, I fear you already esteem me a churlish fellow, obtruding my opinions upon you unnecessarily,—and casting a damper over your mode of enjoying yourself at the watering places. The rumble of the car of time is sounding in my ears and creating a hubbub in my *imagination*—and the thought that a cozy chat or two with you will reconcile us altogether, is fraught with the teasing of a glowing consolation. I reckon we are not so very diverse in our opinions now, are we?

Time (again the same old subject) has hung heavily on my hands this summer, and I have absolutely been lazying—to use Alf's expression: have done very little in the way of business or reading Law. Waded through Greenleaf—wrote a brief or two, two or three bills in Chancery, with several *declarations*, and attended two or three courts.[28] My letters to you and Mr. and Mrs. Smith didn't take up many moments. For several days

---

[28]Greenleaf was the standard text on evidence. Bill in chancery is the initial pleading in an equity case. A declaration opens proceedings in a court of law and usually relates to contracts or torts.

past I have done absolutely nothing; in fact I am tempted to reproach myself for many valuable moments wasted. A serious consideration, when taken in connection with the large responsibilities of life. Who knows what may be suspended on a second?

Clarence left me on Monday last for home, and seemed to be perfectly rejoiced at the idea of going home. I saw him to the yawl first and then safely on the boat, and ere this, I hope, he is with those whose warm and affectionate greetings will remind him of his importance. It's a very dismal "thing" to live in a large house by one's self: boarding forever in preference to that say I. The mind for lack of the salutary influences of social conversation is apt to prey upon itself; to conjure up dusty phantasms; and seek in unprofitable channels relief from its weary burden of repressed emotion. It is not good for man to be alone, and to be content, there must be some peculiar inducement to a solitary existence.

I took a flying trip to Tunica County the other day, and had the peculiar felicity of waiting at Helena, on a *Wharf Boat* fully eight hours for a boat down. The miserable regimen in the way of diet inflicted upon me taxed my philosophy to the utmost. How foolish! After it is all over, the memory of it vanishes and the "fast flitting prospect of a bright future—some passing glimpse of a sunlit valley—tinge all our after years." Our three score years and ten are soon over, and it would seem easy enough to suffer them out, even on a wharf boat. I had "Charley O'Malley" along and read it for the fourth time with great zest. The bold dragoon was a rollicking lover, if he did persevere in his affection for Lucy Dashwood. He had two or three courtships, or flirtations! It would be a sore temptation to me now to bring me into contact with a really interesting young woman—Wouldn't it? I am just in the fix to appreciate any mark of attention; I should feel decidedly obliged to anyone who would amuse me for several hours a day. I have been *hurrying* up the Clerk with my records for several days, in order to *hurry* out to Jackson & Cooper's Well—Maybe I can learn to roll the *balls* too! I don't believe I can make your blood *circulate* any *faster* by a continuance of this strain & will quit. No one can well appreciate the exhuberant happiness which is that man's portion "who weaves out a story of his life and who in connecting the promise of early years will seek to fulfil a fate and destiny." This from "Charley O'Malley." I sometimes think I would make a very good dragoon myself.

For the philosophy of the Law I entertain a profound admiration, for some of the peculiar experiences of the practice of it, I have a hearty dislike. My own opinion is that I shall aspire to the bench as soon as I make a competency. What say you? Would you prefer to see me in the *arena*? The drudgery of so much writing is fatiguing, and the only pleasure attendant upon a professional life is the sense of continual mental improvement. A man can feel himself advancing all the time. But it is a sad reflection to think of making a fortune out of the errors and tergiversations of men. However, I suppose one profession is about as good as another.

I count the days of your anticipated absence & frequently find myself devising expedients to make the hours glide away more rapidly than is their wont. Only think it's a month & a half since I saw you! What changes for the better may not have been wrought in your personal appearance? I hope you will continue to improve in flesh: Somehow or other I always fancied plump girls more than those who were lean and tall.

Mr. Trigg has gone to Virginia. Miss Mag Newman to Bailey Springs Alabama. The Argyle folks haven't yet got off; but expect to leave next week—and so they go. "Friends after friends depart!"

I hope you will have a pleasant trip to the Falls, Saratoga & New York. The pleasurable excitement of travel will well make the moments slip away and make you feel less sensibly my absence—if not for the nonce lose sight of it altogether. You must be sure to write to me from Saratoga & give me some account of your wanderings & loiterings. I got a letter from Alf yesterday as also one from Mr. Smith—who I am glad to hear is improving in health at last. Ike is fixing up the front yard artistically—following out a plan of his own. I haven't interferred because I thought you would like to rearrange it anyhow. All well with us—My health is very good, & I really believe I am "fattening." Here we are at the bottom—and lest my pen may take a pensive turn, I quit. May Heaven bless you with its choicest favors & grant us soon the joy of a happy reunion.

Ever yours
Wm. L. Nugent

Greenville, Miss.
Aug. 21st, 1860

Dear Ellen,

I wrote to you the other day, but didn't send the letter because I was wholly ignorant as to whom I should send it, and after reading yours of the

16th from "Saratoga Springs" I am almost afraid to write any more for fear of marring to a certain extent the pleasures of your journey. I very much question whether or not I should write, but I must, as early as possible, correct a mistake into which I inadvertently led you. I deeply regret that the motive that actuated my last letter should have lain concealed beneath the language employed, and that you should not have understood me correctly. I could bear your heaviest censure in matters not connected so intimately with my heart: when that is subject to your displeasure, a bruised reed could not resist the violence of the tempest with as little success. In all your other letters you have subscribed at least the *yours* affectionately; in this the "yours" is wanting and you tell me that if you are a source of trouble to me now you do hope it will not always be so. Otherwise your letter is all that I could ask, nay more. If in the excess of my love and anxiety—intensified by your long absence—I have said any-thing that has made my darling weep, the sorrow which this inflicts upon me is the heaviest penalty I could possibly be called upon to endure. I hoped my letter to you would not produce anything more serious than a little reflection. From what I heard—*not* from what your Mother wrote me—I was led to *imagine* you had imbibed a fondness for the amusements of a fashionable life to an extent that might cause a *difference* of *feeling* on your part towards me; and my letter, tho' expressed in words that welled from the deepest recesses of my heart, was only intended to get an expression of your mind and real thoughts upon the subject. I doubt not upon a reperusal you will at once detect this. The expressions used were almost all in the interrogative, and I believe I said, I could not think your heart was in the dance. Had you fully understood it, I think it would have afforded you a pleasure to gratify me, not that I wish to annoy you by my importunity or harass you by an unpardonable interference in your plans for enjoyment. So it is, however; I have placed myself in the unenviable attitude of one who has needlessly brought suffering to the heart and countenance of one whose happiness I desire above all earthly blessings; and superinduced a reluctance on her part to continue a correspondence, that has formed an oasis in the desert of my soul. If I have merited this unparalleled misfortune, I shall endeavor to endure it, even though it may increase the isolation that now is creeping over me. In all my efforts to secure earthly happiness, it seems, I am doomed to disappointment, if this be my destiny I will have to endure it; it will hang all around the avenues of my heart a drapery of black—the silent token of an anguish its sable folds can scarcely conceal. But enough—you tell me you love me none the less: and if on your return I may be permitted to press you to my bosom and hear you say that I am forgiven for accomplishing that which was fartherest from my purpose, I will be satisfied. I started out to say that your Mother did *not* write me you had a beau in the light in which you have *understood the term.* My hope surmounts all dismal reflections, and points to scenes of happiness in the future when we shall be united in the mystical ties of a holy wedlock, and have a common sympathy as well as a single destiny! Nor can I, by the strongest effort, blot out the pleasant prospect. I do not think I could bear to meet you with a frown upon your forehead and displeasure in your heart, and I shall not feel at all contented until I hear that I have not lost my position in your affections. To know that I have caused unnecessary pain, has surely affected me for several days past.

Since I last wrote I have had a severe attack of bilious fever: am now well. I hope to be completely restored soon. The School House was burned the other night, and Mr. Hines, the suspected runaway has been compelled to leave.

I have ridden thirty miles today, and it is nearly eleven o'clock.[29] Will Scott has returned in good health and spirits. Love to all: and if I am still as dear to you as ever, will you my dearest Ellen relieve my sufferings by again writing to me? If I lose your esteem and love, I lose all that has stayed, comforted and consoled me for years whose glowing experiences are treasured as the fondest of past recollections. Until I hear from you again please allow me, dear Ellen, still to say I am

Devotedly yours
Wm. L. Nugent

Vicksburg, Nov 26, 1860

My dear wife,[30]

I got here last night "safe & sound" after a rather tiresome trip. The boat was continually stopping to take on cotton, & much to my regret I find

---

[29]Nugent's constant travel is noteworthy considering the primary means were by boat or horse.

[30]The Smiths returned home in September, and William and Nellie were married November 6, 1860. As a wedding gift Nugent presented a sixteen-volume set of the works of Washington Irving. Previously, as a betrothal gift, he gave her the twelve-volume set of Sir Walter Scott's *Waverly Novels.* His gift selections are indicative of his great love of literature, a trait consistently demonstrated in his letters. The two sets are in the possession of LSH.

Portrait of Abram Fulkerson Smith, 1859. Born 1809, died January 1863. Father of Eleanor F. Smith.

myself a little behind time. I will leave for Yazoo City this evening, & hope to reach my destination by Tuesday morning at nine o'clock. Doctor Graham & wife got along bravely on the "Battle", and when we parted appeared to be in a great good humor with one another; albeit I noticed Mrs. Graham crying a little. The old Dr. seemed not to notice this little contretemps. This was a matter of wonder to me; as I do not for the life of me, see how a man could see his wife cry without throwing his arm around her & kissing away the briny tear drop. And who could better console the wife for the absence of home & kindred than the husband: he who solemnly vowed to love, honor, comfort, and protect her in sickness & health, thru' evil report and good report. Your Father left us "Sound in body & mind."

My dear Nell, you cannot imagine how I miss you even now. Your gentle face so long mirrored on my heart is more than ever reflected in my mind, and is an ever present comfort to me. Now that the ties that bind us together are drawn so closely I feel as if to live without you were to live devoid of everything calculated to make life happy; and that existence deprived of the sunshine of your smile, were worse than a desert without its green oasis. I hope, Nell, you will remember to invoke for your husband the protection of a beneficent Providence. I verily believe that Heaven would lend a listening ear to your petition and save from harm & danger the object of your heart's best love. Do not chide me for yet continuing to play the lover; for I feel that I have only *begun* in fact to love you. I did honestly think it was impossible for my affection to become deepened in its intensity, but I have learned that the love one bears a wife is higher & holier than any felt before this high relation exists.

I send by the boat some music for Evy & some note paper & envelopes for you. If I have not selected the proper size, set it down to my ignorance. When I shall have learned more, I will be able to do better. I send up some *green tea*; whether a good article or not I do not know. You can better judge when you try it. The "store" man said it was the *best* in his establishment; but his word is to be taken "cum grano salis"—anglicized with some *allowance* for his disposition to sell.

I find there is a decided tendency to Secession everywhere. Almost everyone I meet has come to the determination to vindicate the rights of our outraged section if need be at the point of bayonet. The Legislature had an informal meeting on Saturday last, and were *unanimous* for secession.

I shall hurry back home to kiss you as soon as possible & renew in person the assurances of my own increasing affection. Kiss *Ma*, Evie & Aby for me. May God in his infinite mercy have you in his most holy keeping & shower the choicest blessings of Heaven upon you, is the prayer of your devoted husband

Wm. L. Nugent

CHAPTER III

Stepping Stone to Higher Places

April 15, 1861–December 13, 1861

V.Burg, April 15th, 1861

My dear Wife,

I reached this place about 4 o'c. this evening, and drop you a line to let you know that the boat didn't blow up with me. No preventing Providence, I shall leave for Jackson on the train tomorrow. The telegraph this evening brings a proclamation of war from the "old rail splitter," with indications from different parts of the North of a warlike spirit. We are evidently in the midst of stirring times with the prospect of a long & bloody war ahead. The feeling for secession is, I think growing in the border states, and they will soon be with us. I send you the dispatches so that you may form your own opinions. You will see in the *Sun* (Weekly) my letter about the presentation of the flag.

Give love and kisses to all. Tell Alf I will try to see what I can do for him in the way of a commission in the Confederate Army—May God bless you is the prayer of your affec. husband.

Wm. L. Nugent

V.Burg, July 19th, 1861

My dear Wife,

I arrived here yesterday about 12 o'clock at night and found Capt. French here this morning, from whom I have received my appointment. I leave for Jackson this evening and will report myself to the Governor. In all probability I will be ordered to report myself to Genl. Dahlgren at Natchez.[1] His jurisdiction embraces, I think, our County and if so I may

---

[1]Nugent was appointed to a civilian position as Inspector General, a post charged with defense preparations. Edmonds, Nugent Family Papers. Samuel G. French and his wife owned Matilda Plantation on Deer Creek. He became a general in the Confederate Army. PWCHS, 246. C. G. Dahlgren headed the early defense preparations.

visit home before the trip is over. I will keep you advised of all my movements.

I feel very well in body and mind at this present writing, and have no doubt the trip will be beneficial to me in a good many respects. I will become acquainted with the people and the position will be a stepping stone to higher places. From present appearances this war will continue for sometime and every man will have to take up arms in defense of his country. The North seems to be as united as we; and the struggle, unless we defeat the enemy at the Virginia battleground will be almost interminable. We have glorious reports from Beauregard in Virginia this morning, tho' from all accounts Garnett has been severely whipped. We cannot, of course judge of the movements in Virginia, but the feeling here seems to be that we have deferred an advance too long. It will take two or three decided victories to put us in an attitude to demand recognition abroad, and we need expect no assistance outside ourselves for sometime.[2] The sheet anchor of our hopes can only be the stalwart arms and brave hearts of our soldiers. They and they alone can achieve our independence. Kentucky is gone over body and soul to the abolitionists and will soon, I fear, be arrayed against us. I would send you the papers but they will reach you by the packet on Sunday morning.

It will be impossible for me to say when I shall go; but you may direct your letters here to care Washington Hotel, or to Natchez care Dix, Nugent & Co.—I suspect I will leave Jackson tomorrow for Natchez and will return to this place in two weeks.

May God have you in his holy keeping & influence your heart to his service here so that you may continually abide in the assurance of a better life in the land of the blessed is, my dear little wife, the daily prayer of

Your devoted husband
W. L. Nugent

N.B.

I enclose a paper which please keep—it is my will & is made out of abundant caution & not that I expect soon to die. Such a step is necessary, at all times, in view of the uncertainty of life. In the will I leave you all I

---

[2]Nugent recognized early the possibility of a protracted war and the necessity for diplomatic recognition for the Confederacy.

have and appoint your Father my executor. Don't take this to heart.—
Every man keeps a will ready, and especially one circumstanced as I am.

Your ever
Will

On Board *Louisville*
July 24th, 1861

My dear Wife,

I wrote you from Vicksburg the other day and will drop you a line to let
you know that I am still in good health. I enjoyed my visit to Natchez very
much, having had the unexpected pleasure of meeting Sister Catherine at
Mrs. W. H. Dunbar.[3] I spent about 48 hours with her waiting for orders
from Genl. Dahlgren, who by the way, married a Miss Vamoy a connection
of yours—one of the Vamoy family of Nashville, Tennessee.

I suppose you have heard of the great victory at Manassas Gap. The
Federalists were defeated and chased for miles. I notice, though, they are
reorganizing and preparing *for a war to the death.* I scarcely think they will
reach Richmond by the first of January next. If God be for us, as I firmly
and conscientiously believe he is—who can prevail over us.

I will go from Vicksburg to Yazoo City—will return if possible in time to
take the *Mary Keene* on Monday next—no preventing Providence—and
hope to embrace my dear little wife again soon. The loss of my kiss three or
four times a day is sadly felt by me. To console myself for the lack of your
society I bo't *"Reveries of a Bachelor"*; but after trying its now nauseating
pages of a few minutes, shut it up in disgust and turned it over to a distant
young lady cousin in Natchez—Miss Mary Miller a pretty and agreeable
young miss—who has promised to come up and see us. I have promised to
show her some beaux, albeit she is yet a *school girl.* I find that all the books
in the world can't supply the place of a wife and especially one such as I
know my own dear Nellie to be.

The ladies everywhere are making socks for the soldiers in Virginia this

---

[3]Catherine was a half-sister of William, the daughter of Amelia (Forman) and John Pratt
Nugent. She married her cousin Richard Nugent, who was in the cotton business in Natchez.
Edmonds, Nugent Family Papers.

winter and I hope you all at home will become imbued with the same patriotic spirit.

I saw Bob Coleman drilling a battalion near Natchez yesterday. He is holding off for an office in the Confederate Army: I do not think he can get it. He is too young and headstrong I fear; hasn't judgment enough nor prudence.

I must close—the boat shakes badly and I have several other letters to write.

Love with kisses to Ma, Sis and Abe. May God in his infinite mercy shield, comfort and protect you is the prayer of

Your devoted husband
W.L. Nugent

Washington Hotel [Vicksburg]
Aug. 10th, 1861

My dear wife,

After quite a pleasant trip on the *Mary* and a good night's rest I find myself engaged in the pleasurable task of a "wee" talk with my little wife. Nothing of any interest occurred on my trip. Except the everlasting and tedious monotony of the River bank, the frequent screechings of the whistle; the repeated landings of the boat; and the hard jolt against the banks,—there was nothing that could have disturbed the equanimity of Dionysius. The grim old philosopher could have slept with dignified quiet in his "tub" and the petty annoyances above enumerated would have simply had the effect to stimulate the circulation of his blood. True it is the wharfboat at Providence may have excited his curiosity unlike as it is any handiwork of man to which his attention had been directed; but further than that his curiosity would have been wholly ungratified. One of my traveling companions was a crazy man on his way to Jackson; a sober, solemn, thoughtful personage who occupied the time by slowly promenading the gentleman's cabin, and staring at the refreshing sight of a sandy haired young lady thumbing the keys of a horrid piano with agonizing pertinacity.

I reached this place at about 12 o'clock P.M. and after a conversation with our friend Frank Valliant, in which the shortcomings of the Legislature were the main topic of conversation, retired to try the virtues of a hard bed.

I got a novel on the boat and passed yesterday pleasantly enough, I suppose, on that account. It was entitled "Philip Rundsfon", or Love on a Cruise—or something of the sort. A nautical story full of incidents, though very poorly written indeed. Anything though, to fill time when a man is separated from the idol of his heart and hammered about on an errand that has little of interest in it. I almost wish now that I had not accepted the position I occupy; but a man must do something, in such times as we are having, for his country & state, and if he doesn't fight he ought to work in other ways.

They have persuaded Madison McAfee to run for Governor and he will, I hope, defeat old Pettus by a handsome majority.[4] We are all getting sick and tired of our effete old Governor—he is a very "slow going coach" and want a little spice of a young Secessionist in his place. McAfee is a clean, intelligent, honest and energetic man; and will, I have no doubt, adorn the position. I shall be very busy during the day, and even until I return to you on Saturday next—which I hope to do, God willing.

There is no news here of interest except the attack made by the *Niagara* on Ship Island along the coast. She was driven off by a masked battery. I have become more than ever satisfied that the Yankees will make a desperate attempt to take Ship Island this fall so as to have free access to New Orleans. I hope and expect we may be able to keep them off.

My health is good—love to all kisses etc. May God in his mercy, have you ever in his holy keeping & protect you from all dangers is the prayer of

Your devoted husband
W. L. Nugent

Washington Hotel,
August 19th, 1861

My dear wife,

After rather a pleasant trip on the packet I reached this place, and have been engaged all the evening looking at the parades & evolutions of several companies that are going off for the wars. The emotions and thoughts that swelled my heart, as I looked at the stalwart frames of those who had

---

[4]McAfee did enter the contest, but withdrew, and Pettus was reelected. Robert W. Dubay, *John Jones Pettus, Mississippi Fire-Eater: His Life and Times, 1813–1867* (Jackson: University Press of Mississippi, 1975), 115–16.

embarked their all in the service of their Country, were conflicting and nearly overwhelming. And along with these feelings there is a kind of vindictive spirit that impels me to want to engage in the service of my Country right away. I feel that I would like to shoot a Yankee, and yet I know that this would not be in harmony with the Spirit of Christianity, that teaches to love our enemies & do good to them that despitefully use us and entreat us. The North will yet suffer for this fratricidal war she has forced upon us—Her fields will be desolated, her cities laid waste and the treasures of her citizens dissipated in the vain attempt to subjugate a free people. Our armies will yet teach the Quakers of the Keystone State that they are not inaccessible. The two boats *Prince* & *Charm* go up tomorrow with the Warren Artillery & Swamp Rangers. They go up the Arkansas or St. Francis River on the way to Missouri, and from their appearance will acquit themselves with credit.

There is no war news here of any movement. Beauregard is gradually advancing upon Washington City, preparing everything for the grand attack, and will level the Capitol to the ground. The necessity for destroying the city is imperative. In Europe it will give us a great advantage, will destroy the resources of the Federal government and conquer a peace. It is useless, I think, to base any calculations upon the reaction at the North; the peace party wants *reconstruction* and not the recognition of the Southern Confederacy. We must whip the North and in my opinion we can do it. There is no use in disguising the truth. The contest is narrowed down to single issue; with us it is life or death. A great many sanguine persons think otherwise; I cannot.[5]

You must not think, my dear wife, that I forget you while my head is so much engaged in cogitations about the war. The persuasion that it will be the cause of a temporary separation from you is very afflicting to me indeed. I cannot think of leaving for the war without sad emotions. I could much more readily die if I had the satisfaction of leaving an heir behind me to take my name and represent me hereafter in the affairs of men. What boots this tho'? One cannot die too soon in the discharge of his duty, and then the chances are rather favorable to escape. The God who protects me in the peaceful walks of every day life, can avert from my person the balls & bullets of the enemy.

---

[5]Nugent's excessive optimism in this letter was not characteristic of his usual somber view.

I leave for Yazoo City tomorrow at noon and will return as soon as possible so as to get the *Quitman* on Friday night & be at home on Saturday. Love & Kisses to all.

May God in his infinite mercy, bless, comfort & protect you is the daily prayer of

Your devoted husband
W. L. Nugent

V.Burg, Miss. Nov. 4th, 1861

My dear wife,

Circumstances have transpired that may necessitate my remaining in Jackson two or three days, and you mustn't confidently expect me home before about Friday.

I arrived here "safe and sound" after a long and tiresome trip, and leave in a few moments on the cars.

Take care of yourself and believe that every moment of my life is gladdened by a knowledge of the excellence and affection of my dear little wife. May God continually bless, comfort, preserve & protect you is the prayer of

Your devoted husband
W. L. Nugent

On Board *Ohio Belle*
Tuesday Dec. 10th, 1861

My dearest Wife,

As we are approaching Memphis the opportunity of sending my greeting and affectionate sympathy in all your little complaints is too good a one to be lost. So far we have had a comparatively comfortable trip, having only about one hundred and fifty negroes aboard. We have moderately fair accommodations on board, have plenty to eat & a mattress, one sheet & a pair of blankets. We will not reach Fort Pillow before Wednesday and will thus, I fear, be compelled to defer our return home until after Christmas—much to my regret as the days at Fort Pillow, away from her who is the nearest to my heart, will seem to be months. Big Charles was a little complaining on yesterday, but I straightened him up with the quinine

I providently procured in Greenville.[6] I have given a dose for this morning and one to take before retiring tonight and he will, he says, be "all right" by reason thereof.

Nothing of any interest has yet happened except that at Beulah we took Eugene Montgomery on board.[7] His lively talk and merry laugh however much it may relieve the tedium of the hour will not compensate our pleasant evenings around our humble hearth. Oh! who would be so blind as to prefer a life of single blessedness?

The River is rising rapidly; but the rapid march of Price upon St. Louis has drawn the Cairo troops back to Missouri. We need, though, have no immediate fear of an attack on Columbus. The troops are going into winter quarters at Columbus and Bowling Green I hear and we may have a visit from Alf this winter the Yankees not preventing.

The lowering clouds portend anything but favorable weather above and I fear we will have some difficulty in working on the fortifications. The people seem to be lulled into a fancied security about Washington County. Bolivar has responded nobly to the call for negroes and has done more than her share. We are yet holding back from pure unvarnished selfishness and may yet have to rue the day we were so backward in the discharge of our simple duty. My humble conviction is that we have not yet seen the beginning of the end of this war. Years will pass ere the smoking of the ruins will disappear. Tears of anguish are yet to be shed, and homes remain to be desolated. May God in his infinite mercy avert the calamity from us. Be brave, my dear little wife, and if you have the assistance of that divine mercy & grace the true value of which misfortune alone teaches us properly to appreciate, "all will be well."

I will write to you as soon as we get up to Fort Pillow—Kiss Ma & Aby for me—regards to all. And now may He who pours the oil of joy & consolation into the bereaved heart & the troubled mind, safely & securely have you in the hollow of his hand, is the ardent prayer of him who seeks no higher honor than to subscribe himself

Your devoted husband
W. L. Nugent

---

[6]Big Charles was a Smith field hand.

[7]Beulah was a Bolivar County landing on the Mississippi River. Eugene Montgomery was of Locust Plantation, and he delivered the Nugent letters after the war to Nugent's daughter.

Fort Pillow
Dec. 13th, 1861

Dearest Nellie,

I wrote you on Wednesday or Friday night from on Board the Steamer *Ohio Belle* and now write again to redeem a promise made to you at that time as well as to advise you of our safe arrival here. We were detained at Memphis all day and didn't get here until Thursday morning. We pitched our tents immediately and went to work. Our negroes are well provided with tents, and have plenty to eat. Since I arrived here, the necessity for immediate and energetic action about here has presented itself to mind in such a manner that I have given out my notion of going to Columbus and have turned to overseeing regularly—and I flatter myself with some small success. We are working like Trojans; and if our planters were aware of the magnitude and necessity of the works here they would respond promptly to the call made upon them. Some of the North Mississippi planters have worked here 100 days with all their effective male force. Fort Pillow is a point of very hilly country embracing three or 4,000 acres of land with batteries in front about two tiers and surrounded in the rear by seven & a half miles of embankment, on the inside of which is a level road 30 feet wide and on the outside a deep ditch say 20 feet deep. When it is remembered that the timber had to be cut and cleaned from the whole route and a mile in front cut down and piled crosswise so as to prevent the approach of an army in the rear, you may well judge of what had to be done. Much yet remains to be done here and *elsewhere*. Those who have sent voluntarily are well off; but I sincerely pity those who will hereafter certainly be *forced* to send maybe to Columbus. The talk among the officials is that Genl. Polk astonished and mortified at the lack of patriotism among the planters intends sending peremptory orders with an officer & an armed squad to execute them. It is calculated that two hundred guns of flying artillery and about 5,000 men can defend this place *if finished* against an army of 30,000 men.

The rumor prevailed here that the enemy were advancing on Columbus tho' it is discredited.

I am writing in my tent with the stub of a pencil on the rough top of a box and with a candlestick made by cutting a hole in the box. We will be home by Christmas. I have to mend my pants tonight and am tired with climbing hills.

May God bless, keep, preserve and comfort you is the prayer of

Your devoted husband
William

Kiss all at home for me.

CHAPTER IV

An Imperious Necessity

March 19, 1862–July 12, 1862

Headquarters Wash. Cavalry
V.Burg, March 19th, 1862

My dear wife,

We arrived here safe & in good condition on yesterday about noon, pitched our tents, stabled our horses and began camp life in earnest.[1] So far everything has progressed finely; a state of harmony and good feeling appears to prevail; and the men generally evince a disposition to be good soldiers. Very little cursing is heard and no drunkenness. Yesterday evening & this morning I offered up my first military camp prayer for the preservation of my own life, if consistent with the will of God, and the assistance and comforting support of our Heavenly Father for my dear wife. I do not know whether I shall be able to return home or not; but as the Company will have some business to wind up, I presume I shall have the pleasure of seeing you again soon. Ma left just as we were landing much to my regret as I wanted to kiss her before leaving for the war and again ask the support of her prayers. I hope tho' to return soon: the prevailing impression seems to be that the war will soon be over—will last no longer than six months—and will be concluded with the coming campaign. I presume we all wish such a hopeful result and the wish is father to the thought I fear. We are encamped in this city and will remain here until Friday, when the cry will be—ho! for Jackson. The people here were much astonished at our having only one officer believing it impossible to control so large a number of men.[2] I believe I can say, without exaggeration, that

---

[1]Nugent enlisted March 9, 1862, for three years or the duration of the war. Early his unit was called Captain George T. Blackburn's Company of Cavalry. Officially it was designated Company D, 28th Mississippi Cavalry. Nugent referred to the unit as Washington Cavalry. Confederate Archives, Chapter I, File No. 82, Record Group 109, the National Archives, Washington, D.C. Hereinafter cited as Confederate Archives, R.G. 109.

[2]The only officer was George T. Blackburn who was elected in Greenville prior to departure. Blackburn had been sheriff of Washington County, and after the war became owner of Oakwood Plantation. PWCHS, 169, 243.

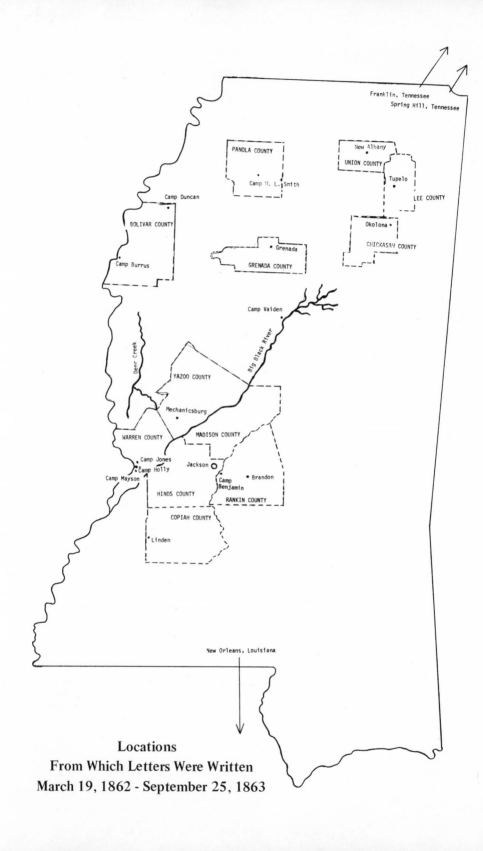

Franklin, Tennessee
Spring Hill, Tennessee

PANOLA COUNTY

Camp M. L. Smith

New Albany

UNION COUNTY

Tupelo

LEE COUNTY

Camp Duncan

BOLIVAR COUNTY

Okolona

CHICKASAW COUNTY

Camp Burrus

Grenada

GRENADA COUNTY

Camp Vaiden

Deer Creek

Big Black River

YAZOO COUNTY

Mechanicsburg

WARREN COUNTY

MADISON COUNTY

Camp Jones
Camp Holly

Jackson

Brandon

Camp Mayson

Camp
Benjamin

HINDS COUNTY

RANKIN COUNTY

COPIAH COUNTY

Linden

New Orleans, Louisiana

Locations
From Which Letters Were Written
March 19, 1862 - September 25, 1863

the members of the Company were better behaved than any I have yet seen. One or two were *slightly* inebriate on the Boat, but none were drunk. I am in hopes they will continue to behave as well; but who can predict ahead the behavior of soldiers, influenced as it always is by a thousand accidental circumstances. Today they are all smiles; tomorrow devils incarnate almost. We haven't yet begun to drill, and the probability is we will not begin until we reach Jackson, Miss. I saw Col. Starke here on yesterday for a few moments, but was entirely too busy to have any protracted conversation with him.[3] I wanted very much to learn the probable destination of his Regiment, and the day of our departure for the seat of war. He doesn't wish to carry an undrilled Regiment into active service and expose them to the consequences of a battle when the fight will be hand to hand & by squads of soldiers who do not support one another. What position we will have in the Regiment I do not know; but we hope we will have that of honor, whether dangerous or not. We cannot all survive; and He who "guides the whirlwind & controls the storm" can as well preserve us in the battle's front as beneath the shade of our own fig tree following in an unpretentious way the peaceful occupations of private life. This is a sustaining thought to me and braces me up to a patient endurance of the inconveniences of my present mode of life, to which nothing but a love of country & a sense of duty would have ever reduced me.

There is nothing new of any great importance. We have evacuated New Madrid, and ascended to Island 10; and rumor has it this morning that the officer in command of Island 10 has lost the fort by being drunk. I do not believe this, however, as the importance of the Post required and I think must have secured the services of the best officer in the Service. Martial Law is declared in N. O. and Jackson and a feeling prevails that the former place will be attacked very heavily soon. Recent disasters can afford us very little hope of a successful termination of the fight for us. "Hope on, Hope ever" must be our motto, and diligence our watchword—By determined action and prompt responses to the calls of our country we will yet whip the Yankees, and thus vindicate the position we have taken.

---

[3]Peter B. Starke lived in Bolivar County. He served as state senator for Bolivar, Washington, Issaquena, and Yazoo Counties for the 1857–61 period. Starke early commanded Nugent's unit. Starke allegedly fell into disrepute after the war for his affiliation with the Republicans. Florence W. Sillers (comp.), *History of Bolivar County, Mississippi* (Jackson: Hederman Brothers, 1948), 107–108.

Remember, My dear wife, to keep up a cheerful, hopeful spirit as much for the child you will soon bear me as for my and your sake. A giving way to grief will have an unhappy effect upon all of us, and will result in no good. I get along bravely and readily accommodate myself to surrounding circumstances. I expect before long to be at home a civilian once more, and to travel over in yr. company the same loved routine of my former life; to while away the evenings around our family hearth and kiss the expected babe. The tracings of the pencil will be effaced if I write much further.

Look, my dear wife, to religion to sustain you, and give your absent husband who invokes them the prayers of a devout Christian. It will comfort and relieve me exceedingly. And now may our Father in Heaven bless, comfort, support & gladden your heart is the constant prayer of your

Devoted husband
W. L. Nugent

Headquarters Wash. Cavalry
V.Burg, March 22/62

My dear, dear Nellie,

I wrote to you a day or two ago and write again by Brother Barton so that you may know I am still well.[4] We have just got our saddles and leave for Jackson tomorrow morning by 8 o'clock. I have been very busy since my arrival and now have only time to write a few lines. I am hearty and getting fat very fast. I am rapidly becoming accustomed to a sleep on the ground, and hope that I will experience no great inconvenience from it. I was defeated by an electioneering scheme for 1st Lieut: but my friends stuck to me and elected me to the Junior 2nd Lieutenancy. When I see you I will explain the matter freely.

Love & kisses. Tell Ma to write to me and write a long *cheerful* letter—I am called off—May God bless & comfort you is the daily prayer of

Yr. devoted husband
Will

Remember my last injunction to be cheerful. I fully believe I will return safely home. I send as good a picture as I can get here and will send a letter from Jackson.

---

[4]Barton was the Methodist minister who performed Nugent's marriage ceremony.

Camp Benjamin
Jackson, Miss. March 28, 1862

My own dear Nellie,

I can heartily, my dear wife, respond to the opening sentence of your letter of the 24th and say Oh! Nellie, you don't know how sad & lonely I am without you. During the day like you I am kept very busy and have very little time to indulge any gloomy thoughts; and even at night there are continual calls upon me for first one thing and then another, that occupy the greater portion of my time. The routine of camp duties is quite onerous and require constant attention. We have comfortable wall tents with flyers, plenty of food to eat, tolerably good water, and enough drilling to keep us healthy. Our company is called the "Washington Cavalry", Ben Johnson 1st, Judge Nelson 2nd, and myself Jun. second 2nd Lieuts.[5] I haven't had an opportunity of visiting my kinsfolk here yet, but hope to do so soon. I imagine that I will get something good to eat by going to see them, and you may well imagine my great anxiety on the subject. I went up town today to take a bath, & have my hair cut, whiskers trimmed and put on some clean clothes. I now feel very comfortable and can go to work *cum amore et vigore.*

I am rejoiced to hear you are so well pleased with Cousin Emily. She is an excellent lady, is well educated, a pleasant companion, and will be a source of immense advantage to you in every point of view. Some of our connections think her an *infidel,* but I do not quite believe it; and besides I hope you are so well grounded in your religious opinions that you may rely entirely upon yourself and not rely upon others. I would have my darling little wife, above all other things a meek, consistent and humble Christian. In my present mode of life, I have great need of the comforting influences of the prayers of a pious wife. They encourage me not a little, & infuse into my heart greater hopes of a safe and speedy return to my home.

I am extremely glad to learn that you are, for my sake, taking a lively interest in my little affairs at home. By taking the rounds of the garden daily and noticing the budding trees, the growing vegetables, and blooming

---

[5]Ben Johnson was a member of a prominent Washington County family who had migrated from Kentucky. John Nelson was a lawyer before and after the war in Greenville. PWCHS, 277, 347.

grape vines, your time will pass pleasantly away. In the evening a quiet talk in the bed room followed by drawing and painting might give you a refreshing sleep.

Our trip from V.Burg to Jackson was tedious & dusty. We rode about 22 miles the first day and crossed Big Black River in a common ferry boat, officers and men working away as common hands. All along the road we were greeted with smiles & God bless yous of the ladies, the presentation of small flags, and the hospitality of the planters whenever we stopped. As we rode thru V.Burg on the Sabbath the Congregation of the Episcopal Church came out to see us pass and the tears filled up my eyes as I looked upon the House of God. When shall I again be privileged to go up to the Church to worship?

I wrote to you from V.Burg twice & sent as good a picture as I could. I will have another taken here as soon as I get my uniform and will send it up to be shown to our little son (?) after while. Don't be angry with me for again reminding you to be cheerful. A sad heart and a saddened countenance are never good for a person in your condition.

Wash is getting along finely; makes a good servant and seems to be very contented. He hasn't been sick a day. I enjoy my life very well and will like it better when I make the acquaintance of all the officers in the Regiment. Capt. Scales is a kinsman and a thorough gentleman. He has invited me over to see him, and I will go as soon as I can get a little leisure. I am endeavoring to familiarize myself with the duties of my position and with those that belong to *higher* positions—who knows what I may be before long.

My candle is nearly out. I must close as I rise before day. Be cheerful, my brave little wife, I will come back to you if I can. I am getting along well—May God Almighty bless & cherish, & protect you in the hour of peril is the prayer of

Your devoted husband
Will

P.S.

See Cousin Betty Shelby and ask her to make me a mattress like Dr. Talbott's.[6] I am privileged to carry it now. Tell Mr. Smith to send down to

---

[6]Betty Shelby was Mrs. Thomas Shelby and a close friend of the Smiths. PWCHS, 96.

William Lewis Nugent in Confederate uniform. Letter of April 10, 1862, stated that he turned the coat collar down to look less military to please his wife and suggested that she might color it, which she did.

Mr. Blackman's & get my Bridle bit; he will have a chance to send it to me soon. Kiss Ma & Cousin Emily for me.

Good night—

Camp Benjamin
April 1st, 1862

My own dear little wife,

Poets have often spoken of the winning influence of pet names, and I never feel that my fond devotion can be so adequately expressed, as when, to relieve the misery of our necessary separation, I call you my own little wife. Not little in the sense of a precious consort, & agreeable companion; for in this you fill every sacred corner of my heart. Nor in those qualities of mind & heart that make a husband lose the enjoyment of the present in contemplation of a long life of prospective happiness; for there is no thought more frequently uppermost in my heart than that which in imagination places us after this fraticidal war is over, beneath our "own vine & fig tree:" cultivating the gifts which God has given us for usefulness & happiness and cozily brushing away all points of divergence between us. Little only in that best & to me dearest of all senses, *Size.* I scarcely think I do right in thus speaking in a way to draw to your eyes the pearly tears that, I am satisfied, are swimming on the brim of your heart continually; but it may be some compensation for my absence to know that thoughts of loved ones at home constitute the refrain of my waking songs & burden of my nightly dreams. At evening when the duties of the day are over, I sometimes feel oppressed with sympathy for you in your present delicate situation; and leaning against my tent pole I invoke the narcotic influences of my pipe to carry my mind far away into the ideal pleasures of dreamland. And the picture I always paint has one grand central picture around which I fondly love to delineate all that is beautiful and bright. Verily there is "no place like home," especially when the home is the abode of the partner of one's bosom. To it the mind ever reverts when the cares of life burden us.

I am now in the very objectionable position of Lieutenant of the Guard, and have a fussy, drunken man in the Guard Tent to watch. Every now & then he gets sick and affords me some relief; but it is truly annoying to be bothered with the continued mouthing of a brute. If he were sober it would be different, and the annoyance of guarding him might be relieved by an occasional nap. Tonight I will be compelled to sleep in the Guard Tent or on some boxes and be up every two hours. As it is only for one night though I do not care and besides I didn't go "a soldiering" for the fun of the thing. Nothing but an imperious necessity drove me into the ranks of the army, and I expect to remain in the army until the necessity for an army of volunteers ceases to exist.

I have worked hard since I came here with a double purpose—to acquire the information necessary for my position and to get a furlough to go home about the middle of April. I don't think this will be refused unless we receive marching orders, which is now very unlikely for sometime. Col. Starke says he is determined not to move until his Regiment is well organized and drilled. There are here encamped at present six companies & others are daily expected. We get our water from Pearl River and eat baker's bread & pickled beef. Strange to say I am fattening on it.

I sent you a picture from V.Burg; but as it is not a good one I will have a new one taken here and forward it to you at the earliest opportunity. Capt. Blackburn has returned from N.O. and will send up also five hundred dollars to keep you going for twelve months in these days of economising. Please say to Mr. S. that he can get the Treasury notes here to pay his taxes in lieu of Gold & Silver and get an advance on his cotton. The cotton money is circulating very freely here and is regarded as our best currency. Write to me & tell me all about *yourself* and *home*. Love & Kisses—May God Almighty bless, comfort, & protect you is the prayer of

Your devoted husband
Will

St. Charles Hotel [New Orleans]
April 10th, 1862

My own dear Nellie,

I have been here for several days on business for the Regiment and had hoped to reach Jackson in time to send you a letter by Mr. Haycraft who leaves for Greenville Friday; as it is, however, I am compelled to remain here today. A boat goes up this evening & I snatched a few moments this morning before business hours to write you a short letter. I sent up by Mr. Haycraft a very good photographic likeness, which you and Cousin Emily may be able to color if you like; I turned down my collar in deference to

Alfred Cox Smith, brother of Eleanor, served briefly with the Mississippi Cavalry, fought in the battle of Shiloh.

your wishes to hide the *soldier* & display the civilian in all his *charms*, but I noticed the "high falutin doings" on the sleeve showed itself a little. I send up along with this, another print in which nothing of the soldier appears at all. I think the likeness very good; a little *paint* might make it better; and if you desire a portrait I can easily order one to be painted. The artist has the negative and can supply as many prints as you may wish either plain or colored. As soon as I reach Jackson I shall apply for a short furlough to go home and see you, and have very little doubt of my success. Col. Starke will give me one if he can possibly do so. Judging from the present pressure and seeking for arms, we will not be equipped for a month and hence will remain at Jackson Miss. for that length of time. The mosquitoes are becoming somewhat annoying already, and will trouble us exceedingly unless we can get netting enough to make us bars. Please ask Ma to get the netting at Penrice's and make a bar for me and Clarence immediately.

My health continues very good, thank Providence, and everything so far has worked auspiciously. I believe that God in his goodness, will bring me safely through the present troubles and give me a happy deliverance from the numerous perils with which I am surrounded; but you, my darling one, have no unimportant part to play in it. May God abundantly bless, & comfort you & gently lead you, by the influences of his holy spirit, to a closer walk with him. Prayer is the most powerful lever known in the administration of the moral government of man, and can secure to us all blessings consistent with God's will.

I regretted very much to hear of Will Scott's death; he has gone to reap the reward of the faithful as he died in full hopes of reaching Heaven. May we all so live as to join him hereafter. Mrs. Sallie Cox is dead, and her family, including a five months baby, is in town at Judge Cocks. . . .[7]

Kiss Ma & Abe for me—Love to all. Be cheerful; look ahead; trust in God; & pray continually for your absent &

Devoted husband
W. L. Nugent

---

[7]The Yazoo County members of the family spelled the name Cocks; the Washington County members spelled it Cox. Cox Bible.

Jackson, Miss. April 17, 1862

My own dear Nellie,

I have had a full conference with Col. Starke in reference to going up home, and he says he will let me go and see you. There are so many applications for furloughs, however, that he thinks the example will have a bad effect; and if you can get along without me, he would prefer it. If you think it better for me to come and your time will come off in a few days, send a special messenger down. Mr. Haycraft would come & I would pay his expenses here & back. Don't fail in this as I wouldn't like to be the cause of any unpleasant feelings in the Regiment; for Col. Starke has treated me with uniform kindness since I came and will I have no doubt, do all he can to promote my interests. I want to go home and that with a *good excuse* and for a *sufficient reason*. Send down a special messenger as soon as you think the time is at hand, and I will come up by first opportunity. It is next to impossible to get a boat down stream now and I might be detained a long time. We are now taking lessons daily in the saber exercise and Col. thinks I had better remain here until I can ascertain in the manner proposed the time when I should come up. The justice of this thought is apparent and now especially when I am compelled to learn the men everything new. I had to drill them at the start and will have to keep it up! This is *hard* when considered from a selfish standpoint; but then I went into this war not for personal emolument. The only motive was to do my country some good. And when such a man as Genl. Beauregard has achieved such renown when acting as second in command, there is some room for me to acquire some credit even as 3rd Lieutenant, a post which my enemies now admit is far below my deserts. Better far, tho' to begin low, to take the lowest seat and be invited higher than take the highest & be invited *lower*. It is a source of some consolation to know that the members of the Company have bitterly repented putting me low down. If God will but protect me thru' this war and bring me safely to my dear wife's home once more, I will be satisfied with the humblest offices.

My health continues to be very good, albeit I have for the first time, had one of my headaches today. This hasn't troubled me very much; and you will believe it when I tell you that I have been drilling & being drilled the entire day. I have become reconciled to a soldier's life, for I believe conscientiously that I am in the discharge of duty and that God will, out of his abundant mercy, grant me a safe return home to the embraces of her who is dearer to me than life itself. I feel when I pray that a merciful Providence is over us and that all things will work together for good if we are only righteous. I have but a few moments to write and the messenger is waiting for this letter. Be cheerful; write often and just as you feel; your letters distil into my heart the very essence of a sympathetic consolation. Love & kisses. And now, my more than precious darling, may He who "tempers the wind to the shorn lamb" have you in his holy keeping is the daily prayer of your devoted husband

Will

All well; will write to Ma soon.

V.Burg, Miss. April 19th, 1862

My own dear Nellie,

I am sent to V.Burg today on special business to return this evening. I send you by Mr. Montgomery four hundred dollars to buy anything you may need.[8] Mr. Smith can put it in the safe for you.

I am in fine health and as good spirits as possible under the circumstances. I long to see you safely thru your hour of trial. May God bless and give you a safe deliverance. Let me know if I must come up. The difficulty of getting back is so great that Col. Starke doesn't want me to go unless it is absolutely necessary. Love & Kisses.

Pray for me.
In haste
Yr. devoted husband
Will

Camp Benjamin
April 24/62

My own dear wife,

I send up by Mr. Archer a letter from Mr. Smith giving all needful information in reference to Alf.[9]

---

[8]William P. Montgomery.

[9]Stevenson Archer was a Methodist minister who served well the people of Washington County during the war. He conducted the funeral services for Abram F. Smith and wrote a newspaper account of his life. Clipping in possession of LSH. Alf enlisted in the service in January 1862 and fought in the Battle of Shiloh. Smith Diary.

I still continue well as does Clarence. Wash is a little complaining. We are getting along well. And hope to become perfected in drill soon. When we will move is a matter of great doubt—The news that N.O. is in danger may hurry us up a little but I scarcely think we will leave for a month—I will be up next week & will write by Mr. Smith who goes thru' here in a day or so—

May God bless, comfort & preserve you is the prayer of

Yr. devoted husband
Will

Jackson, April 28/62

My dear wife,

Your Pa is here now and leaves for home tomorrow, and I have thought it better to write as my failure to go home may occasion some alarm. Since my last I have been appointed as Adjutant at this Post, a place of great responsibility & importance. I am, therefore, kept continually at work, and Col. Starke says he cannot spare me. Lieut. Col. Ferguson says he can't spare me well from the Regiment;[10] & the consequence is that I am not permitted to go home; The Army Regulations limit my absence to seven days and I could hardly go home & return now in less than eight days. The assault of the Yankee Gun Boat has so interferred with navigation that I would be compelled to return in a skiff by way of the Sunflower River. I need not tell you how much I feel the ill-effects of Col. Starke's refusal, and I am only constrained quietly to submit because of the persistent disposition manifested by officers generally to shirk their duties. There are others in the Regiment similarly situated with me, and they have been refused a furlough. And besides I occupy the enviable and unenviable position of *knowing too much.* If I were less acquainted with my duties I would stand a better chance. I feel assured, however, that God will answer my prayers and bring you safely thru' with all your troubles. The feeling is impressed strongly upon my mind at everytime I kneel before the throne of Grace, and I feel a sweet assurance that God will grant us, in a good time coming, the boon of a blessed re-union. To the familiar scenes of home; my mind

---

[10]Samuel W. Ferguson was a prominent Washington County citizen who succeeded Starke as commander. He later was a general, and his unit was called Ferguson's Brigade.

continually reverts with the longing of a schoolboy after the hearth stone of his mother, and around one little room I find my eye yet traces the handiwork of my brave and gentle little wife. Her image is stamped in living colors on my heart, and with each recurring day, she becomes the dearest object of my heart's fondest hopes: without whom 'twere vain to suspect anything of enjoyment from the future. And when I think that my dear little wife will soon become a mother, I am truly proud in anticipation tho' exceedingly anxious withal. I would give anything to be privileged to be with you in your hour of trial; but as this cannot now be, for my sake & your sake & the sake of your expected offspring be cheerful, be brave, be hopeful, trust in the goodness of God and "all will be well!" The dangers are not so many as you imagine and with the assistance of a skillful physician, I do not think you need be alarmed. I am enjoying fine health, and get along as well as possible under the circumstances. I shall not feel entirely relieved until I hear from home once more. Evie is in Baton Rouge and I will have to make some arrangements to get her here.[11] I will take care of her until an opportunity offers to send her home. Mr. McKatten sent me a telegram to go after her, but I couldn't do it. We have no arms here yet and there is no telling when we will get them. We are drilling, however, and hope to be soon placed in a situation to do our Country some service.

Love & kisses. Don't be afraid of the Yankees; they won't be apt to hurt you. May God Almighty bless, preserve & protect you is the prayer of

Your devoted husband
Will

Camp Benjamin
Jackson, Miss. May 2/64

My darling wife,

I received your letter this evening and write a reply tho' I sadly fear it will never reach you until this war is ended. Your Pa & Alf who went up home a few days since will acquaint you with the condition of things here; and more particularly with the brevity of my letters. We rise at 5 o'clock in

---

[11]Nugent demonstrated a protective attitude toward Evie on several occasions. He was especially fearful of travel by the teen-ager.

the morning, drill nearly two hours, are recalled at 7½ o'clock, get breakfast, guard mounting at 8, at nine I am compelled to go to my Post
Adjutant's Office in Town where I am generally kept as busy as a bee until
3½ o'clock P.M., when I return to Camp & drill until Dress Parade at Sun
Set. Frequently I am kept busy until eleven o'clock at night; and being
compelled to study my tactics I have, as you will doubtless perceive, very
little leisure. In fact I feel generally wearied and tired to death at nightfall
& am more disposed to sleep and dream of the loved ones at home, than to
do anything else. On this account I am fearful that I will rather be tiresome
than otherwise. You need not attribute this to any lack of affection, for my
affection is rather deepened than lessened by absence. I feel a kind of
yearning after home scenes, home joys & particularly my little wife. Mrs.
Theobald gave you rather a gloomy account of me. The truth is that seeing
her & hearing the boys sing "Annie Laurie" made me feel anxious and
uneasy about you and you will hardly blame me for the feeling. I would be
dead to the better feelings that move the souls of the patriot Soldier, if I
did not constantly feel solicitously about the welfare & safety of those for
whom I have bared my arm in the struggle. We are getting along very well;
and if we only had arms could be of some service to our Country. Gen.
Beauregard has ordered us to report for duty as soon as we can obtain arms;
but we find it very difficult to do anything. Genl. Lovell interrupted the
shipment of arms to our Regiment, or we would have had some five
hundred sabres in the hands of soldiers. As it is we are compelled to "labor
and to wait." This does not worry me much, because I am used to it, I
think we need greater efficiency in drill. Soldier's fare is better than that at
the Hotels in Town, & hence we hear very little complaint in Camp, tho'
some will grumble occasionally. We are in daily expectation of a fight at
Vicksburg and Corinth—at which points we are fearful of the results. The
capture of New Orleans has had a very disastrous effect upon us. It will
open the whole River to Northern Vandals, and you may expect to see
thousands of flatboats coming down the River loaded with produce. As you
will have nothing but Confederate money to buy with, however, I do not
see that it will help you any. I greatly fear that you will have a hard time of
it if the water goes over you. I can, I feel, humbly trust you in the hands of
Providence, being satisfied that all things will work together for good.

I send this letter by Tom but am fearful he will never get home. Rest
assured that I will keep so busy that the blues cannot hurt; and that amid

all the labors & vicissitudes of life I am ever & will be to the end devoted to you. You have my *whole* heart & reign supreme in my affections. Love & Kisses. May God bless & have your all in his most holy keeping is the daily prayer of

Your ever fond & faithful husband
Will

Camp Benjamin
May 11th, 1862

My dear wife,

Your letter of the 5th May came safely; and to say that I occasioned excessive pleasure, would convey a very faint idea of the real enjoyment I experienced. The numerous reports which you have heard of my being sad, doubtless originated in my always wearing a look of anxiety superinduced by the delicate state of your health. If I only knew that you were safely through with your expected trial I would be very happy, indeed. The separation from you I could well bear without a murmur, from the fact that a sense of duty to my Country bears me up; and I am also well satisfied that we will soon have the good fortune to greet one another again "under our own vine and fig tree" "with none to molest or make us afraid." I do not look forward to an interminable contest. We will know the worst before the expiration of a twelvemonth, and will either be defeated or prevail over our enemies. The issue of the battle on the Potomac and that near Corinth will go far towards reconciling the conflicting interests. I do not think that England will permit the re-establishment of the Union. Her interests are diametrically opposed to such a consummation, and her actions usually follow the leadings of her interests. The power of both governments manifested in the present war has amazed foreign nations; and induced the well-founded belief, that unless lessened by the division of the country and the protraction of the war, it would seriously jeopardize the balance of power in Europe.

I did not go to Greenville because Col. Starke said he couldn't let me; that my assistance in the Office in Jackson was necessary for the public good; and that my place couldn't be supplied. As I had sworn to do a soldier's duty, honestly and faithfully to the best of my ability, I could make no further application when approached in this manner. You need not feel, for a moment, that I will not go home until the war is over;—opportunities will offer before long I am satisfied and when offered I shall gladly avail myself of them. We have been separated not quite two months; and how many thousands are worse off. I do not say this to remonstrate with you at all, because the anxiety expressed in your letter to see me is a sure indication of your devoted affection, the expression of which in your letters affords me more true heart-felt gratification than everything else besides. You will before long tho', I hope, have an opportunity to see me. Events are hurrying one another along so rapidly that we cannot tell what a day may bring forth. It may be that the seat of war will be transferred to the Mississippi Valley, and our Company be called upon to operate in Washington County. Our Company is ordered to Vicksburg, but Col. Starke intends retaining me at Jackson as Post Adjutant. As the fighting will be pretty lively there, I presume you will prefer my being out of harm's way; I would prefer, however, being with my Company. The men seem to want me with them and express a remarkable confidence in me. They say they were fooled in me by third parties, and doubtless they were. I am satisfied, though that everything will work out right in the long run.

Mrs. Theobald has little to do to tell you I was the saddest man she ever saw.[12] The anxiety that preys upon my mind on your account and will continue to prey upon it, until you are over with your "trial", doubtless keeps me from appearing in a good humor continually; but it is not correct to say I am sad. I have never concealed one thought from you, and never will knowingly. The experience of more than a year of married life ought to have satisifed you that I would not conceal a cause of sadness if it existed. At one time I was rather unpleasantly situated in the Company, being junior Commissioned officer & compelled to see my superior committing errors in drilling which I could not correct. The Company saw it and were continually telling me of it. How to steer clear of the controversy was a source of continual thought to me, and gave a great deal of annoyance. The Captain took the matter in hand, however, and we are getting along smoothly. Rest assured, my darling, little wife, that you never occasioned me anything but pleasure. Your long and confiding letters are like a soothing balm to a wounded heart. Whatever of real trouble I have I shall let you know, but I cannot at present trouble your mind with little petty

---

[12]Nugent protested on several occasions erroneous reports of his personal or professional activities.

trifles that distance would magnify into mountains. You are not the cause of any trouble to me at all; on the contrary I am kept up by the hope of seeing my little wife again "when the war is over" or sooner.

Dr. Finlay had very little to do to force you in your delicate condition away from home on a tramp to the plantation. It was, I think, a rare exhibition of selfishness. Of what advantage would a trio of masons be against a Yankee gunboat. I scarcely think they would have risked it; and the trepidation of the people resulted, and could result in nothing but harm. I hope when Alf's health is better you will enjoy yourself in his society better and now that Evie is at home you will doubtless get along better, at least I believe so.[13]

Cheer up, my dear wife, and bear the privations which the exigencies of our Country have forced upon us bravely—And now may God bless, comfort & preserve you is the prayer of

> Yr. devoted & own faithful
> husband
> Will

Kiss Ma & Evie for me—Love to all. Clarence is well & Wash.

[On the back of the page]

This letter was written to be sent up by Penrice. He forgot all his promises, however, & went away without it. You perhaps know the reason of his forgetfulness.

> Jackson, Miss. May 18/62

My dear wife,

I began this letter on yesterday & was cut short by continued calls upon me. In consequence I only wrote "My dear wife" and quit. I regret it the more because Mr. Morris was going direct to Greenville and would have carried the letter to "headquarters" for me.[14] Here I am stuck down hard and fast as the saying is, a Post Adjutant with plenty of hard work, hard fare, and no glory,—except what comes from diligent attention to my duties. Our Company has gone to V.Burg to repel the enemy if landing and will have a very arduous duty to perform. I was anxious to go with them,

---

[13]Alf had developed chronic dysentery, "the soldier's complaint," and had been furloughed. His illness had made him restless and irritable. Smith Diary.

[14]Christopher Morris lived on Goshen Plantation. PWCHS, 117.

but Col. Starke opposed it on the ground that he could find no one to fill
my place & that the public service required my continual presence here. It
is strange that with so many Lieutenants around I am the only one qualified
to fill the position. The fact is, however, almost all are Volunteer officers
from Colonel down and generally are very ignorant of their duties. They
give no attention whatever to the details of the service—a very important
thing I assure you; and don't seem to have any concern about the effects of
their ignorance. In fact the want of capacity among our Company and
Regimental officers is terrible. Some Captains can't read; others there are
whose chirography would shame the heiroglyphics that bedeck the slopes
of the Egyptian pyramids. Regimental officers are scarcely any better; and
thus we go. I wish we had a Genl. Bragg in every Division of our Army so
that we might make a clean deal of all incompetent officers. The service
would be benefitted greatly, I assure you.

The enemy's gunboats are at Vicksburg and a fight is momentarily
expected. What the result will be God alone can tell. My fear is, the
Yankees will take our Batteries and add another to the long list of our
defeats by sea & land. Our people lose a great deal by attempting to
remedy the suicidal policy of our Government in dilly dallying with what is
a very momentous struggle. I am hopeful, tho' that the war will soon be
over. The Yankees must fight at Corinth soon and will fight to great
disadvantage unless we allow them to take Memphis. If we resist them
successfully at V.Burg or keep them in check for any length of time we will,
I hope & pray, defeat them at Corinth & drive back the hordes of invaders.
A disaster to their army at Corinth, or even a hasty retreat will give us free
passage through Tennessee & Kentucky. I also confidently expect that the
last measure of the Lincoln dynasty,—the abolition of Slavery in the
District of Columbia,—will open the eyes of the Western States to the real
nature of the fight & disorganize the army North. Already, I am told, there
are symptoms of disaffection existing among them; and if suffered to *fer-
ment* in the minds of the Western troops for any length of time, they will
produce a surrender of the whole army to Genl. Beauregard. The Tennessee River is falling rapidly and the Gunboats & Transports must soon be
compelled to land. If this happens, the Federal Army, being without
transportation, is bound to fall back; and my opinion is, when commenced
it will be a second retreat from Moscow. As the author of Armageddon said,
the Mississippi Valley is to be the scene of a mighty contest for Empire, the

70

result of which will be felt for years. If in the Providence of God, we are destined to become the victims of a Despotism, we must submit, tho' Freemen scarcely may be subjected to unjust & uncharitable epithets if they disbelieve the possibility of such a result. While we have a foot of soil unoccupied or a hundred men to repel the invaders, standing like the Spartan band in the pass,—we must look aloft and fear not. Sacrifices must be made, blood and treasure must be freely poured out until the problem is fairly solved. The surrender of New Orleans is a great disaster—But when we think of our large armies in the field, of our gallant general & brave troops—yet unsubdued and sullenly facing the foe, we may well have courage. In my humble judgment Genl. Beauregard will be the instrument in the hands of God, to work out our salvation and redeem us from the polluting tread of our Vandal invaders. Thus much, my ever dear wife, for the war.

Four Federal officers have been here for a week in Col. Starke's care.[15] Three of them are "Germans" and the other is from Missouri. I have had several conversations with them and the only reason they give for their unusual war is, that we intended to close the Mississippi River and prevent them from having access to the ocean thru' this great channel of communication. And when I informed them that the first act of our Confederate Congress stipulated for the free navigations of the River they were seemingly very much astonished. One of them, the Missouri Captain appeared to be a man of more than ordinary intelligence; and remarks in a letter I have before me, "I do not wish to be exchanged, I would prefer to remain in prison in the South to returning to my Regiment and fighting against my will." This is very proper language if it is not used with a mental reservation; and from the character of the officer I judge he is sincere. I hope there are a great many other officers influenced by the same feelings; I am told by these officers that if we defeat the armies at Corinth and in Virginia, the Lincoln Government cannot supply their places, having neither the men nor the money. How this will be, we, of course, cannot determine.

I learn this evening that the bombardment of Vicksburg has commenced; the battle is opened; and the Hill City will evince a determination that may

---

[15] Nugent's Service Record includes several receipts signed by him in accepting prisoners. Confederate Archives, R.G. 109.

do Memphis some good. Look out for glorious news from below soon or *sooner*. My impression is the Yankees will try to reach Jackson & cut off Beauregard's communication from below. If they do this, they will injure us seriously. The war is now reduced to the point, where we can fight to a better advantage. Yielding the River, we fight upon our own soil and can defeat any number which the enemy can bring against us. So mote it be say I; and a "pull altogether" will pull us thru' the war successfully.

My health continues to be very good and my spirits as pleasant as possible in view of the fact that I am so far separated from my darling wife. What would I not give to see you & fold you to my bosom; to feel your head reclining confidently upon my bosom and your fond heart bounding with delight & beating its warm pulsations against my own. That time will happen—when? Not long, I believe and hope.

Cheer up, my brave little wife, we have a great deal to live for yet, and will have the good fortune to enjoy one another's society at home sur-rounded by home joys & home comforts. Look aloft and ahead,—days that try men's souls are upon us,—and the bravest must draw inspiration from above.

Kiss Ma, Evie, & Abe for me. Love to Mr. S. & Alf & all inquiring friends. And now, my dear wife, May the Father of all mercies and the God of all love, gently clear your pathway thru' life and protect you in this your hour of trial is the ardent prayer of one whose heart's fondest affections are centered upon you.

Will

Jackson, May 21st, 1862

My dear wife,

I wrote you a letter this morning and handed it to Mr. Brown to carry up; since then I have received a letter from Ma conveying the intelligence that you had been confined and had a pretty little daughter,—our first born.[16] The news was exhilirating indeed, and lifted a load of anxiety from my mind. Instead of feeling older as I anticipated, I felt a great deal younger, a kind of toploftical sort of sensation, that creeps over a man when he is half-sloughed or half-seas-over. Let me congratulate you upon your

---

[16]The child, named Myra, died within two months. The infant mortality rate was high. The Smiths had eight children with four dying in infancy. Smith Bible.

happy good fortune, and express the hope that our daughter may be the prototype of her mother. Teach her infant lips to lisp her soldier Father's name as soon as she can articulate, and learn her to love me well. Let me have a full and fair description of her;—are her eyes heavenly blue, and her hair as dark as the plum of the raven's wing? Has she the pouting lips of her mother or the *Grecian* mouth of her Father? Does a dimple beautify her cheeks and has she pencilled eye brows? I know she must be a "great" young lady—and that she gives promise of being a very handsome & accomplished creature. How could it be otherwise with such parents? If you give her the looks and I the genius or *vice versa*—we may entertain strong hopes of her future.

I am glad you have so many fine strawberries, would like to drop in and help you eat them—but fear we won't have that happiness very soon.

Mr. Brown leaves in a short time and I must close.

May God speedily restore you to health & bless you abundantly is the prayer of

Your ever devoted husband
Will

Jackson, May 25/62

My dear wife,

Dr. Beden goes up to Bolivar County tomorrow morning, and I avail myself of the opportunity to send you a little garment handed to me by Cousin Emily, along with a letter. For the past two days I have been a little unwell, being affected with a slight attack of Dysentery. I believe I have checked it now and feel no other bad effects from it than a little weakness and an indisposition to locomotion. I am very sorry Penrice didn't carry my letter up to you as it would have relieved your mind of all uneasiness on my account. The powers that be seem determined so far, to keep me out of harms way, and if they continue I have no fear but that I shall go thru' with the war without a scratch. We have very dull times here now. Business of all kinds is at a complete standstill. Merchants, lawyers, planters, & clerks meet in crowds on the street corners, and converse glibly about the war prospects, while far down below the ragged slopes of the hills behind the Capitol, the weary soldier lounges out the day and sighs for a good *musket*. How different the avocations and how unthankful the task of the Volunteer.

Our Regiment has nearly all gone to Vicksburg; four companies remain here waiting for some kind of arms to fight with. We have all been compelled to come down to shotguns, it being impossible to get pistols; and were compelled to go off with guns badly in need of repairs. If I had been let alone we would all have all been splendidly rigged. Others thought they knew better and were finally compelled to give in to my arrangement at last. There are a great many wise men in the world, but I have discovered that ordinary men are always called upon when any particular service is needed. I believe I could have armed two regiments in a better manner, at less expense & in a shorter time than Col. Starke armed his. The condition of the country precluded the possibility of getting the pistols we wanted, and he might have known it. The sabres we have got are, as a general thing, no account; and but for our shotguns we would be in an awful predicament. I have two good pistols and a fine sabre and can do good service.

I am called off on important business. Kiss & pet the baby for me. Kiss Ma & Evie—

May god protect preserve & comfort you is the continual prayer of

Yr. ever devoted husband
Will

P.S.

Dr. Beden deferred his departure another day and I thought I would write a Post Script especially as you abuse my short letters so much. To a man cast away from the pleasures of home life and launched upon a sea of troubles, dangers, toils he knows not of, everything is so unreal that he can hardly realize his condition. The painful fact of my absence from the partner of my bosom & the light of my life, is the only thing vividly impressed upon my mind. I can hardly realize anything else. And even now, it is difficult to conceive that a ruthless enemy is so near our very door. And yet their acts of vandalism at Warrenton is enough to frighten any one. Killing negroes & white men, stealing chickens, cattle & everything else they needed. I am hopeful, and ever think, they will not stop at Greenville on their way up the River, if they pass Vicksburg. If they do pass and attempt to land at Greenville, every man in the County ought to turn out to prevent it. Take double barrell shotguns & pepper them like smoke. Kill, slay & murder them. Give them no peace; for unless we do, we do not deserve God's mercy.

I have another batch of Yankee prisoners under my charge and am instructed to keep them confined until further orders. I suppose they will be exchanged for some of our men soon. In a conversation with a Yankee prisoner just escaped from Tuscaloosa, Ala., some one asked him why Lincoln didn't exchange prisoners. Because, said he, he has got some of you *in the Union* and wants to *keep you in it.* Very good for a Hoosier boy just turned of eighteen.

Alex. Brandon has escaped from Indianapolis and got thru' safely. He saw Mrs. Hunt & Mrs. Brenham coming down and says all are well. If you see Major Hunt say to him that his wife and children in Ky. are well.[17] From Brandon's statement I am inclined to think Kentucky is on the verge of a terrific revolution in our favor. Exiles always tell good stories of the sort tho', and evince hopes that are groundless. Kentucky will rise only when it is too late I fear. The coming battle at Corinth, tho', will be the harbinger of future events. If we give the Yankees a good beating there our cause is safe, and the war is virtually over. The large armies in the field must be brought together and have a grand fight before the North will give up. We never did believe this; and if our leaders will only let reason have its way, they will see the great propriety of such a course. If successful, we conclude the war perhaps. If not, we fall back, increase our numbers, rally recruits & at them again. Fight large armies & fall back is the motto:—draw them in & turn upon them with the spring of a tiger at every opportunity.

Great hopes are entertained at V.Burg of our beating back the Yankees. The gunboats are evidently afraid of our batteries at present; and, in my humble judgement, intend to make a flank movement by land upon them. Let them come, they little think we are prepared for them even on land, and if they come out, God willing, we will bag the whole of them—and sink their boats.

I intend to call on Mrs. Dr. Cabaniss as soon as I can.

Feel well this morning; am relieved of my disease. Don't forget to Kiss and pet the baby for me.

Will

<hr>

[17]Mrs. Hunt had gone to Kentucky for protection. Major William Hunt served at one time as commander of the Washington Cavalry. PWCHS, 169.

Horace Fulkerson is in town & desires to be kindly remembered to you all. He is going to Richmond to submit to President a plan for building Gun Boats.[18]

Jackson, Miss.
May 26, 1862

My darling Nellie,

Judge Yerger has arrived, and although I have forwarded you a letter & a baby dress by Dr. Beden this evening, I have concluded to send along a few lines more. I am in hearing of the voices of fifteen Yankee Prisoners, who are singing "Nellie Gray" and the thoughts suggested by the music are not of the best. These poor deluded victims of a false and aggrandizing policy, far away from home, in the hands of enemies and hedged in by bayonets, are singing to relieve the dull tedium of the day. And while I am listening to them comes obtrusively the thought will I ever be in a like predicament. There is no telling; but my faith in the watchful care of a beneficent Providence of the least of whose mercies I am altogether unworthy, precludes the possibility of such a thought. I feel as if I will be permitted to return to my own quiet home soon, to caress the dearest idol of my heart, Kiss my baby and eat strawberries from the vines which have yielded you so rich a harvest this spring. As to the peaches my mouth waters when I think of them, nor do I dare to think the Yankees will have the audacity to destroy my favorite trees. Well, Nell, what are the folks doing with my trees, my *fig* trees, my vines, &c? The grape vines are your Pa's exclusive vanity, and I presume he pays every attention to them.[19]

Jackson is the dullest of towns—I won't dignify it by calling it a city— nothing indicates any activity but those things connected with the war. Generals, Colonels, Captains, and Lieutenants flock in and fill up our Hotels, talk of plans & fighting battles, sieges, gunboats, wars, policy, and scrupulously eke out the last moment of their furloughs away from their commands. I suppose it is a failing of soldiers, who are very similar to school boys during a vacation. But then, at Corinth, we need every officer

---

[18]Nugent often inserted material above the dateline. This was especially true in the latter stages of the war, when stationery was limited, or writing conditions were adverse. Horace S. Fulkerson was a cousin of A. F. Smith. His activities were later published in *A Civilian's Recollections of the War between the States.*

[19]Nugent's great love of fruit trees appears throughout the letters. His Jackson home included a large city orchard. The last of the trees planted in Jackson died in 1930. Recollections of LSH.

and every available man. The enemy do not appear to fancy a fight at all.
Twice have we offered battle and twice has it been declined. They are
concentrating their forces from every available point & preparing for a
desperate struggle for Empire. With Beauregard for our Leader, and a
good God for Protector, our armies will prevail over theirs, and terrible
will be the retribution for all their devastation. Stonewall Jackson has given
them a tremendous whipping in Virginia and is driving their routed legions
back into Pennsylvania, Beauregard, by the blessing of God, will defeat
them at Corinth, Johnston at Richmond and Smith will check their onward
career at V.Burg. Altogether we have all to be thankful for to Providence.
While we have had reverses, we have had successes. Sleeping upon a
fancied security at New Orleans we were suddenly aroused from our
fancied security and are being taught the hourly lesson that liberty is the
price of ceaseless watchfulness. In fact we needed some lessons that only
defeats could teach us. Men learn nothing but by experience, and nations
composed of aggregated individuals, labor under the same infirmity.
Donelson, with all its sad results taught us the necessity of prompt united
and vigorous action. This action is being taken and in time, I think, to
effect the object of our revolution. In the army there is none of the
despondency manifested by the non-combatants at home. The homespun
volunteer feels a patriotic ardor which reverses cannot dampen; and the
people at home must not complain, if they are called upon to suffer
inconveniences. Privations are ennobling to any people if willingly endured
for the sake of a public good. Eternal shame should mantle the cheek of the
skulking coward, who hopes nothing and does nothing; and while his
nerveless arm is not raised in defence of his Country, his croaking voice
should be palsied instead of breathing its dolorous accents into the ears of
the timid. God bless the women of the South, God bless them! With
delicate frames not made to face the pitiless storm of battle, they yet
uncomplainingly bear the brunt of privation at home, and hover, like
ministering angels around the couches of those whom war has crushed
beneath the iron orbs of his intolerable car. Rallying from the effects of
each reverse they gather courage in misfortune, and inspire us with the
ardor of their patriotism and the enthusiasm of their souls. If our men of
stout frames had but the staunch hearts of our women, Nell, we would
indeed be a nation of heroes worthy of the name. We have too long "laid
supinely upon our backs and hugged the delusive phantom of hope to our

77

bosoms." We have well nigh suffered ourselves to be defeated. The wonder
is that God has blessed us so wonderfully,—even beyond our deserts.

I have penned enough. Here's to the health of the "bonnie Ladye" far
away & the little baby. How much does she weigh, Nell? I hardly think
tho' you had the hardihood to attempt weighing her: the mother is small &
I rather suspect the baby is small too—say a three or four pound fairy.

Everything is quiet at Vicksburg now. The Gunboats have dropped down
the River & the impression prevails that they will land a force of some
three or four thousand men and attempt to take the batteries at Vicksburg
by a bold push from below. If they do land we will welcome them with
bloody hands to hospitable graves. Everything indicates tho', a speedy
termination to the present war. The battle at Corinth will decide the
duration of the present contest and if entirely successful there our enemies
will be disposed to cease their attempt at our subjugation. They will be
satisfied with war and will like to try the cultivation of peaceful pursuits for
a time; to which end let us all unitedly lend our prayers and ceaseless
efforts.

My health is good now. I have got rid of the Dysentery, I think, and feel
very well tonight. Love to all. Kiss Ma & Evie for me & the baby until you
are tired. Kiss my picture and imagine it to be me.

May God Almighty have you, my dear Nell, in his watchful care and
keeping & keep you secure unto the perfect day is the prayer of

Yr. devoted husband
Will

Jackson, Miss.
May 29th, 1862

My own dear wife,

The quasi poetic sentiment that strikes me at times, broke out on
yesterday and I send enclosed the result.[20] Keep it until baby can read,
and write, & let her learn it by heart. To discuss the critical merits of the
piece when it goes before such partial eyes as yours, would be altogether
useless. Its merits are few; its defects glaring; but I scarcely think it will be

---

[20]Throughout his life Nugent wrote poetry—fragments of which are included in the letters.
The last record of his writing was a poem to his daughter December 8, 1892. A copy of the
poem is in possession of LSH.

subjected to the scrutiny of many who are well posted in criticism. It is intended for our baby and you. You will perceive there is a blank left to be filled by the color of her eyes. By the way, what name do you intend to give the baby? Myra or Eleanor? Myra, I reckon, is the best. She is the first grandchild, and should bear her grandmother's name. However, of course, I shall leave this small matter to your better judgment, believing that you have the better right to name it.

The weather is becoming warm here now and the dull monotony of the times is equally oppressive. Genl. Beauregard is preparing for an active campaign in the west; Johnston has taken his position for fight in Virginia; Stonewall Jackson is driving the enemy before him into Maryland; and the Yankees are checked at Vicksburg. A check to an invading army is tantamount to a defeat, and especially is this the case when summer is coming on apace & in a Southern climate. I feel very very hopeful now. God has blessed us even while we were undergoing Chastisement at his hands, and opened our eyes fully to the nature of the contest in which we are engaged. If we make good use of the means within our power, the whole North can make but very little impression upon us. We may suffer severely for a season but man's extremity is God's opportunity. When all appears dark and gloomy we may hope most; for we are told "there is a silver lining to every cloud."

Our boys have gained all the credit so far at Vicksburg. They had the honor of the first brush at the Yankees and came out safe. Fowler had a hole shot through his coat; & Terrell's canteen was smashed in: with these exceptions and the death of Bailey Bradley from the effect of measles, all are doing well.

My health is good now. I believe I have entirely recovered from the Dysentery, and feel very well today. I look for peace within the next ninety days and a happy return "to home"—Beauregard is preparing for a bold movement, & keeps out of camp all newspaper correspondents. Kiss the baby, Ma & Evie for me. Love to all. May God bless you, comfort & preserve you: & grant us soon a happy reunion is my prayer.

Your devoted husband
William

P.S.   Mr. Tull came in yesterday after I had finished the letter herein enclosed, and while I was anxiously looking out for an opportunity to send it to you. This morning business is dull and I thought I would chat awhile longer with you. The balance of our Regiment leaves this place for Vicksburg on Saturday next and will leave me here, the only representative of Col. Starke's Regiment at this Post. Gen. Lovell declined relieving me at present, and how long I shall remain I do not know; wouldn't be surprised if I staid all summer unless the Yankees drive us all away. The news, this morning, is that they have left Vicksburg declining to take it, until after the fall of Fort Pillow, which is looked forward to as a very easy matter. A Federal army is marching down on the other side of the River without opposition at present, but if Price & Van Dorn get after them they will move backwards. Unquestionably the grand object of attack will be the Mississippi defences. The Yankees fondly imagine that we will be whipped as they get control of the Father of Waters. Cotton is what the Lincoln Dynasty wants. The distress & suffering in England and Ireland consequent upon the failure of the cotton supply is opening the eyes of England & France; and unless soon pacified, there will be some demonstration from across the water that will astound us all. The war must be ended soon. The commercial interests of the old world inwrought in our social fabric require it; the dictates of humanity require it; the happiness and material prosperity of the whole world almost absolutely demand it. Lincoln will sooner or later be satisfied of this & rest in his career of anticipated conquest. If the news that one of the New England States has refused to send any more troops to the army without abolitionism engrafted into the war policy of the Federal Government as its peculiar characteristic be true, the signs are hopeful. That this will be the result I have no doubt; & then we will see of what material the great Northwest & the border states are made. Things are rapidly culminating & there will be a general explosion in the Northern Camp soon. Not all the adhesive and cohesive power of the great national debt will save it: and when that time does come, as come, I pray, it may soon, you may hear of Southern & Western soldiers together marching to the proud emporium of Northern trade— New York. If in the Providence of God, abolitionism be put down, the design will be accomplished in some way or other. "God moves in a mysterious way, His wonders to perform"—and we may expect a deliverance from all our present woes in a way we little dream of.

The weather still continues to be warm, and the prospect for a dreadfully hot summer is brightening. Yellow fever will invade the city of New Orleans, and will entail a vast deal of suffering on the vandals.

There are a great many sick in our army at Corinth and a Northern trip is the most efficacious remedy for it. From Genl. Beauregard's recent orders I incline to the opinion that he is meditating some bold movement into Kentucky; where he will gather an army of determined men who will march wherever he orders.

My health still continues good. Have a pleasant time with the army officers all of whom I find to be gentlemen.—Wouldn't be surprised if we are kept here all summer. Love & Kisses.

Your affec. husband
Will

Jackson, June 1, 1862

My own dear wife,

I was heartily rejoiced at the reception of your letter by Mr. Penrice; I was expecting a treat & was highly gratified. To know that you are alive & comparatively well, & that the baby is doing well even tho' it has the colic continually, affords me an immense deal of satisfaction and induces a large outpouring of heartfelt gratitude to God for his unspeakable goodness & mercy. In a devoted wife I feel that the bountiful giver of all good, had "doubled my store," and the climax of my reasons for glorifying his precious name will be reached, when we and all of ours shall meet around the Mercy seat unitedly to hymn the praises of our blessed Redeemer. You recollect, Nell, my advice to bathe your breasts in cold water to prevent sore nipples: the same advice might, if followed, do you good now. The water should be mixed with a Tincture of Arnica, a weak solution. Consult the "Homoeopathy" Book and endeavor to follow the prescriptions contained in it.[21] You will find that though slow, the remedy assisted by nature & rigid dieting will do you incalculable good. If the war should terminate soon, or if the enemy is driven back so that you can come in safety down, you & Alf both had better spend a month at Cooper's Well. In fact I suggested to Mr. Smith the propriety of taking Alf to the Well. The water

---

[21]In the late nineteenth and early twentieth centuries, two schools of medicine were practiced. The Allopathic theory was to treat disease with an agent having the opposite effect and to give large infrequent doses. Homeopathy methods recommended like remedy for like causes, and small doses given frequently. Nugent and his descendants followed closely the Homeopathic treatment. Recollections of LSH.

[illegible] would cure you both. I have seen the fatal consequences of large doses of medicine since I have been here. Soldiers are taken sick, heavily dosed, become convalescent and are reported for duty so soon that nine of twenty relapse and die. Officers get along very well, but the poor privates suffer amazingly. It makes my heart bleed to see how generally the soldiers are made the victims of the treatment of incompetent surgeons; here, however, we have an efficient kind-hearted & humane Surgeon Dr. Cabaniss, whose wife is an old friend of Ma's. The soldiers notwithstanding their wounds & diseases are hopeful and high-spirited. I heard one poor fellow the other day with a broken leg, cry out as I passed him, "Hurrah for Jeff Davis & the Southern Confederacy!" and yet there are timid timeserving non-combatants who cry out "we are whipped." Beaten we may be, but we are not destroyed and never will be until our armies are dissipated. Happy it is for us that the soldiers are hopeful otherwise the furloughed sick rendered timid by croakers would never return to duty. The press must be, to a certain extent muzzled. It has heaped abuse upon Gen. Lovell, a loyal tru-hearted & able officer. I know all the facts & he is not responsible for the fall of New Orleans at all. Gen. Beauregard has written him expressing entire confidence in him and offering him the command of a Division of his army. This wholesale, premature & uncalled for abuse of an innocent & deserving officer is shocking. The gaping public are ready to wreak their vengeance on the first man who is abused without regard to truth. The cry is begun by some irresponsible man and is immediately taken up by the people generally. The consequence is soldiers lose confidence in their commanders & we lose faith in our cause. My health still continues good.

May God bless you & have you in his holy care & keeping. Return you quickly to health & grant us soon a happy reunion.

Your devoted husband
W. L. Nugent

Camp Mayson
June 8th, 1862

My beloved & constant wife,

The affectionate tone of your letters has so far overpowered me that I feel a good cry, unmanly as it would appear, would be a considerable relief. Not that I have not patriotism enough to bear me up amid all the trying scenes thru' which I may be called to pass, but the thought is a painful one that I am not privileged to be with you and bear the heavy responsibilities and great anxiety in reference to our darling baby. I would fully give all I am worth to see the war ended, peace declared, and ourselves reunited around our family hearth. Wealth is worthless when compared to the pleasures of a happy home; and could I but be present to pour the oil of a tender sympathy into your bruised and anxious heart, I would be more than willing to begin the battle of life as bravely as ever I did before, poor as the poorest peasant on Earth, but a little more confident in my own ability. But be of good cheer, Nellie, all will yet be well. The war will soon be over. Things are assuming that sanguinary character which ever evinces the coming conclusion of the war. It is now an effort of futile anger to destroy our property, when the enemy sees we cannot be destroyed ourselves. Trust in God and fear not. I feel, when I pray, for you as I do every day, that a good Providence will watch over and protect you & your little babe from all harm and danger.

My health is, I believe, entirely restored again. I relieved myself from the Dysentery with Homeopathy and find that Nature is a great thing in relieving disease if left to herself. I have removed to the camp upon the order of Capt. Blackburn and am getting along very well, am now acting as Adjutant of the Regiment, a very *safe* & lazy position. You must, however, learn to trust me in the hands of God. How I wish that in your troubles you could rely upon the strong arm & protecting & comforting influences of the Holy Spirit. You would feel that all afflictions are light if they result in working out for us a far more exceeding eternal weight of glory.

We will in all probability, move from here in a few days, and may be ordered to Washington Co. to protect you all. Col. Starke told me he thought of sending us up there.

There is nothing new from Corinth yet, and the Yankee Army in Va. is driven back. Summer is coming on apace, and the Feds can't stand our Summers very well.

Mr. Haycraft leaves pretty soon. Clarence & Wash are well.

And now, my dear wife, be brave, cheerful & contented; Know that you are the object of my heart's best affection and that my thoughts and strongest love are constantly on and with you & our babe. The devotion of a heart which has been constant to you so long may be relied upon. Be hopeful; don't let croakers induce a painful thought or reflection; remember it is a long lane that has no turning. Love & Kisses—and May God bless comfort & preserve you is the prayer of your devoted husband

Will

Camp Mayson near V.Burg
June 10th, 1862

My own dear Nellie:

Your letter by Thomas came safely to hand and I replied somewhat hastily. Today I have a short respite from labor, and avail myself of the opportunity to reply now at length.

I do not wonder at your great uneasiness about the baby. Unaccustomed as you are to such things, you will be alarmed at every symptom of approaching or present disease, and you will always be more or less alarmed. I would advise you though strongly against allowing yourself to give way to your feelings. Strong nervous excitement, or emotional agitation of every kind, has from the necessity of the case, a great influence over your milk, will injure the character of the secretion, and thus make your baby's health worse. I would guard you against the indulgence of feeling, not in a spirit of scolding or upbraiding; for, God knows my heart, and I would much prefer folding you in my arms and relieving you, to the extent of my ability, from the grave & novel responsibilities devolved upon you. Be hopeful, feel that everything is for the best, imagine the future to be full of joys however painful the present may be, rely upon the strong arm & protecting care of Providence & you will find that your spirits & health will both improve. Give a trial to that religion which is so fully exemplified in the daily walk and conversation of your Mother, and you will be enabled more bravely to bear your present ills and more happily to anticipate the future. I would not thus write, but cut off as you are from Him, who is your best comforter on earth there is no Source to which you can look other than the Author of all our happiness and the giver of all good things. If I could upon the polished surface of this paper whisper a word into your ears that could at once banish all your anxiety, or breathe a sigh responsive to your own—I would cheerfully & gladly do it. The trouble of discovering the one or the other would be nothing if success would but crown my efforts. Alas language must fail when the writer cannot be present. Be cheerful, Nellie, for our dear baby's sake; things may look hopeless & dreary, but fear not; calm your feelings, and go to your Ma for comfort & advice. Trust to her judgment & opinions in all things, be governed by them, and, I feel satisfied, you will never regret it.

I didn't mean to speak slurringly of the baby. What I said was in jest & merely said to banter you a little. You know I have always said I would prefer my first child's being a daughter. I like little girls more than I do boys. They are more innocent and lovable, and generally better company. The responsibility of raising boys is terrible in our Southern country. Their tendencies are all towards the evil side of everything, and it requires a great effort to bring them up properly. Hence I think it is better for a mother to raise one or two girls before she tries her hand at a boy. Don't you think I am correct in my judgment? I still think I would like to have a dozen children, and yet I would not relish the idea of seeing you suffer any more than absolutely necessary. In things of this kind where you are more immediately concerned, it would be a pleasure to me to yield to you as I am determined always to do. I do not wish or purpose that the after years of our married life, shall be any less pleasant than those thru' which we have passed. Nay, on the contrary, I propose, God assisting me, that our affection for one another shall deepen every day and that in my person I may exemplify the doctrine I have always taught, that a married life should be a continously happy one. Unless we are trusting and confide our cares to those with whom we are brought in the relation of husband & wife, how else can we make a proper use of the means of happiness within our reach. If the sturdy oak does not protect against the storms the tender vines that creeps & clings so lovingly around it, how will it gather support in after days, when its limbs are blasted and its trunk gradually crumbling from the affects of time's corroding tooth. I may protect you now, but when old age creeps on apace, I feel that I shall derive immeasurable comfort from you. Let us then make good use of the present, and gently loving and sustaining one another look the future boldly in the face: for God has said, "I will *never* leave you nor forsake you."

Today we learn that Memphis has fallen, Sad though it be, I think it all for the best. We must be taught, it seems, by severe lessons the utter futility of scattering our forces in a thousand directions. I think it would be a fortunate thing if all our seaport towns, cities & forts were taken; because we would then be compelled to concentrate our armies and strike for the enemy's country. The policy we have been pursuing is & must be ruinous in the extreme. All the valor of our troops and the skill of our Generals cannot counterbalance. The motto should be gather your forces and strike for peace by one grand battle. V.Burg still holds out. The gun boats have gone below, it is thought, to New Orleans—& probably to attack Mobile. The fighting is still going on at Richmond.

[The letter is unfinished. The fragment which follows appears to be a continuation].

. . . but we cannot ascertain the result. I hope we may route McClellan's Army and turn westward on Buell's flank. If this could be done the war would terminate. If Buell's Army is routed and Beauregard could turn & help Johnston the same likely would follow. We are too timid and trust too much to a time worn policy of wasting the enemy by checking him. This may have done, heretofore, it will not answer now. I still feel, however, that we will soon see the end of the war. Summer will work much in our favor and the existence of yellow fever in New Orleans will decimate the Federal ranks. God will assist us in our extremity and furnish a new exemplification of his dealings with man.

Cavalry cannot operate in this country and we will, doubtless, fall back if the enemy attempt to land: and unless the Yankees advance into the country more boldly than they have been accustomed to do the war will terminate with the defeat of McClellan and Halleck. Love and Kisses to all & especially the baby. Say to Mr. Smith that Tom couldn't get home & was compelled to return. I will supply him with what money he needs. Let him have any of my clothes that suit him & you are willing to give up. And now, dear Nellie, may God bless, comfort, & preserve you & our baby is the prayer of

Yr. devoted husband
Will

No paper in camp or would write more.

Hd. Qrs. Camp Mayson
Near V.Burg June 13th, 1862

My own dear wife,

I wrote you the other day by Mr. Wolfe of our Company, and learning that there will be another [opportunity] tomorrow of communicating with you, avail myself of it. And I do this with the greater pleasure since the news from all of our armies is of an encouraging character. Maj. Gen. Stonewall Jackson has defeated three columns of the enemy's armies, Gen. Johnston has driven back McClellan, Gen. Beauregard has completely checkmated Halleck by his retrograde movements from Corinth, and Gen. Kirby Smith is prepared for them at Chattanooga. Our Gen. Smith is confident of his ability to drive the Federals back from this city, and we are looking out every day to hear that the Yellow Fever has broken out in New Orleans. Butler's infamous proclamation is thought by the *New York Herald* to be a forgery, and the English papers are denouncing it as unparalleled by anything that ever emanated from Nero himself. These flagrant, unwarranted & demoniac violations of the usage of a civilized warfare are having, as they should have, a recalcitrating effect; and if the rebound doesn't accomplish some good in our favor, I don't know what will. Every calculation, has however, up to this time, been more or less defeated; seemingly and really, as I believe, to teach us to rely more upon Divine aid than human foresight. Our armies are getting into the best possible fighting trim—discarding all superfluous baggage, accustoming themselves to physical endurance by rapid marches and learning the art of fighting with their legs—an art much practiced by Napoleon, tho' sorely neglected in these latter days. Gen. Price has adopted the idea that breastworks in the open field are useless, and the idea is a good one. If an army is kept busy it will not have the time, nor will the enemy have an opportunity of making regular approaches by parallels & all the other trenches & ditches known to engineering art. Give me an open field, rapid marches, heavy blows, constant skirmishes, incessant annoyings, and I will be better pleased than now. I have no possible fear of the result, however, my mind is fully impressed with the belief that all things are rapidly culminating towards a speedy & successful end to this war: and when the crushing blow falls upon the unprotected shoulders of the North, the effects will be terrible. The Yankee Despotism will be utterly annihilated and a new Empire will spring up in the West.

We have received intelligence that France, Spain, & England have determined to intervene in our war, and have submitted to both Governments a proposition to arrange the whole matter. The propositions are,

1st. Reconstruction of the Union upon primitive principles—2nd Cessation of hostilities—3rd General Amnesty—4th Evacuation of all Southern ports & 5th The Decision of the question of *Secession* by an election in all of the Southern States. These propositions have all been accepted by our Government, but the last has been refused by the United States Government, thus leaving the matter to be settled by the foreign Governments; and the result will be the annihilation of Northern commerce & her navy; and the speedy establishment of Southern independence. England & France are bound to play their hands openly very soon, and no one can doubt that they will indirectly favor a severance of the Old Government. United the old union could have defeated the world in arms, and had really grown too powerful for the good of the human family. Strength brings in its train lust of power and disregard of the rights of the weak; and the preservation of the balance of power is necessary to the security of nations. Here let my lucubrations terminate.

We are encamped in a pleasant Magnolia grove, have enough to eat and plenty of good cistern water. The health of the Company is better than usual, there being only some four or five sick. Several of our men are absent on sick leave of absence just recovering from the Measles, and will return to camp soon. We have an excellent Company—nearly all good, gentlemanly attentive soldiers. They are the best drilled men in the Regiment, moving on foot nearly as well as on horseback. The Colonel is very proud of us and has often said we are the only Company that drills like soldiers. We will maintain this character in future and if we can go into battle will show that we may be relied upon.

Paper is very scarce here now, the Adjutant's office is "plum out" and none can be readily gotten anywhere. I am writing this letter on a piece of *borrowed* paper, with a borrowed pen & ink.

I think of you Nellie *all the time* and long to see you, and pet you & kiss you till you would make me quit: and I hope to see you soon. Kiss our dear little baby often for me & show her my picture when she is old enough to notice it. Tell her I love her now, and will love with all the fullness of a Father's heart when I see her. I am proud of her because I hear every one speak of her beauty. Tell Ma I would write but have no paper. Kiss her & Evie for me. Tell Abe he mustn't forget to look after things as he promised to take care of the fruit trees, carriage, horses & everything else. Give my love to Mrs. Finlay, say to her I have always had a very exalted opinion of her goodness & virtues, but cannot now find words to express my deep and abiding gratitude for her goodness to you. All well. Give love to Mr. S. and

Alf; and may God Almighty bless, comfort & protect & preserve you & our baby is the prayer of

Yr. devoted husband
Will

Camp Holly near V.Burg
June 22d, 1862

My beloved wife,

I wrote you last week by Mr. Tull, and write again now by Mr. Fall. I hope you may be fortunate enough to receive both letters, as I am debarred the privilege of seeing you.

Since I last wrote I have been somewhat unwell, and am just now recovering from an attack of intermittent fever. My diet is *mush* & broiled mutton, not much better than you all have at home. I have taken nothing but Homeopathy & quinine, and will, in consequence be all right in a day or two more. So I hope & believe any how. Don't fret yourself into the belief that I have been very sick. If such had been the case I would have gone to see you to a certainty. The only chance of my going home is in getting sick; but while I am as homesick as the veriest schoolboy you ever saw or heard of, I don't like the idea of being sick in Camp. Soldiers get careless of one another; and in fact the idle habits of a camp life are enough to deaden one's moral sensibilities entirely. And then, too, the men are usually required to do all they can in the way of ordinary duty. When relieved from duty, the poor weary private feels like stretching himself out & resting. I, for one, didn't expect much sympathy, and not getting it, was not disappointed. We have moved our Camp to a cool shady walnut grove, where we have an abundance of good cistern water to drink & enough to eat of its kind. The people around here charge outrageously high for everything a man is compelled to get in the way of eatables. Mutton at 20¢ per lb.—a good average sheep $12.00, cabbage 25¢ a head, chickens bring 60¢ a piece, butter 60¢ a lb.—& other things in proportion. I am persuaded there are a great many people who will feel relieved when Vicksburg falls. The Yankees will never take it except by a flank movement on land. We learn that they are coming up the Jackson Road to take or attack Jackson; and if this is the case unless we have force enough to protect the line between Jackson & V.Burg, why, of course, we leave this point for the

interior. General Beauregard is sick, and has gone to Bladen Springs
leaving Bragg in Command at Tupelo Station. The Federals have Holly
Springs, Miss. and are coming on down in some force. A recent order from
the Medical Director has dispensed with all hospitals except at Meridian on
the Mobile & Ohio & Southern R. Road indicating that as the basis of
operations for our army, which leaves the Mississippi Valley open to the
Yankees. You need not therefore fear on account of starvation because
Memphis will be well supplied with everything and maybe more of everything than will be well for the enemy after awhile. They may occupy all our
cities & towns: this is just what we want. While it may occasion individual
suffering, it will diminish the Federal ranks and we will dash at them while
they are dispersed. We will just keep guns enough along the River to
trouble transports and the ordinary navigation of the River, and thus
prevent the speedy concentration of an army at any given point. The large
army of the Yankees cannot be kept together during the summer. The
Generals for fear of epidemics will scatter and quarter their forces and then
we must work and work like Trojans. God will soon, I believe, deliver our
enemies into our hands if we will only avail ourselves of the opportunity
presented. Gen. Bragg is not the man to let an opportunity pass without
being improved. I am afraid Gen. Beauregard's health is very much shat-
tered by his stay at Corinth. The water was bad enough to kill a dog much
less a man. G. M. Helm was with us a few days and gives some very
exciting incidents of the Shiloh fight.[22] He acted as a reconnoitering engineer, was exposed to the fire continually and saw a great deal of the
fighting on both sides. He is promoted to be Captain & desires to be kindly
remembered to all. He is just recovering from an attack of Bilious Fever,
and looks a little thin.

I have been complimented very much of late on my good looks, Nellie,
and did I not place more confidence and repose a much greater judgment
& preference in yr. good opinion I might have become vain. A very nice
young lady inquired particularly whether I was married or not; and when
told yes, said she was very sorry as she intended to set her *cap* for me. To
relieve anything savoring of jealousy I may as well tell you here that I
haven't been to see a young or old lady since I left home except one or two

---

[22]G. M. Helm became a major in the Confederate Army, and after the war was chief
engineer of the Levee Board. His plantation, Helm Station, was located on the border of
Washington and Bolivar Counties. PWCHS, 255.

relations. Indeed, indeed, my individual heart is in the lowlands clustering close about those of my darling wife & daughter, and nothing but death can ever separate it. The separation will be hard for you & harder for me; it can't last long, however, and we will all be privileged to assemble around our family hearth ere long and enjoy one another's society to the full. We will be prepared to appreciate one another's society more and will have an abundance of leisure for that purpose I hope. I would like, after the war is over, to go somewhere, where I cannot be at all disturbed, and pet you & the baby to my heart's content. I have sometimes imagined a home in the interior of Texas would be best. No Yankee army could ever get there and we would be healthy to say the least of it. The solid food of life is in great abundance, and with health we could jog along very bravely. We might get close along by the side of Brother Perry and raise stock.[23] What do you think of it?

Our Company is in very good health generally. Clarence is troubled with a bad cold, but is otherwise well. Wash is well, much to my satisfaction.

May God Almighty bless, comfort, & preserve you & your baby is the prayer of

Yr. devoted husband
Will

Kisses to Ma, Evie & *Myra*, love to all & especially Mrs. Finlay—Tell the negroes howdye.

Lindin, July 6th, 1862

My dear, dear Nellie,

I arrived safely this far on my journey & leave in a few moments for Deer Creek. Alf says he is better this morning & feels strong enough for the trip. I feel satisfied that a stay at Cooper's Well for a month will relieve him altogether. You had better call in Dr. Finlay unless you are willing to risk Homoeopathy. The fever you had was produced by the flow of milk. I feel well. May God bless, comfort & preserve you is the daily prayer of

Yr. devoted husband
William

Cheer up. The news is McClellan's whole army has been taken.

---

[23]Perry was William's older brother, born 1831, who did civilian work during the war. Edmonds, Nugent Family Papers.

Camp near Blake's
July 10th, 1862

My own dear Nellie,

I arrived here safely on Monday night after a very fatiguing trip down. The road was very good the most of the way, but the last fifteen or twenty miles were quite bad. I fear I lost a horse on the road. The horse I bought from Mr. Gregory fell down from exhaustion & "foundered" and I presume will die.[24] I left him in charge of a negro on the plantation of Mr. Harden & promised to pay him well if he relieved the poor suffering animal. I feel very well with the exception of a disagreeable headache with which I have to go on picket duty this evening; a duty necessary but extremely inconvenient just now. We are encamped here without tents & few cooking utensils and as a necessary consequence are rather roughing it just now.

I went in town yesterday & had a long conversation with Gen. Van Dorn. I wouldn't be surprised if he sent some forces up on the River to protect you all against Yankee violence. This you must keep *secret*. In view of this probability you had better move to the plantation as soon as your health will allow. A general order has been issued pronouncing the penalty of death upon all who trade with the enemy, and our people had better take warning for Genl. Van Dorn will do what he promises to the very letter.

The news this morning is that Genl. McClellan has been reinforced & has made a stand at Berkley. Our forces have pierced and divided his army and will cut it up in detail. The report of the arrival of commissioners from England, France & Russia demanding a cessation of hostilities on the part of the United States lacks confirmation, but is generally credited. Gen. Beauregard is relieved of all command by the President, a certain indication of spleen and dislike, contemptible in a man holding the position Jeff. Davis does. Halleck's Army is demoralized & retreating; Bragg is advancing on Memphis; Hardee is at Chattanooga & Polk's at Holly Springs. Gen. Hindman has an army of 35,000 men & has surrounded Curtis in N. West Arkansas. Altogether I think our affairs look very cheering now. We are daily mounting guns here and will give the Yankees more trouble the next time they attempt to pass the city. There has very little injury been done

---

[24]P. W. Gregory owned Elmwood Plantation. PWCHS, 327.

by the enemy's shells as yet, tho' they have thrown a great number of them.

Alf's trip, I think, rather improved him. I got him a letter from the Medical Director authorizing him to go to Cooper's Well where I have no doubt he will get well. He is very imprudent, however, and it took all my persuasions to induce [him] to ride down in an easy carriage instead of *open top* buggy. He wanted to ride down with Jim Smith.[25]

Send me down some paper by first opportunity, as I am entirely out & can't get any here now. The mosquitoes are a little troublesome here now. Kiss Ma, Evie, and baby for me; Love to all friends. May God bless, comfort, & preserve & restore you & baby to health is the prayer of

Your devoted husband
Will

Camp Jones near V.Burg
July 12, 1862

My own dear Nellie,

I am again installed in the office of Acting Adjutant of the Regiment for one month, Sam'l. Starke having gone home for one month on sick furlough. The office is a comparatively lazy one and is very comfortable to an inactive nature. Col. Starke, in my opinion, discovered that he could save Sam'l. from conscription only by appointing him Adjutant in his vacillating course and gross nepotism. He still remains at Jackson in command of the Post and his Regiment is in the field. I think, however, it would be a good thing for us if he were to remain where he is. The men have lost confidence in him and would not fight well under him; at least not as well as under Col. Ferguson.

A Yankee Transport went up the Yazoo River this morning, and we hurried down expecting a fight. In this, happily, maybe for us, we were disappointed. The Federals are in a terrible commotion over the Richmond fight, and are beginning to blame all hands at all connected with the Grand Army. Secretary Stanton, Old Abe and Genl. McClellan are all accused of utter incompetency. A call has been made for 300,000 men volunteers. Verily the Rebellion is a terrible thing to deal with and it is not yet quite played out as our enemies first imagined. Vicksburg is thought by our

---

[25]Jim Smith was a resident of Egg's Point, Mississippi. PWCHS, 284.

enemies and they have need to [illegible] and failing to take it by storm, they are endeavoring by a cute Yankee trick to cut us off. They have finished the ditch across the point opposite the city and have nearly completed the cut off above; hoping to straighten the River and leave [Vicksburg] in the lurch on a Lake; with what success time alone can develop. One thing is certain they can never take the place, and may as well cease shelling us.

Alf left for Cooper's Well today apparently much better. At least his looks indicated it. The Medical Director here said his name ought to be placed on the books of some Hospital and ordered him to put it on the books at Mississippi Springs Hospital giving him the privilege of going to the Well, where I have no doubt he will recover his health. I will endeavor to have him transferred to this Regiment and think he will get along better with us. He promised me when he left to be more prudent and to diet himself. If he does this he will certainly recover. We have a good many sick in our Camp. Picket duty among the mosquitoes & sleeping on the ground has done us no little harm. No news of any consequence from below. The Road from here to Greenville will soon be in fine order and you needn't be surprised to see me at any moment. Love & Kisses; and may God bless, comfort and protect you & our baby is the daily prayer of

Yr. devoted husband
Will

CHAPTER V

On the Move

August 11, 1862–May 6, 1864

Camp Burrus, Aug. 11th, 1862

My dear, dear Nellie,

I wrote you a letter by Fielding the other day, since which time we have moved to Judge Burrus's, about twenty miles from Greenville, and fifteen from our place on Black Bayou. You can come up and stay at Dr. Gibson's who is a relation of your Pa's or at Judge Burrus's.[1] The trip can be made in three or four hours. I will come down myself if Colonel Starke's *in* becomes relaxed enough to allow a man to leave camp. He swears he won't let anybody leave, and intends to keep us here until frost. Never mind, I will have a fair swing at him after the war is over, and will make him render back the debts he justly owes and has long witheld without cause or provocation. It is still very warm & there is a great deal of sickness in Camp. We have about forty for duty out of one hundred and eight. I am in very good health, tho' on the road up here I was compelled to stop at R. M. Carter's & take medicine again.[2] We are here in the woods, and the Colonel intends, I believe, to keep us *until frost* for which I presume, you are very thankful to him.

Say to Carnes that I want my mare well taken care of as I may need her this winter. We may have some hard service to perform. If Mr. Smith would come up he might make arrangements to get all the brine & salt out of the pork barrels, and could make good use of it.

We are all enjoying ourselves but poorly compared to our living near Greenville. Better times will come when the weather cools off a little—

---

[1]J. C. Burrus was a prominent Bolivar County leader and friend of the Smiths. The Gibson home was located near the Burrus home. PWCHS, 235.

[2]Carter owned the Nomini Plantation in the northern part of Washington County. PWCHS, 169.

There is no news on hand here. We have no late papers from below.—
Love & Kisses, & believe me to be as ever, your fond & devoted husband

W. L. Nugent

Bolivar Co.
Sept. 17, 1862

My own dear Nellie,

We have been for the last eight or ten days running about from pillow to post to prevent the landing of the Yankees & the consequent destruction of property. They did, however, land at Prentiss in the night & destroyed the whole town, leaving only one small tenement unburnt. They avowed the intention of burning Greenville, and I presume as your Pa has not, in all probability, moved our Law books all of them will be destroyed besides his house & everything else in the village.[3]

I am enjoying very good health and would have been down but that I hate to leave the Company when about [to] march. We have a great many sick and are encamped where we are getting "no better fast." The Colonel still persists in operating about & below Prentiss from an opinion I suppose, that our presence is more needed here than elsewhere.

We will leave here for Greenville pretty soon and I will then get a few days leave of absence to go and see you. I heard that Alf was coming up to see me and was very sorry he was unable to do so. If he wanted the bay horse you might have given him away. I heard Alf was looking very well & hope he is nearly restored to health. It would be a very advantageous arrangement for him to get a position under his fast friend as an assistant. I have got a bottle of excellent quinine for you; it cost 25$ and I understand there is an abundance of it in Jackson. If we do not come down in the course of the next ten days send up for it.

Love & Kissess & believe me to be in haste

Yr. devoted husband
Will

---

[3]Indeed, the house was burned. However, some of the law books were saved and became the possessions of Lucy Somerville Howorth, who subsequently donated them to the Law School, University of Mississippi.

Camp Duncan, Bolivar Co.
September 19th, 1862

My own precious Nellie,

A day or two since I wrote you a few lines informing you that I was in good health and the reasons that prompted me in not forcing a temporary leave of absence. An officer has to be very careful of his reputation for courage; for upon that in a great measure depends his efficiency & ability to command the soldiers under him. When once the troops lose confidence in the bravery of their Commanders they necessarily have an utter contempt for him, and will not cheerfully obey his orders. I know I would dislike to have a cowardly Captain over me, and I presume my *Subs* are pretty much like me in disposition—human nature being the same the world over.

The camp is pretty lively over their recent fight. On yesterday the gunboat *Queen of the West* came up by this point having in tow abreast and on her larboard (left Hand) side and abreast of her [?]. Captain Winston's Company of Rifle men were dispatched below some four miles to fire into them and engage their attention. When the boats arrived opposite Bolivar Landing they fired into a Squad of men killing one or two; and galloping up behind the Levee, under a storm of grape & minie balls, renewed the attack at their several places. The boats advanced slowly up the river, and were greeted by the lower supports of the battery with another volley of balls doing some little execution. The battery then opened fire and the noise became terrible. Anon our shotguns opened, the enemy replied, and one could hardly hear his ears. The rattle of small arms, the roar of the cannon, and the crash of the boats timbers was truly electrifying. The balls from the enemy's guns passed almost altogether over our heads. One shell loaded with ounce balls however, exploded right under the noses of two of our men about three feet below the edge of the bank. We were lying about eight feet from the edge of the bank behind the natural embankment made by the deposit, and were in comparatively little danger. The enemy admitted a loss of *three* killed: put this at ten & treble the number for wounded, and you may possibly have the correct estimate of their loss: our own loss was one wounded, belonging to the Artillery. This poor fellow's leg was broken just above the ankle by a minie ball. I was lying down most of the time behind our men, who occupied the same position in front of me except when they were engaged shooting. This was a bold attack especially

97

when it is remembered that all our shot were discharged at a walled up Gunboat and against men who were almost all entirely concealed; a few gunners at the bow alone showing themselves at intervals when our fire slackened. If the Colonel will follow this up a few times he may add to his own reputation and retrieve his lost ground. The citizens here are very much "down on him," speak quite harshly of his conduct which cannot be wholly justified & predict everything evil of him. The officers of the Regiment feel that they have not been treated with courtesy & respect due them, and hence do not take the same interest in the management of their commands as they otherwise would. My own private opinion is, the whole Regiment is no better managed now than it was at the start & scarcely as well organized. This is a sad fact, but a very obstinate one indeed.

The health of the troops is very bad, and the fevers are beginning to result fatally.—Our own Company is doing well. Dr. Talbott seems to be remarkably successful in managing the cases under treatment. We have much, however, to be thankful for to the Author of all good.

Love & Kisses to all: and may the God of all mercy and the Giver of all good abundantly bless, comfort, & preserve you, and at last bring you into his haven of rest with him who delights to feel that he is

Your devoted husband
Will

[Reverse side]

Please forward with *one bottle of Quinine* which Tom has. My wife needs it very much just now.

Nugent

Mrs. W. L. Nugent   Care
Black Bayou,   C. A. Brown, Esq.
Washington Co. Miss.[4]

∽✚∾

Camp Burrus
Sep. 28/62

My own dear wife,

I dropped you a note a few days ago by Lesiecki, who went down on Company business, to let you know I was still in the land of the living, &

---

[4]Nugent's address of Black Bayou indicates the removal of the Smiths to the Oakwood Plantation on Black Bayou.

wanted to see you dreadfully; a contingency that seems to keep itself very distant. Poor Ben Johnson has, at last, lost his wife, and Mat has returned: so I presume we shall soon have our senior officers back again. In that event I shall certainly go home for a few days to rest and enjoy myself in the sunlight of your precious society.

The only word I have heard from you for a long time was that you had been ill but were well; and even this came through third parties. I didn't get a letter as I hoped, for I should then have known the true state and condition of your mind & heart & body.

The Yankees seem to have left us for awhile to take a little repose, but whether to gather strength for a more terrific blow, or because they are called off above I do not know. The health of our Regiment being so bad I am inclined to think we will remain where we are for sometime, & then move to Vicksburg for the winter. I must confess that this arrangement would suit me very well personally. I have no desire to go to Tennessee or Kentucky for the winter. Glory amounts to very little in itself; and I must say it is not to be considered at all when a man's duty allows him to remain near his home even tho' there is not much fighting to be done. I would prefer places where the dangers to be encountered were comparatively few; though I should not hesitate to head a forlorn hope if called upon to do so. We have only 250 men out of 1,056 present for duty, and have buried a good many recently. The cases are principally chills and fevers which, in the absence of quinine have resulted fatally. We have in our Company nearly 1/3 of the fighting strength of the Regiment, & have in the last month consumed about two hundred dollars worth of quinine. By the way, did you get the bottle I sent you by Mr. Brown?

The Col. is quite sick at present & will leave us as soon as Lt. Col. Ferguson makes his appearance, which will be in a few days I sincerely hope. The whole command is in a state nearly verging on utter disorganization.

Clarence & Jack are both up & about having missed their chills for two days[5]—I am well. I wish you would inquire around for enough Linsey or

---

[5]Jack Cox (Cocks) and his sister Kate lived with the Smiths after the death of their father, Seth. Mrs. Smith, Seth's sister, protested Jack's enlistment because he was underaged. However, the youngster did enlist. Kate married Wilson P. Kretschmar, a Greenville banker. Smith Diary and Bible.

Jeans to make me a suit of clothes. Love & kisses—and May God, the giver of all good ever bless, comfort, & preserve you is the ardent prayer of

Yr. devoted husband
Will

Camp M.L. Smith, Panola
November 2nd, 1862

My darling,

On Friday evening a little after dark I arrived at this place safe & sound and not much wearied with my long jaunt. If you will take any map of Mississippi, you will soon be able to ascertain our route from Greenville via Judge Yerger's & Bogue Phalia. The distance is much greater than you would imagine by looking at the map, owing to the many crooks, and turns in the road, which winds about thru' the *bottom* like a "wounded snake." It seems, however, not to have wearied the crowd much.

A few days, Nellie, away after a short stay at home (how sweet that dear old word sounds) appears like an age: and how fast time stole by when I was with you![6] I used to sit and in my dreamy way count the strokes of the pendulum and regret that each pulsation marked an interval of time less of that in which I was privileged to sit and talk with those I love. And while thus counting how warm & tender my heart grew, and how it clung about the remaining space of time allotted me; as fondly as the wayworn traveller across the desert views the green oasis sleeping on the desolate waste of sand about him. I cannot well express my feelings towards or affections for you, for when I begin the tear drops well up & glisten in my eyes and the pen staggers over the traced lines of my paper. To love you dearly and consider you as the "idol of my affections" requires no effort: it is natural as it is for me to breathe. Every breath I draw is perfumed with the holy incense of this sacred affection, and every wish invokes the protection of a thoughtful Providence upon your head. But enough of this, I shall wake to tuneful action the melancholy longings of your own precious little heart, and make the "melancholy days" of the year indeed the saddest.

We are encamped near the Tallahatchie River upon the first range of hills, and I believe, are considered to be in a healthy location. The water is

---

[6]The Muster Rolls of the 28th Cavalry record Nugent as on sick furlough for October, 1862. Confederate Archives, R.G. 109.

very good being pure and cool. We have so far had an abundance of forage for our horses & have plenty to eat. Flour of an inferior quality can be had for fifteen cents per pound & chickens at twenty five cents a piece. Coffee has effectually "played out"—sugar is abundant & a tolerably fair stock of bacon on hand. The Colonel wanted to make me Adjutant, but I will & have politely declined the appointment under him. What I formerly would have gladly accepted, I now feel would be a clear disgrace. He foisted upon us his ignorant and utterly incompetent son, and seems to want other persons now to "cleanse the Augean Stable" & retrieve the Regiment from the odium under which it rests. This is an ungracious task at best; and under Col. Starke would be hopelessly impossible. He pursues a course of toadyism towards the Generals which keeps him in favor; but with his Regiment he has sunk far beyond the hope of redemption. His field & staff do not even approve of his course, and the men are fond of cursing him. He carries things with a high hand and actually threatens to sacrifice the lives of his men because of their abuse. I shall ascertain, soon I hope, upon what basis his claims to the position of Colonel rest; and if we can reorganize we will lift him out of his boots.

My health is very good at present and I trust will continue to improve.—

The news now is, that there is a probability of recognition and intervention soon on the part of France & England. This is believed here by many and may be true, but I must confess I am not hopeful. Van Dorn had been superseded several days before his fight and was only notified; but fought anyhow in a sheer fit of desperation—We get the daily newspapers here by Rail Road. I will write by Lake Bolivar unless I can find someone going thru'. Love & kissess—May God bless, comfort & preserve you is the prayer of

> Your fond & devoted husband
> Will

> Camp M. L. Smith
> Panola, Miss. Nov. 16th, 1862

My darling wife,

I am again blessed with an opportunity to write you and to draw you nearer to me in a short communion of heart, by the speechless flow of letters:—all of which do not equal the ardent kiss & close pressure to my bosom of your loved form. The playful, affectionate smile that lights up your countenance when we meet and the fondness with which you linger about me are far dearer to me than other terrestrial blessings. I am not as you know, much of a hand to talk;—my forte is in the outward manifestation by action of the inward feeling—the expression of which is impossible. The deep & almost ever present heart yearning for home—its light shades—its quiet & perfect enjoyment—its hopes & fears—its plans for future pleasures—its joys & alas! its sorrows—too often swells the fountain of my tears, until the effervescing drops are dropped in quick succession down my cheeks. It may be a vanity—but I like the quick susceptibility to feeling that is almost a characteristic of my nature; the facility with which I can weep with those who weep and rejoice with those who rejoice—might not be a very good trait of character by some. I suppose, though, you prefer a wild exuberance of feeling to that cold, passive selfishness that is a characteristic of a nature directly antagonistic to mine.

The present position of our army is not very flattering. We hope for the best, however, and look forward to a victory in the neighborhood of Abbeville, which will relieve us of the presence of one army at least. The removal of Genl. Beauregard was unfortunate, leaving as it did no general in the field who had the sympathy & confidence of the people; for say what they will, soldiers cannot & do not fight successfully under an inefficient or unsuccessful officer. Their instincts very soon teach them whom to trust, and a firm reliance upon the commanding General superinduces a self confidence that is absolutely essential to victory. Bragg, I do not think, is capable of leading a large army. He is a good tactician, an able disciplinarian and a good Major General: beyond this, I do not suppose, he could be relied upon. There are few men of genius at the head of our armies. Beauregard is one, so are Lee & Johnston. There is no news from Virginia except that McClellan is displaced & Burnside put at the head of the Army of the Potomac. I hope & believe this will result in good to us. The Yankee army is again advancing upon Richmond, in a different way though. They hope to come down the Valley above Manassas Junction, or failing in this to come up in the Peninsula on the south side of the James. At last accounts Bragg was pushing on towards Nashville as a feint to cover the withdrawal of supplies; and by a rapid countermarch to take the Yankee army in the rear when they shall have advanced considerably into the State of Mississippi. This is a good idea—only a surmise—if it can be carried out successfully. Napoleon could do it if he were here:—alas! we have no Napoleon in genius. We hear nothing from Arkansas, The people here are becoming alarmed and are leaving rapidly every day: some for Texas & others for the Arkansas hills. The whole Northern portion of the State will soon be a wilderness.

We are still under orders to move below, and will I hope move soon. I do want to be near you, so that in case of danger you can be removed to some place of security. My health is pretty good. I have been troubled for several days with a bad cold & neuralgia that have given me some pain and trouble. Am better now. I received a letter from Tom yesterday. He is in tolerable health and had some prospect of being appointed Quarter Master in some Texas Regiment. He didn't say a word about his sweetheart & I judge *"she has played out"* & kicked him. Clarence got a letter from Mother the other day. They were all pretty well at home, and intended if possible to move out to the hills.—

We have a triweekly mail from Grenada to Bolivar, Miss. and if the Post Master at Greenville could make the proper arrangements, you could get letters & papers both. Love & kisses and may God bless, comfort & preserve you is the prayer of

Your devoted husband
Will

Send your letters in the most convenient way and make any arrangement you please about it—

Hd. Qrs. 28th Regt. Miss. Vols.
Camp Vaiden, Nov. 24th, 1862

My darling wife,

Your affectionate letter greeted me on my arrival in camp tonight from an extended tour of observation through the Northern portion of this County, whither I was sent to examine its topographical features and obstruct all roads converging at this point. The task is onerous, trouble-some and highly responsible; but I find pleasure in roaming through the country & eating "home made victuals." Only think of fresh butter, splen-did biscuits, sweet milk, honey, fried chicken & *real coffee,* if you please, and then add fresh pork, beef steak, &c—"as well as other things too numerous to mention." I have twenty men from my Company and eighteen

& a Lieutenant from another under me. The men are delighted so far at their comparative freedom and are clamorous to be kept at it a "little" longer. I think I shall be detained on the work for a week longer and then return to await something new to turn up.

From the movements of the enemy, we are induced to think they will move a column of troops down the roads from Memphis, and another from Helena, converging their lines at or below this place. There are strong reasons for a contrary opinion, however, the item of transportation being the strongest. Added to this is the difficulty attendant upon a march through the swamp over the obstructed roads. My own impression is that they will move along the Memphis & Tennessee & the Mississippi Central R.Roads and effect a junction at or near Grenada to which place a few thousand men could march from Prentiss or Greenville very handily. They will make a desperate effort to take Jackson & Vicksburg this fall; and unless almost superhuman efforts are made by us Mississippi will be lost. Gen. Pemberton is a man of activity & enterprise I learn, though I must confess I should prefer Beauregard, who, you know, is my pet General. I find everything here in abundance, and really think it criminal that the tremendous surplus of corn &c. has not been removed before. The R.Road is carrying it off every day in large quantities, but the Quarter Masters are dillydallying about *Sacks*.

It was reported that Bragg had reached Holly Springs with fifteen thousand troops. The report is not generally credited here, and I am inclined to disbelieve it. The wish is not father to the thought either.

I take great pleasure in informing you that Capt. Blackburn has not resigned, nor do I think he ever intends doing such a thing. If he does Ben Johnson will be Captain ahead of me. I do not aspire to high position, not coveting the "short lived glories of war," and I shall endeavor to do my duties as Second Lieutenant to the best of my skill & judgment. A good many of our men, doubtless, would like for me to be Capt. but I do not want it. The responsibility is very great when a man conscientiously endeavors to discharge his duty faithfully. I find one thing to be the case: *big* men know very little more than I am confident I do. This has astonished me very much indeed.

You forgot to tell me whether Carnes succeeded in getting you any flour or sugar. I hope he did, as I should dislike to see you out of both, and sugar will become very scarce this winter.

I suppose Kate goes to school with Evie, and that you find some solace in endeavoring to impart instruction to the girls. Give her my love & tell her I hope she will be prepared to love me as a cousin "when the war is ended." Jack is a noble, little fellow; a fearless, brave good boy and deserved all possible encouragement. By keeping him with me I hope to give tone to his morals & impress correct ideas of duty upon his mind.

I am heartily glad to learn that Alf is improving. Tell him for me that he owes it, at this juncture as a high duty to himself & others to take particular care of himself. You all may have soon to rely upon him for protection. I will be so busy that I cannot well leave the army for sometime to come, and your Pa is getting old.[7]

You don't know how it rejoices me to know that you can realize the extent of my affection for you; for I again assure you, you constitute the polar star toward which all the wealth of my love gravitates. Love & Kisses & May God of all mercy love, cherish protect & preserve you is the prayer of

> Your ever devoted husband
> Will

> Grenada
> Dec. 4, 1862

My darling Wife,

Mrs. Nelson goes home this evening so I avail myself of the opportunity to drop you a few hurried lines.

We arrived here today from our former encampment in hopes in this of having a brush with the enemy, as it usually is however we are only doing picket service. Things are looking gloomy enough for us here. The Yankees are advancing from Holly Springs, Helena and Greenville and will unless something is speedily done, result in the fall of Vicksburg and the opening of the Mississippi River. This plan of the campaign is just such as I anticipated and our Generals do not seem to have anticipated the movements of the enemy at all.

---

[7]On January 6, 1863, while riding unarmed and dressed in a dark blue civilian suit, Abram F. Smith was shot in the back by a member of a Federal platoon. He made his way home, but he died the next day. Reportedly, he was Washington County's first civilian casualty. Newspaper clipping written by Stevenson Archer, in possession of LSH.

The possession of all our principal towns by the enemy will be useful to us if we only take advantage of the opportunity afforded us. We had a dreary time marching from above here sleeping in the open and with the rain pattering down upon us, eating a little cornbread and bacon not enough for a baby. [Illegible] and although it is hard find that I am fattening on it. I am now under a *rail tent* made thus and covered with a few blankets, with the cold rain pattering down.

I am well and doing tolerably well. We will have to give up Mississippi and move to Tennessee I fear. Still I am hopeful and doubt not we will eventually succeed.

Love & kisses & may God Bless, comfort, protect & preserve you is the prayer of your devoted husband

In haste
W.L.N.

✆✶✇

Hd. Qrs. 28th Regt. Miss. Vols.
March 24th, 1863

My own dear little wife,

Excuse the diminutive, but it has, when taken in connection with your darling self, a tinge of endearment about it so attractive that I like to use it. I know, too, that you are somewhat sensitive on the subject; tho' with the gallant explanation above given, you cannot feel offended without doing violence to your feelings of affection for your absent husband.

Here we are after a very worrying time camped a mile or two north of Spring Hill, Tenn; and about twenty five miles south of Nashville. To describe my trip from Columbia to Spring Hill & thence by way of White's Bridge back to Columbia, would be tedious and uninteresting. Over mountains and through Cedar Brakes; across creeks nearly swimming & ploughing through mud nearly saddle skirts deep, we went riding for about twenty hours right ahead. We have been driven around so much that one large Regiment is reduced to about three hundred & twenty effective men, for duty. Our number is dwindling down every day; and my belief is, we will be sent back to Mississippi soon to recruit. I hope this may be the case, as I am heartily sick of the Volunteer State. We have had very little good weather since we came here, and rains when a man has no shelter are quite disagreeable. The Soldiers, however, manage to protect themselves by making shelters and apparently fare tolerable well. We have had a very good supply of provisions so far, tho' after the recent raid of the Yankees down to Rutherford's Creek, we can find little or nothing. The Yankees took all the flour & bacon from the people, and burnt all the fencing around the wheat fields to prevent the raising of another crop in carrying out the idea of attempting to starve us to death. The supply of subsistence for the coming winter will be very short indeed unless something unexpected happens. The darkest hour is, however, just before day; and it may be, and I fervently pray will happen, that after we shall have been sufficiently humbled, a merciful God will open the way for our escape.

The news from Bragg's Army is very favorable; and if rumor be true, Rosecrans is now falling back & Bragg pursuing him. The wily Yankee may be making a feint merely, to draw us upon his entrenched position on Stone River and thus, by gaining a decided advantage at the start, defeat our well laid plans. We learn that Longstreet & Marshall are marching into Ky. with a view to drive Rosecrans back & open a high road for supplies from the dark & bloody ground. I fear such a move is absolutely essential. The Confederacy is getting pretty well drained and there are manifest here no symptoms of a disposition to "pitch a crop" this year. In fact so much fencing has been destroyed by both armies that it is almost impossible to plant or raise anything.

We are under old Bragg now and are forced to work like everything. Yesterday we were drawn up in line of battle all day long: & a day or two before after swimming Duck River in part we were drawn up all night long & travelled until 5 P.M. the next day. It would be tedious to enumerate the utter folly of our different movements as a general thing. Our Generals appear not to know what to do at times, and the fun of it is, the men frequently see it. I have no great confidence in our little General as yet. He is a Northern born man raised in Kentucky. I do not believe he can manoeuvre a Regiment on the field. I may judge him harshly, however, and if I do, shall be more than pleased to recant. His staff officers are a drinking, rollicking, set of men, and profane as pirates. General Van Dorn still maintains his reputation for *gallantry!* and you can see at times some fine looking *ladies* driving about in his splendid four horse Ambulance. I do not relish such an officer and am only reconciled by the ability he displayed in capturing those Yankees at Thompson's Station. The fight was a well conceived and well executed affair, and would have been still more success-ful had we pursued vigorously after the infantry was caught. We could have captured the Batteries & all the Cavalry. Genl. V.D. was, however, ordered not to pursue, and bit his teeth, doubtless, with vexation. We could have made a clean deal of the whole Yankee force.

Col. Starke is, I firmly believe, more than a match for the most of our officers; and that we can be successful with our present Generals & Colonels is wonderful. There are very few of them who know anything about tactics or the management of troops in camp; the consequence is, our Brigade some 4,000 in number, only musters some 800 for duty. Just *one-fifth*: only think of it. The General officers are all the time giving their attention to parties, balls &c. and neglect their troops. They can give as many orders as their Adjutants, by hard labor, can transcribe, and beyond this they do not extend their efforts. Regimental Commissaries are turned loose and instructed to grab all they can get for their commands, while the Brig. Commissary enjoys his *otium cum dignitate* in a private house over a canteen of whiskey & a pipe. Col. Starke not inaptly remarked the other day that this Cavalry Corps was rapidly going to the Devil.

I am in pretty good health; and am not as much exposed as the balance of the Regt. Acting as Adjutant I sleep in the Colonel's Tent and get an abundance of forage for my horses. I could not otherwise enjoy these great blessings in such a campaign as this: and besides I have no scouting or picketing to do. You do not know what a relief this is; but Alf can tell you.

I haven't heard from home since I left and am consequently very anxious. I take it for granted, you are all well until I learn the reverse, and am thus enabled to keep the blues away. I would like very much to go back to Mississippi where I could hear from you all and hope soon to see you once more. Clarence is well & sends his love & respects. For me Love & Kisses. And May God Almighty bless, comfort, protect & preserve is the daily & hourly prayer of

Yr. devoted husband
Will

Hd.Qrs. 28th Regt. Miss. Vols.
Near Spring Hill, Tenn.
May 2nd, 1863

My Darling, cherished wife,

Since my last letter to you nothing of unusual interest has transpired here. Beyond the ordinary excitement of picketing at intervals, and a hurried saddling up of the Command when the enemy made a raid upon our *videttes*, we have had a dull, dreary desolate time. We are encamped upon a succession of slopes whose sides are bathed in sunlight from "dewy morn" to "stilly eve." A few beeches, clothed in the green & fresh garb of Spring, relieve the tedious monotony of the landscape around us; but broken & burnt fences, pillaged houses & untilled fields remind us of the presence of war in our midst; a war so devastating & dreadful. Horror of horrors is not a term expressive enough for war. But enough of this; from all accounts you are now completely hemmed in by the enemy, and will soon learn by heart, as a child, the oft told tale, the recital of their outrages and the invocation of divine punishment upon them. I have given up all hopes of ever saving anything from the crash that will inevitably follow close upon the heels of the termination of the present contest. If famine should not stalk abroad throughout this once-happy land we will only have the beneficent ruler of a wicked world to be grateful to for it. War, pestilence & famine usually succeed one another in the order named; and are doubtless intended to remind us that the first is utterly inconsistent with the duties we owe the Supreme Being. For myself I am perfectly satisfied that war is altogether an unmixed evil, and can never be justified unless in self-defense; and the only thing that can at all reconcile me to our war is the fact of its being for our homes & friends, our altars & our liberties.

How I long to hear from you and read the lines [Page torn] the privilege of folding you in my arms as in days "lang syne." Since I came to Tennessee, I have not seen or visited a lady, except casually, and content myself with thinking of you by day and dreaming of you by night. I have heard a sermon once or twice only & then enjoyed the word spoken excessively. You have no idea how demoralizing camp life is and how difficult it is for one to preserve his consistency of life and his inward purity of heart. Oaths, blasphemies, imprecations, obscenity are hourly heard ringing in your ears until your mind is almost filled with them; and the difficulty is to guard against suffering them to dwell within your mind. Still, by the grace of God, I am enabled to live somewhat up to my professions, tho' not as much as I would desire.

Continued rumors reach of Bragg's advance; and cavalry raids towards Kentucky. I am not disturbed much in my equanimity by these reports, knowing from experience the regularity & tardiness with which large armies move. Bragg may advance to about thirty miles beyond Tullahoma; but I do not think he will get beyond a day's march of his entrenched position. Meanwhile the Yankees will advance up the Cumberland and threaten his left flank & force him, unless he displays better generalship than heretofore, to retire even beyond Tullahoma. We do not hear nowadays of sudden & rapid movements; the destruction of one wing of an army by combined & concentrated massing of troops; and the sudden hurling of a mass of troops against the flank of the center & the other wing; the steady yet swift strategy that characterized the motion of Napoleon's troops, nor the irresistible weight of Cromwell's columns. These are things we read in history and are [Torn Page].

I hear we will go to Mississippi after the anticipated fight here. Which I hope may be the case, I cannot promise you a speedy return however, unless I can be released from the army. Present my kindest regards to my friends and particularly Judge Yerger's and Judge Devine's families. Can never forget their disinterested kindness.

May God bless you always.

Your devoted husband
Will

Camp near Big Blk.
Madison Co. Miss. June 8th, 1863

My darling wife,

I wrote to you regularly from Tenn. and having heard nothing from you take the opportunity to write a few lines by Mr. Paxton.[8] My health is very good just now and I hope will continue so; and that God will nerve my arm for the coming conflict and prepare me for the dangers of the battlefield. I believe & trust that I will be protected in the "perilous edge of battle" and that I will yet be enabled to embrace you again. Mr. Paxton gives very gloomy accounts of the depredation of the Yankees in Washington County and I fear that you are involved in the general ruin. Nevertheless be in good heart and trust in Providence, and we will come out all right in the end. We may be straightened in circumstances & compelled to live on short rations—but the good Lord will not forsake us nor will he see us

---

[8]A. J. Paxton owned vast new lands along Deer Creek in southern Washington County. PWCHS, 320.

begging bread. Our revolutionary forefathers suffered worse than we—& were compelled to run for their very lives.

Our forces here are ready to strike an effective blow and when Genl. J. gives the command for an advance the columns will move and woe betide the Yankee army. We are all confident of a complete success and I firmly believe will raise the Vicksburg Siege and destroy Grant's Army.

Genl. Bragg is momentarily expecting a collision with Rosecrans and is also confident of success. If we succeed in our efforts with the Tenn. & Miss. Armies we will move forward towards the North and drive the Yankees before us.

I would prefer, if possible, that you all move away from Washington County, Mississippi to some place of security. At the present juncture it is impossible for me to render you any assistance & you must rely upon Alf whom you must, at all hazards, keep out of the army for your protection. Write me by first opportunity and give me full particulars of your condition & the state of things generally in our County & particularly as regards our immediate family. Don't be despondent—look up & aloft—Tell Ma to write me a long letter & be very particular to do so yourself. Love & Kisses—& may God have you in his most holy care & keeping is the daily prayer of

Your devoted husband
W. L. Nugent

Camp near Mechanicsburg
June 18th, 1863

My darling Nellie,

I received your letter of the 4th yesterday and was lifted up by its perusal notwithstanding the sad tenor of a portion of it. I am pleased to hear that we are not altogether ruined, tho' somewhat pinched for the necessaries of life. Of these we may always confidently expect our due & have relying upon the promises of Him who never fails. We are now undergoing the "Experimentum Crucis"—the experiment or trial of the cross—and when we are purged by the fiery trials surrounding us, will be astonished at the good luck that has attended us.

I was in the Franklin charge—had the honor of forming the Regiment for the Charge and rallying it when the fight was over. I was acting Adjutant at the time. I escaped by the good providence of God; and feel that the shelter of his wings will still attend me. To this end we must all, however, unite our petitions to the rich throne of Heavenly Grace. I must confess to a very hopeful condition of mind. Our affairs all around look more cheerful than ever, and the Confederacy is better off in the way of supplies for the army than ever, and our soldiers are becoming better satisfied of our ultimate success. This will prevent straggling and keep up our numerical strength.

My health is pretty good at present. Will write at every opportunity and expect you to do the same. Letters can be forwarded from the creek here almost regularly. If directed to me at Canton—Co. D. 28th Regt. Miss. Vols. Cosby's Brigade, Jackson's Division—Haven't time to write more— Will Yerger is now waiting to carry this letter to Jackson for the purpose of being forwarded.

Love & kisses—Jack and Clarence both well & send love. May God bless comfort & protect you is the prayer of

Yr. devoted husband
Will

Camp near Mechanicsburg
June 24, '63

My own darling wife,

Again I have been exposed to the missiles of the enemy, and again, by the blessing of God, have escaped. A *spent* grape shot struck my right arm but didn't hurt me at all. May our all wise & all merciful Providence continue this protection to me ward and preserve me to rejoin you before long amidst all the blessings of peace.

We left camp at nine o'clock at night and rode all night resting about one & half hours the next morning—After feeding our horses and sleeping a short while we mounted and rode some nine or ten miles in a circuitous direction in the direction of the enemy's pickets. We were jogging along at an easy gait when the outpost pickets made their appearance. Adam's Regt. in front raised the shout & dashed after them. These Yankees retreated upon their reserve in a very hurried manner, and their whole reserve was drawn up in line of battle in and across the road that runs along a ridge which only occasionally expands sufficiently to afford room for a small force even to deploy; generally the road runs along & completely occupies the

112

ridge. Image one of these places with deep gullies on either flank & the woods just thick enough to cover skirmishes & you have the enemy's position. The road approaching this place runs parallel with it for some distance within easy range of rifles & cannon, & then directly perpendicular, the only protection being the growing corn. As we dashed up the small field piece the Yankees had opened upon us with grape and wounded a good many horses—Two of Adam's Squadrons were engaged, Cleveland in front & Yerger on Right. Our Company & the 1st Squadron were on the left to turn their flank. Co. *D* went in with its usual spirit and took the Yankee Cannon, five horses, several prisoners &c.—We charged with such a yell that the Yankees left the field in a run and didn't take time to shoot at us at all. The result of the fight was four killed about a dozen wounded on our side—Yankee loss 40 prisoners, 45 killed & a good many wounded. We captured some 30 horses.

When Genl. Johnston will move it is impossible to tell. He is preparing to raise the siege of the Hill City as soon as possible and I have every reason to think he will accomplish his purpose. He is confident of discomfiting Genl. Grant. Genl. Lee is reported to be at or near the Capital of Pennsylvania with 90,000 men. Business is suspended in Philadelphia and the whole state is in an uproar. Genl. Bragg is near Nashville and Rosecrans retreating; and now if we can only defeat Grant the Yankees will, I hope, let us alone for awhile. At least I earnestly hope so.—Matters are becoming very complicated up in the Northwestern States, and there will be a civil war soon between the Democrats & Abolitionists. I confidently look forward to a cessation of hostilities as soon as the next Congress meets; and if the war fever has a short time to cool off the Yanks can never revive it.—They are keeping up the drooping spirits of their soldiers by exciting their fears of our vengeance and encouraging hopes of the speedy capture of our stronghold. This, I trust, they will never accomplish.—

My health is pretty good, tho' I have for several days past been afflicted with the camp diarrhoea that gives me a little trouble. My greatest discomfort arises from the want of the means of Grace. I hear no sermons, hear none of the Songs of Zion, and am verily a stranger in a strange land. I find it almost impossible to *enjoy* religion surrounded by everything that is evil, and cheered by very little that is good.

Clarence & Jack are both well & hearty and send their love to all. I learn you have all moved back to the plantation; and on this subject am very much of Judge Yerger's opinion. I scarcely think Alf can succeed in taking the negroes to Texas. If not he had better move them to the interior of the State and behind our army. I think it would be better to take them all to Texas & dispose of them there if practicable. I understand they command very *high prices.*

I heard from Jefferson yesterday. None of your relatives have been disturbed at all. The Yankees didn't reach them. By the way, Howell Hinds was very badly injured by a wound through the fleshy part of the back.[9] He is suffering a great deal but will, I think, recover. Capt. Yerger was badly wounded in the thigh. He is cheerful, however, and says he will give them another turn.

Our camp fare is limited in the number and kind of food. Cornbread, bacon & beef generally rules the roost. Occasionally we have chickens; now & then butter & eggs—Biscuits are a rarity; but the incoming wheat crop will remedy this defect. Love & Kisses and may God bless, comfort, direct & preserve you is the ardent prayer of

Yr. devoted husband
Will

Have Maria, Agnes & Uncle Frank deserted you?[10]
Let me know the names of all who have gone.

Mrs. Wilson's near
Mechanicsburg
June 28th, 1863

My darling wife,

Mr. Sutton two or three days since conveyed a letter from me to you, and Mr. Shanahan will carry this.[11] Nothing of interest has occurred since Mr. Sutton left. We went out to *ambush* the Yankees, but they wouldn't be drawn out at all. Our Company ran up on their picket camp and endeavored all in vain to invite pursuit. The Yankees anticipated an attack on our

---

[9]Howell Hinds was the son of General Thomas Hinds of Plum Ridge Plantation on Rattlesnake Bayou. After the destruction of their home, the Smiths lived with the Hinds family. The baby Nellie of these letters was born on the Hinds plantation. Smith Family Bible.

[10]Servants of the Smiths. Many of the former servants were departing during the heavy Greenville fighting of March, April, and May 1863. Newspaper clipping in possession of LSH.

[11]James M. Sutton had extensive land holdings in Washington County along the river. PWCHS, 65. Shanahan was among the first Irish to come to Greenville.

part and had ambuscaded their force to give us *issue*. Both sides were thus outwitted without any intention on their part. We struck them a tolerably heavy blow in a small way the other day, and they do not intend to be caught napping again.

Old Grant is moving all his heavy baggage across the River preparatory to a fight or a run I scarcely know which. The news now is that Gen. Lee is within ten miles of Harrisburg, the Capital of Pennsylvania, driving everything before him and making every Dutchman, woman & child take the oath of allegiance to the Southern Confederacy. This is done, I suppose, for the purpose of exchanging them for our Southern men who have been forced to take the Lincoln oath, and is a very felicitous idea. Our Virginia Army is now feasting on crackers and cheese, coffee, bacon & everything else that heart could wish. This dash will open old Abe's eyes. He has left Washington and is removing the public records and archives. He will doubtless leave Washington to its fate and establish the capital at New York or Chicago one. Bragg has sent his cavalry into Kentucky and Maysville, Lexington and Frankfort are ours. If our army now advances we will soon have the whole State of Kentucky under our control and with it about 20,000 more fighting men; a great desideratum every way. I have greater hopes than ever of an early termination to this war and think I will be at home again before January for good. Don't you wish this could be the case? Magruder is reported marching on New Orleans and Banks has left Port Hudson in disgust. I don't think Grant will get more than ½ of his men back north from around Vicksburg, and what he does take away will be worthless as soldiers. The chills & fevers & mosquitoes will kill them off by hundreds.

My health is good & Clarence & Jack. Am ordered on camp duty immediately which will take the whole of the evening & must close—Love & kisses & May God bless, comfort & preserve you is my prayer—

Yr. devoted husband
Will

Deer Creek, July 8th, 1863

My darling Nellie,

A carrier brings me [news] that Vicksburg has fallen; *no particulars given*. I am ordered to work my way out by the most practicable route.

This sad catastrophe will have the effect to paralyze our army, and if Grant follows up his success vigorously there is no telling what the result will be. One thing is sure the River must be surrendered to the Yankees and our country now belongs to them by right of conquest. I presume you will be safe and secure where you are; and if not inconvenient the safer policy is for *as many as possible* to keep together. When you can remove with safety to yourself you had all better go to Texas where Brother Perry will give you a home & living is cheap. The war will soon be terminated one way or another this year, and we will either be defeated absolutely or some compromise made that will restore the old Union as it was. In any event wherever you go, if advised, I shall follow you & your & my fortunes shall be identical. Do not be alarmed; as far as your personal safety is concerned you will be better off now than you were before the fall of V.Burg—The Courier waits—Love & kisses & May God Almighty bless comfort & preserve you.

Yr. devoted husband
Will

Camp near Brandon, Miss.
July 28th, 1863

My own dear wife,

Corporal Robb of my Company has been furloughed, as well as several men from the Bolivar Company, and I take advantage of the opportunity to write you a letter, which I hope may serve to relieve you, in some measure, of the great anxiety that is superinduced by the present condition of our public affairs.[12] Recently after the fall of V.Burg I entertained the most gloomy forbodings of the future; and indeed the great demoralization produced in our army thereby added to the submissive spirit of the people generally, was enough to make one dispirited. The enemy have, however, ceased pursuing Johnston and have withdrawn their army to the hills of Warren to recruit. This will afford us an opportunity to reorganize and rediscipline our army and to call out our reserve: thus bringing us somewhat upon an equality with General Grant, whom, I hope we may hereafter successfully encounter. If I am not greatly mistaken the possession of

---

[12]Joseph H. Robb lived in the Lake Lee region, and in the Grover Cleveland administration served as postmaster of Greenville. PWCHS, 326.

the River will prove a conquest barren of results. The west will soon discover that the trade upon which they heretofore throve has been ruined and that there are few or no customers for their redundant supplies. The fertile valley of the Mississippi has been desolated and the millions of dollars once realized by Western men thru' the trade along the banks of our mighty River will be entirely lost. Our people have no money and no exchangeable commodity; and must be the recipients alone of bounties if they consume Western produce. The consequence of this state of things will, I hope, produce a state of indifference to the further prosecution of the war. We are now driven to fight to the bitter end, if conquest itself be the result. The ruling majority are contending to emancipate our slaves, and if the negroes are freed the country, as a general thing, is not worth fighting for at all. We will all be compelled to abandon it and seek some more congenial climate. Pemberton's Corps will be reorganized & placed under command of some more efficient General, who may succeed in bringing a little order out of a great deal of chaos. This being accomplished, we will have a pretty big army out here, which will be hard to whip. I have no idea we will attempt to hold the state west of the Mobile & Ohio R.Road, and believe our efforts will be directed to Genl. Rosecrans' Army first. In fact, we ought to be going there now as fast as possible. Our force added to Bragg's would enable to whip the Army of the Cumberland, and this would accomplish more for our cause than the retention of Mobile. Jeff. Davis, tho', I fear will continue his old policy of endeavoring to hold fortified places and seabord cities to the great detriment of our cause. We need *concentration*. Charleston ought to have been left to take care of itself & Beauregard should have been sent to Lee's assistance. Johnston ought to have sent all possible reinforcements to Bragg and beat the life out of him while Grant was driving away at V.Burg; Why it is our Generals can't see through a campaign I cannot discover. Their penetration does not extend below the surface and they are moving about utterly unconscious of the great issues now pending or of the magnitude of the task imposed upon us.

We are now lying here roasting in the sun, eating roasting ears & vegetables in the main. A little beef, an occasional leg of mutton and a boiled ham now & then constitute our bill of fare.—Still we enjoy ourselves very well, and think our time is passing away pleasantly enough. We are daily in anticipation of orders to move—where no one knows unless it be Gen. Joe's confidants, who are few in number. Like our brethren of African

117

descent we doze away the hours of noon under the shade of the broad oaks around us on a blanket, utterly oblivious of the morrow. We are fast becoming soldiers indeed. The other night I slept in the open air during a considerable rain & awoke in the morning very much refreshed. The rain didn't even give me a cold. Ben Johnston, Fowler & Capt. Blackburn are all absent sick and I cannot get a furlough.[13] As soon as two of them return I will make my application, and try to get to you: I would risk capture to be allowed the privilege of remaining with you a few days. They are now giving two weeks furloughs allowing travelling time in going to & returning from home.—I had an amusing time with the boys drawing lots for furloughs. John & Tom Dunn *drew blanks* much to my regret. They have both become good soldiers, and by the steady attention to duty are entitled to some favor of the sort. The policy of giving furloughs should have been kept up from the beginning. It would have saved a great many of our men to us & prevented them from running off to see their families & make the necessary provision for them.

From the policy pursued by Genl. Sherman around V.Burg I judge you will not be in any danger at home. They will compel *you* to [give] him your slaves, perhaps, but will compel *them* to obey & respect you. You will be enabled to live, I hope. I gave Alf 50$ in La. money with which you can purchase the necessaries of life along the river, and will endeavor to procure more current money for you. As long as you are quiet & the country is not invaded by either army you can get along well; and being now within the lines & power of the enemy you will have to be politic.

My health continues to be tolerably fair—and promises to continue good during the balance of the summer. Our men are generally healthy, tho' we have a good many cases of intermittent fever, which readily yields to treatment. The shirts you sent me came in the nick of time; I had been endeavoring for sometime to get me some shirts. If Alf needs money and can come down I will let him have it; and as you may be driven out of the Yankee lines it might be as well to have some Confederate money. I have some 1,500$ at my immediate command. There is no telling what emergency may arise and Alf had better be in a position to aid you. Hence I would not approve his going into the army just now. Tell Sis I regretted

---

[13]Fowler appears to be the man designated in 1864 to clear Washington County of looters. Instead, he was captured by Union troops, executed, and buried on Swiftwater Plantation. PWCHS, 224–25.

very much not being able to see her before I left and I am sorry she didn't remain at home especially as she knew I was going to return at the time appointed.

Good fortune & a kind Providence have attended me thus far and I hope this war will soon end and permit our reunion once more. Love & Kisses to all; and May God Almighty bless, comfort, direct & preserve you is the prayer of your

Ever devoted husband
Will

In the Field, Aug. 4, 1863

My darling wife,

I wrote you a long letter the other day by Ben Offutt and as Corp. Robb's furlough has just been forwarded to us I am enabled to write you a few lines more.[14] Since I last wrote we have been hurrying around in this county [Hinds] making a reconnoissance in force in front of the Yankees. As usual found the Yankees too strong for us and are now going back to Brandon where we will go into camp again & roast for several weeks. As soon as we return and another one of our officers comes back I will get a furlough and be at home for two or three weeks. My health continues to be tolerably good, and I am beginning to hope that I may escape having an attack of bilious fever this summer.

I received a note from Col. Ferguson the other day in which he has invited me to accept the position of Adj. Genl. Added to this I am highly recommended; without solicitation on my part for the position of Major of the 12th Miss. Regt. Cavalry and that you may know your husband is not unappreciated by some I send the letter of recommendation enclosed herein.[15] I will accept either position tendered because it will place me in a position to do my country more efficient service and I will not be cramped. I dislike excessively inciting my mind and capacity subsidiary & tributary to the inability of my superiors, and will escape from my chains as soon as possible. I feel that if I have an opportunity I can render important service:

---

[14]Ben Offutt lived on the Ashbrook Plantation owned by his father Dr. Zack Offutt. PWCHS, 240.

[15]Ferguson's request stated that he knew "of no officer as capable of assisting" him as Nugent, who was "a most competent officer." S. W. Ferguson to B. T. Ewell, July 27, 1863, Confederate Archives, R.G. 109.

but no matter what I do in the 28th Miss. I can never get credit for it. This is a source of continual annoyance to me, and makes me to a certain extent discontented and unhappy. This discontent, however, does not make me unhappy except for a moment, because the natural elasticity of my mind raises me above all trivial disappointments. I am more in heart now than I was some days since. Our absentees are returning and our army is gradually swelling to something like its usual size. I hope when U.S. Grant, Esq., pays us another visit, he will find a force more numerous than those at Jackson. In this Department, however, things have been badly managed, and we want a brilliant victory to inspirit our soldiers. The people, though, are much to blame for the desertion of the troops. They are almost ready now to *submit absolutely* to old Abe's will and kiss the rod that strikes them. It is now too late "to retire from the contest; there is no retreat but in submission & slavery." We can never get any honorable terms unless we continue fighting, and dishonorable terms I hope we would never consent to receive. Grant's inactivity at V.Burg will save us if we take the proper advantage of it: and I hope our people will respond bravely to the call. Meanwhile do not be discouraged, but with a firm reliance upon Almighty God, be trustful, hopeful. Love & Kisses and May a kind Providence ever bless, comfort & preserve you is the prayer of

Yr. devoted husband
Will

Hd. Qrs. 28th Regt. Miss. Vols.
Near Brandon, Aug. 7th, 1863

My darling Nellie,

I wrote you a hasty note by Corp. Robb; and now having the opportunity write by Capt. Gay for the purpose of convincing you that you are ever present to my thoughts & that the *oak* is supported by the *ivy*.[16] The soft & pleasant sensations engendered in my heart by the reflection that the constant outgushings of your early affection, ripened by the subduing experiences of married life, ever steal their winsome way into the depths of my bosom, beguile the wearisome toil of many a long and tedious day. As when the cooling zephyrs cheat the dazzling summer's sun of all his

---

[16]W. L. Gay lived near the present town of Winterville. PWCHS, 247.

blinding heat and woo the way worn soldier's frame to a gentle rest, so do these sensations instill a mental quietude which is alone worth worlds of wealth. You cannot imagine, my kind & gentle Nell, how gratifying the reflection is that I have a "little wife" at home whose courageous heart is braving the tedium of separation for my sake and weaving many a tale to blend our lives in one by a common suffering and a common lot. I would not be without a wife for a mint, however much I grieve because of the exigencies of our situation & the necessity of surrendering almost everything upon the altar of our country; without which we must make our minds to become, like the scattered tribes of Israel, without a *national existence* but preserving our identity as a people alone. Things are brightening up, though, now and we appear to have at last become aroused to the necessity of a rapid concentration of our armies and suffering our seaboard cities to take care of themselves for the interim. Since the fall of Vicksburg I have reflected a great deal, and am now satisfied that the calamity will result in ultimate good & force us to the adoption of some more decided plans of action. I have no doubt the President has, to a certain extent, mistaken the plans of the enemy and been probably misled thereby. I hope, now, that he will adopt a different policy. Had we concentrated all our movable forces under Genl. Johnston at Tullahoma and pressed Rosecrans to the wall, we would [have] gained an advantage that would have amply compensated for the loss of the Hill City. The tardiness of Rosecrans' movements was proof of his cooperation with Grant, and we could have defeated the whole arrangement by whipping the Army of the Cumberland. When we had forced the enemy to concentrate so many thousands at V. Burg an opportunity was afforded us which we will not soon have again. They will now attempt to take Mobile and force our armies out of Alabama by moving a large army on the left flank of Bragg, cutting off his supplies and dividing him & Johnston. This can be done by sending Johnston's army to Bragg who with this & Beauregard's army can crush out Rosecrans, force him to retreat & follow him swiftly & surely. When this is done the armies can tack about and press Grant to the wall, & in succession play the game out upon the whole set of thieves.

The science of war is the science of numbers, and while we are carrying into rapid effect this system, we must rely upon our cavalry to protect our rear & keep down raids. This we can do if we only place active energetic officers in charge of this army. We must get rid of the slothful, gold-laced &

thin-strained gentlemen & let young America have a swing at the *cannibals*. Our war-policy in reference to our officers must be changed: there must be no dilly-dallying, no tardiness, no timidity in our counsels. We must fight ever, fight bravely, and contend for every inch of ground, falling back only when our warm and patriotic blood shall have watered & dyed the soil of the sunny South in many an unaccustomed spot. We must awake to the realities that are pressing upon us. The enemy cannot move without railroads & steamboats & we have learned to do so. And our men, too, must learn that battles are won oftener with a soldier's legs than his gun.

There is a rumor that we move to the Swamp soon. I hope so if we go in strength sufficient to teach the River openers that V.Burg is a conquest but not a victory complete, and that in its ultimate results, it will not compensate for the blood & treasure expended in its capture. I can learn nothing positively as to this; though, and only give the rumor for what it is worth.—

I haven't heard from War Department & do not know whether the recommendation for Major of the 12th Miss. Cavalry had been favorably acted on or not. I am not very keen for promotion. If it comes, unsolicited, I shall accept it and endeavor to render my Country more efficient aid in a higher sphere of action; feeling assured that all things are ordered for the best. I have a feeling at times that I will render my name famous; but then you know we all have daydreams and I am sometimes given to a little air castle building. I would like to do something distinguished for the purpose of evidencing my ability to do more good than I have already accomplished. Meantime I have learned—"to labor and to wait."—

My health continues very good. I have the *Camp* disease slightly but it easily and readily yields to a Homoeopathy and does not at all disturb me. Clarence is well, and I presume Jack has been with you before now, and has, by his own proper person, answered for himself. We made a reconnoissance the other day, rode four or five horses to death & captured one poor miserable specimen of a Dutch Yankee. Love & Kisses to all. May God Almighty ever bless, comfort, protect & preserve you is the prayer of

> Your devoted husband
> Will

Tell Agnes *Bally* is well, lively as a cricket and sends his love to her. Give my howdy to her Uncle Ned, Frank, Lucy, Hetty & Nutty.

Hd.Qrs. 28th Regt. Miss. Vols.
Near Brandon, Aug. 10th, 1863

My dear wife,

I wrote you by Capt. Gay on yesterday. I was busy all day long yesterday & until late at night paying off the Company, making up descriptive lists &c;—and in consequence had no time to write again. We are on the move this morning for Raymond, and I hope will find some place where can get something to eat. Our Commissary fails to supply us, and we go on a possibly long tramp with nothing in our larder. This is no new thing, however, in the history of our war and we will have to learn the useful lesson: to live without eating.

I am well & cheerful, however, and feel very hopeful of the result of our Contest. A more healthful tone of public sentiment is prevailing among the people, & I hope the ladies everywhere will force the cowardly recreants from duty into field—

I am in a great hurry and cannot write any more—

Love & Kisses—and may God bless, comfort, protect & preserve you is the prayer of your devoted husband

Will

Camp near Brandon
Aug. 11th, 1863

My darling Nellie,

While on the march today a peremptory order from Gen. Johnston overtook me relieving me from all command here and ordering me to Col. Ferguson as Asst. Adj. Genl.[17] This will soon give me the rank & pay of a Captain of Cavalry, and will place me in a position where I can render myself famous, if I choose, and ascend the ladder of promotion very rapidly. The berth is a very comfortable though laborious one. I will have all the conveniences & comforts of home, as a general thing; and in the field will have the shelter of a tent: As it was I have frequently slept on the ground during a rain, and one night in a chair leaned against a tree with my overcoat wrapped about me and the rain pelting down upon me all the time. In this Regiment while Col. Starke commands I can expect no

---

[17]Nugent's rank was effective August 15, 1863. Confederate Archives, R.G. 109.

promotion & no favors. The reason alleged by him, that the Regt. can't do without me. This, I fear, is not the honest truth. With Col. Ferguson my opportunities for a furlough will be greatly facilitated when I shall have become *warm* in my new berth. If the exigencies of the service require my constant attention to my duties, I will send for you as soon as you are in a condition to travel and bring you near me, so that I can see you at any time.

Columbus, Mississippi is one of the most pleasant places to sojourn in you ever saw, and I can soon make friends who will esteem it a privilege to render us a service. The active influence of an Adjutant General is almost unbounded, and you [know] that folks generally like to pay court to influential persons. What may be in store for me I cannot tell. Of one thing, though, I feel assured, and that is that I shall act an important part in this war before it closes. I have always felt I was filling a station altogether below my deserts and in consequence was cramped. I am now compara-tively foot loose and will do better. I shall, very soon, get Clarence transferred to me and we will both enjoy more satisfaction & ease of mind than here. I will help the boy along & hope to see him an officer soon. He is quick, unexceptionally moral, and intelligent; is vastly superior to those who command him and must come out of the ranks. Say nothing of this, however, as others may throw obstacles in the way if they knew my intentions and might thwart my good intentions. Clarence has a sneaking fondness for Evie, I discover, and if she likes him, must make himself worthy of her. This he can easily do if he but exert himself properly, I can, if God spares me, easily educate him after the war sufficiently to study law or medicine & thus place him in a position to marry her with the prospect of rendering her life a contented & happy one. But I am taking a long look ahead and speculating upon probabilities which, perhaps, exist only in my imagination.

My leave-taking of the Company was a very affecting one. Very few words were spoken and each man appeared to feel as if he were losing a warm friend. Soldiers easily get over these warm outgushings of emotion, and my place can be very well supplied by others, if the Company only select the proper persons. This, I think, they will do in all probability.

Jack Cox brought me word that some idle gossips are reporting, upon authority of Evan F. Jones, a discharged member of our Company, that I refused to go into Franklin. This is a most unmitigated lie, and I have in

my possession a written statement from Jones that whoever says he made
such a remark is a liar. You may say to any one who asks, that I was on the
right of the Regt. acting as Adjutant and went into Franklin & to within a
few yards of the River beyond the town when I hauled up on account of a
deep cut in the railroad track and two or three plank fences—and that I
returned rallied & formed the Regiment thus saving it from discharge and
stood under a heavy fire of the siege battery for nearly an hour. I was
furthermore complimented on the field for coolness and gallantry.—Say to
my friends, I authorize & request them to denounce all such statements if
any have been made. If anyone has acted braver than I, I would like to see
him. I have been in every fight & skirmish the Company ever had except
one while I was recently in Washington and have always been where duty
called me. I do not intend to throw my life away uselessly for the gratification of anyone, and only wish that they, who circulated & credit such idle
tales, may shoulder their guns & go as far as I do.—

I have missed having the fever this summer and hope my change of
location will greatly benefit. Say to Alf that Mr. Green the banker at
Jackson, Miss. has my money, and if he needs it, I send enclosed the
necessary authority to draw. It would be advisable for your Mother to
follow her negroes if she can reconcile herself to the trip when you are in a
condition to travel. If not, when things quiet down along the River she may
move to the plantation. There is a probability that the war will not be
conducted altogether in a civilized way hereafter. Lincoln demands that we
treat the negro soldier upon an equality with our *whites* & threatens
retaliation if we do not. This will bring about some dire results & may
provoke the abolitionists to a ferocity unparalleled. I would prefer to see you
all removed beyond their reach.

Love & Kisses & May God Almighty bless comfort, protect & preserve you
is the prayer of

your devoted husband
Will.

Okolona, August 15th, 1863

My darling Nellie,

I came to this place on yesterday, and find the change from the sunny
woods to a house very agreeable indeed during the dog-days. I am now in a

condition, without any solicitation on my part, to enjoy some few comforts along with the disagreeable experiences of a soldier's life, and shall take advantage of it I assure you. Dr. Talbott is here and his "old ways" remind me of the days of yore when we all enjoyed life so much together.

My health is excellent & from all I can learn will continue so in this country, by the way one of the best farming countries I have ever seen. The people, though, are like Mississippians generally, rather lukewarm in their feelings. This abnormal condition of things will not continue long, because it was, at the outset, so great a reaction that nothing else could have been anticipated. Men's minds will very soon acquire a healthy tone, and if they will only exert their influence to keep stragglers in the army we will soon conquer our enemies, achieve our independence & have *PEACE*.

My trip on the cars up was not very pleasant, which was owing to the fact that I was compelled to travel on the baggage train. I met *Ike* at one of the Depots.[18] He seemed delighted to see me & gave me an excellent supper, that came in the nick of time, considering I had nothing for twenty-four hours previous but a little piece of corn bread not a very nutritious diet except when a man is starving. He said nothing about wanting to go home. Jno. Webb is now a *Major* Quarter Master, lives high, dresses finely and dispenses his money freely I reckon. Will Campbell, *Sergeant*, came out to see me and looks in a decided state of preservation.[19] He has become very industrious and thereby has astonished his friends not a little.

Frequent rumors reach us of the advance of a force of Yankees; but we sit in our office perfectly quiet feeling that these canards are engendered in fevered brains, & are the result of fear. You know, however, how a story once set afloat increases in intensity; in compound ratio with the distance it travels. I regretted very much to hear of Carnes' death, as it will throw the negroes in the hands of some person who does not know them. Alf will now be compelled to look after them and you. *Jack Cox* wants a discharge since I have gone out of the Company and can get it if *Ma* writes a request therefor.[20] I do not know whether he will be profited by it or not. If you

---

[18]Ike had previously served as a body servant to Alfred C. Smith and Nugent, but he apparently was not hostile to Nugent.

[19]John Webb and Will Campbell were Washington Countians in the Erin Guards. PWCHS, 171.

[20]The basis of the discharge was that Jack Cox was not of military age.

have the opportunity please send me a good blanket (can you spare it?) & two or three linen shirts if you have them. I am now in a position in which I am compelled to dress neatly all the time. I write a note to Billy Blanton in reference to the hire of a negro who can bring the things out unless you have a better chance.[21] Send them to Capt. R. H. Smith AQM 28th Miss. who will forward them to me. One or two pair of socks would not be out of place. If you have cloth, a jacket for *Bally* would fit.—
Direct to W. L. Nugent, A.A. Genl. Ferguson's Staff, Okolona, Miss. care Capt. R. H. Smith AQM 28th Miss—*Post Quartermaster Meridian.* Love & Kisses—May God bless comfort & preserve you is the prayer of

Yr. *devoted* husband
Will

Head Quarters Ferguson's Brigade
In the Field, Aug. 20th, 1863

My darling Nellie,

Mr. Sutton came up here this evening and I hasten to write you a note by him as I am to write a letter. Since I last wrote I have entered upon the discharge of my duties as Asst. Adjt. Genl. and if my appointment is confirmed will have the rank of Captain. My position is a very agreeable one indeed and I do not think I shall accept of anything else short of a Colonelcy. The Genl. and I will get along finely together and my associates all appear to be gentlemanly officers. For the past few days we have been hurrying around in search of Yankee *raiders*. But haven't come up with them yet. We make a move tonight which will I think check them, and in all probability will crush them out entirely: at least I hope so. They are burning all the mills in the country and endeavoring literally to starve out everybody. I ardently hope they may be frustrated in this and meet such a reception that they will remember it to the latest days. The Yankees say they intend to force into submission that the people are already disposed to submit, and a little starvation will soon do the work; and in a great many instances they are not far wrong; as much as I regret to say it.

---

[21]Billy Blanton was the son of Dr. William Blanton and Mrs. Harriet (Blanton) Theobald. PWCHS, 167.

We move again immediately and I have no time to write any more. My love & kisses to all & believe me to be as ever—

Your devoted husband
Will

Hd. Qrs. Ferguson's Cavalry
Okolona, Miss. August 27th, 1863

My own darling wife,

Bride I was on the point of writing for with the thought of you in my mind insensibly recurs to the days *lang syne* when first I "wooed & wed"; and were it not that the flashing flame of my affection some years agone had steadied to the burning glow of a continually increasing love, and the youthful bride become the gentle, trustful & confiding wife I would so have written it: as it is, my darling Nellie, let me always call you wife; and let that endearing appellation continue the watchword of my life and the conservator of my purity of purpose & constancy of love. May the remembrance that I have so gentle and noble a creature for my life companion ever buoy me up amid the many trials through which I am called to pass and nerve my arm in the dread hour of a battle. Dear is my country to me, yet dearer far in that I have a treasure in a little woman who bears her trials bravely far away surrounded by the invading foeman. Let the legions of our relentless enemy come on. Their graves dot many a hillside between the muddy waves of the rolling Mississippi & the limpid waters of the Pearl River, and many more shall "sleep the sleep that knows no wakening" before their hostile tread shall disturb the quiet of the rolling Alabama. There will we rest, and gathering our poor & ragged soldiers around us, will strike "till the last armed foe expires." In God's own good time, the day of retribution is coming, and when it does come, woe to the worthless invader, who has had no mercy. Our people may become lukewarm, defeat may follow defeat for awhile; but we will always [have] a brave & gallant army to contest every inch of ground. And they will contest it stubbornly under *Genl. Jno.* Let U.S. Grant, Maj. Genl. U.S.A. try them. We whipped his army at Jackson badly and retired in good order, without the loss of a gun & but few men. Their cohorts returned to V.Burg, the most woebegone set you ever heard of. This their General admitted. Their armies faltered before a little ridge of dirt, which, had the difference been on the other side, our soldiers would have instantly stormed. They tried a charge and failed; and then like a parcel of burrowing owls commenced to dig. One thing they understand thoroughly and that is the use of the shovel and spade. Put them in a parallel, a trench and they work like Trojans: they far excel us in manual labor, and are no mean antagonists. They count time & men & money as nothing, esteeming the length of the war as of no moment. Well, if it is necessary, so be it. If they are determined to fight it to the bitter end, let them go ahead. It is difficult to conquer and possess so widely extended a country as that which we hold. They may & doubtless will impoverish the people as they go along; but this only leaves a thousand foes behind them who will rise upon their stragglers and put an end to their useless lives. Every hollow will resound to the alarm of the Guerilla's gun, and every bush by the roadside will conceal a relentless pursuer. They might avoid this by a different policy, but their maxim is rule or ruin and they haven't judgment enough to pursue a different course. If they would respect private rights & private property, abolish their unholy alliance with our negroes, put them back upon the plantations and make them work as heretofore, they would do more to end this war than by five years hard fighting. Of this, however, they could not be persuaded "though one were to rise from the dead"—What good will it do us if we submit? Our land will be a howling waste, wherever it has been invaded & we will be forced to abandon it to the *freed negroes* & the wild beasts. The humble tiller of the bleak hillsides in the interior may manage to eke out a miserable existence, but the growers of cotton & sugar, the staple products of the country, will be forgotten as a class—The commerce of the South will be nothing and certainly no one, unless his pretensions be very humble, will be content to live in a land where the inter-mixture of races will breed a long train of evils which were fairly illustrated in the history of Jamaica. What the end will be of course no one knows. Of one thing, I feel assured, if we pursue the proper policy all will yet be well. I think our authorities are beginning to see that I have been right in my opinions all along; and that they will let Mobile & Charleston take care of themselves for awhile, concentrating our different squads of armies into a solid phalanx and moving along with a crushing force. The enemy already feel that they can do nothing unless they have a large increase in their mounted force, and they are planning extensive raids for the purpose of burning our factories, arsenals & mills & thus leaving us to *starve it out*. Let them know there are men who can look every calamity in the face, and whose arms are never nerveless. Be hopeful still—let the lessons of history cheer you up and the memory of our revolutionary fathers comfort you.

You cannot imagine how comforting your letters are, and how great a satisfaction it is to me to know that you are a patriot still, when your husband fails to gird his sword upon him gladly to meet the invader, you may then feel disheartened.

As you are situated you have no other alternative than to trade for your clothing and the necessaries of life, and I would have no hesitancy in doing so. You are in their lines virtually without the ability to get beyond them and have to yield to an imperious necessity. I am fearful though you will not have the *means* to buy anything. Mr. Courtney has some *greenbacks* and I could pay him or Lou Gay in Confederate money if they would consent to it.[22] I sent you 50$ in La. money by Alf & 10$ in South Carolina money by Mr. Sutton which I hope reached you safely. I will pay the hire of servants for you if you can make any arrangements. If not you had better endeavor to get a white servant from Memphis.

I do not think they will conscript Alf if he has his discharge—No surgeon would refuse to give him a certificate of disability and he has our [The remainder of this letter is missing].

Hd. Qrs. Cavalry Brigade
Tupelo, Miss. Aug. 30th, 1863

My darling Nellie,

I wrote to you the other day and having a remote chance of again reaching you I have concluded to wish you another moment's enjoyment. The news of hostile movements around us convinces me to use a trite saying "that somebody will be hurt very soon;" and that the Yankees will either be defeated or drive us further into the interior. Cut off as you are from direct communication with "our side", I suppose you hear sad tales of destruction and disaster to our Cause. The newspapers are considerably down on Jeff. Davis just now, and I fear that their ill-timed abuse will serve to encourage the despondency of mind which is afflicting a large number of our troops. I am confident, however, that the Yankees will find it impossi-

---

[22]Tom Courtney was the uncle of Captain Gay and lived on Oakland Plantation. PWCHS, 247.

ble to behave themselves; and will, by flagrant violations of the rules of civilized warfare, open the eyes of our whipped citizens & soldiers. There are, I am sorry to say, a great many whipped curs among us; and they need some artificial stimulus, some outside application, to open their eyes. This will, sooner or later be done for them by Ulysses Grant.

We now occupy memorable ground and it makes the war-feeling creep instinctively over us. Beneath this soil there sleeps many a martyr to the sacred spirit of liberty. From their graves comes up an all-prevading sense of our ability to accomplish our independence. Our military family is increasing; and if all the applications made for positions were favorably listened to, we would have quite an extensive staff. Jno. Tomlinson is the General's Aid-de-camp, and will do very well, I think. We live very well though it costs like the mischief. Everything we buy is sold at outrageously high figures, and our pay is consumed before we are aware of it. Mrs. Ferguson will come up soon, and will give us a little sunshine. Our labors are somewhat arduous, though, and will continue so until our command is organized better. Soldiers here have a great fancy to go home every now and then and it seems almost impossible to prevent it. We are endeavoring to rectify things somewhat.

My health is good and I hope to be freed from the chills & fever this year. Did Alf ever get the money for the carriage horses sold to the Battery?

When you write, send your letters to the care of R. H. Smith, AQM. 28th Miss. Regt. He will forward them. Give my love and kisses to the dearly remembered ones at home. Respects to inquiring friends. Be cheerful, hopeful, confident. Trust me in the hand of the Good Lord & pray for me often. May the Lord of all Mercy bless and keep you is my prayer

Your devoted husband
Will

Hd. Qrs. Cavalry Brigade
Tupelo, Miss. Sept. 7th, 1863

My darling wife,

The hour of your trial is approaching and I feel very very uneasy on your account. I hope and trust in the Giver of all good, though the thought that you are so far away, so near the enemy's lines and surrounded by so many dangers makes me feel quite blue at times: and were it not for the elasticity of mind & heart which characterizes me, I should have long since grown utterly despondent.

War is fast becoming the thing natural, tho' abhorrent to my feelings. I go at it just as I used to go at law-suits. Still I am not by any manner of means fond of the profession. The idea of being continually employed in the destruction of human life is revolting in the extreme. Necessity imperious and exacting, forces us along and we hurry through the dreadful task apparently unconscious of its demoralizing influences and destructive effects both upon the nation & individuals. I wish *Uncl. Saml.* would recognize his nephew and give us peace. I do not desire a reconstruction & a hollow truce, a servile place in the family of nations and to eat the bread of dependence while I am denied all the privileges of a freeman. The Yankees say, that when we are conquered they cannot afford to let us have the right of trial by jury, because they say a "secesh" jury would clear us all, neither can we have our own judges or exercise the elective franchise. This is the doctrine held by their main supporters and is the one which will be practiced by them if they are successful. And yet our weak-minded friends are willing to lick the hand that would smite them and pay court to the hardhearted minions of abolitionism. I own no slaves and can freely express my notions, without being taxed with any motive of self interest. I know that this country without slave labor would be wholly worthless, a barren waste and desolate plain—We can only live & exist by this species of labor: and hence I am willing to continue the fight to the last. If we have to succumb we must do it bravely fighting for our rights; and the remnant must migrate. If the worst comes, we must go over to England or France, and become Colonies again. Never will I be content to submit to Yankee rule. The Russian yoke would be preferable. The close fisted Yankees would filch our pockets at every turn—France I would prefer. Her policy is more enlightened than that of England and she would give us the rights and privileges of freemen. It would be her policy and doubtless when her affairs are straightened in Mexico, she will recognize the importance of a more decided policy in American affairs.

I hope the enemy now discovers that the possession of the River is a barren victory. Their western produce finds no market and the foreign demand will not be very large or extensive either at New Orleans, Their commerce is fettered by childish restrictions & the Southern *privateers* keep them uneasy. Cotton cannot be found and *flour ᴗ bacon* is not a commodity of much exchangeable value. A few men, *in authority*, may make fortunes; but the poor man who brings his flat load of corn & potatoes expecting to return with a pocket full of money will be utterly mistaken. The Yankees won't see this until too late to remedy the evil. They are not far seeing enough. If they only had the negroes at work on the plantations under their masters, they would have realized some beneficial results.

We are now camped at a place memorable in this war, and whose name will live in history. We are occupying Genl. Bragg's old Hd.Qrs. and have a cozy time of it—and if the enemy don't disturb us soon we will be quite comfortably fixed. Dr. Talbott is as fussy as ever, and speaks of trying to go over to the Swamp this fall. He is a surgeon and the enemy will not take him up, or make a prisoner of him.

Old Pillow is conscripting every man in the whole country. He is no respecter of persons. There is in consequence a terrific quaking among the noncombatants and substitute men. Judge Handy has just decided that the principal is liable unless his substitute is over 45 yrs. of age; and is in any event liable for *militia duty.* This will make the nice young gentlemen quake in their shoes, and force them to "come to the centre."

My health continues good—I am endeavoring to get Clarence promoted so that he can come up here and be with me, and, I think I will succeed in due course of time. The Company, is, I am sorry to have to say going to pieces, numbering now only some twenty nine men for duty.

Give my love & kisses to all. Do the best you can, and ever remember that you are supreme in my affections. May God Almighty bless, comfort, protect & preserve you is the prayer of

Your devoted husband
Will

Hd. Qrs. Cavalry Brigade
New Albany, Sept. 20th, 1863

My dear wife,

I have just learned that our Company had gone to Washington County and thinking the opportunity a favorable one write, I have left my old command permanently I think, and will in consequence not have such frequent opportunities to write to you. I will, however, write whenever a chance presents itself. The General will have a very fine command soon if he is allowed to go ahead and obstacles are not thrown in his way by the numerous aspirants for position in this deserted region.

Here the country presents, as ours, a dreary uninviting spectacle. Fields grown up, houses deserted, churches pillaged & the people plundered generally. The condition of things is very bad indeed. A large majority of the farmers have taken the oath of allegiance without a particle of benefit. After they have foresworn themselves, they awake to the sad truth that their Yankee friends do not regard it as entitling them to any protection. The *pill* when swallowed does not lose its bitter taste. We "harnessed" a trader's wagon the other day and I bought a *bolt* of calico which I would like to send to you if it were possible. I find it almost impossible to get any clothing for myself up here; am in hopes, though, that I can make out.

We went up to Ripley the other day and created so great a stir along the Rail Road that the Yankees have kept close in ever since. When they do venture out again, my impression is they will be taught a very useful lesson and receive some punishment. They are all of the opinion they will whip us this fall & winter, and are disposed to be somewhat haughty. It appears to me, tho', that the difficulties multiply as the Yankees leave the R.Roads & rivers—They do not relish the idea of leaving behind them a country exposed to raids. Old Rosecrans is now at Chattanooga fortifying and collecting supplies for another campaign; and if allowed to remain in his present position will give us much trouble. I hope Johnston will cut off his supplies and starve him into a *fight*. If a battle follows soon we will have a terrific fight and with prospects for a grand victory. There is no telling what the result will be though I am still very hopeful. Old Abe is very stiffnecked and will prolong the war to ensure his reelection to office. I fear, too, the Northern Democrats are becoming somewhat unsteady in their devotion to Constitutional right and will lend their aid to Lincoln. If this is so, we will have a long war of it unless foreign complications are such as to necessitate a change of policy.

My health is very good just now and promises to improve considerably with the incoming cool weather. If the river remains low for any length of time I will try for a furlough to visit you and if possible move you out of the Swamp and in striking distance of me. I would like very much to have you near me so I could look after your wants. It is true I could not be a great deal with you but then I might go to see you now & then. As it is, you are so far off and so close to the Yankee lines I hardly ever will have a chance to visit you. I will get things to moving right up here and will apply—Let me hear from you by every opportunity if it is only to say that you & the balance of the folks are well.

Say to Mrs. Shelby that Mrs. Moore, formerly of Issaquena, saw *Bayle* going with a Yankee Battery from V.Burg to Jackson when the Yankee army advanced, as a Lieutenant, Tom Shelby's mulatto boy (house servant) was along & said his *Mas Bayle* was a Lieut. in the Battery. Mrs. Moore is positive but I think *must be mistaken.*[23] Bayle could hardly be so recreant to his duty & so false to his country. There are strange things transpiring around me so often that I hardly know what to believe and it may be that Bayle has played a base trick. If so—Alas! poor Yorick—The men who were heretofore considered substantial, sturdy & patriotic, are giving up all hopes and going even to Memphis to take the oath. They exhibit their oaths with the *"old flag"* flaunting over it with perfect sangfroid and esteem their perjured opinions & statement as entitled to credit. I hope the time may soon come when a reckoning can be had for all such outrageous conduct. To take the oath under compulsion is bad enough and hardly excusable:—to take it freely & voluntarily is an evidence of guilt that would warrant hanging. We live in evil times and can have, from experience, some idea of the effects of a civil war. I have frequent opportunities of reading the Memphis *Bulletin*—a most abominable abolition sheet—and am inclined to think we will have an ironclad Navy afloat very soon. The Yankees are terribly alarmed on the subject. They fear a blockade of Northern ports and the bombardment of New York & Boston—I would like to hear of it.

I do not know how the Yankees intend to deal with you all on the River. I hear, however, that all restrictions upon trade are to be removed and that the people will be invited to buy at cheap rates. They have not the means to do so, and the sight of plenty around without the ability to buy is quite annoying indeed. I suppose you can make meat enough to do for the *winter* and if you can get *salt* you will manage to live. I would advise you to keep the old negroes together at home or turn them adrift entirely. I regret Agnes' desertion; it is what I expected. When last at home I advised Alf to

---

[23]Bayliss Shelby was the son of Tom Shelby and lived in the Princeton area. PWCHS, 339–40. Shelby did return to Greenville, and there was no indication of his serving in the Union Army. Recollections of LSH.

sell her, or run her off. Old Nelly & Lucy can do little jobs of work and Frank & Ned can get wood. I suppose you can all manage to survive the repeated blows of the enemy—Whenever I think of your defenseless condition I take the blues; it requires all my courage to bear it bravely—Good bye—May the Everlasting God bless, comfort, & preserve you all is the prayer

Of your devoted husband
W. L. Nugent

Love & Kisses.

Hd. Qrs. Cavalry Brigade
New Albany, Miss. Sept. 25, 1863

My darling wife,

I am quite uneasy, despite my fortitude on your account as rumors reach me from time to time of the Yankees holding Greenville and of their probable intention to make it a negro camp. This being the case, I hope you will all not delay a moment in getting out of the way. Either go across the River into the interior of Texas or come over here: anything but being kept in close proximity to a camp of demoralized negroes. I hope at least that you will move out to the creek and get under Judge Yerger's protection. As soon as you are in a condition to move I can provide you a comfortable home out here and keep you from starving. Nay I can give you a tolerable fair livelihood. Let me know as soon as you can move with safety and I will so manage it, if possible, that you can be removed without any trouble: if necessary I will procure a flag of truce from Vicksburg and either go up the River after you or come over through the Swamp. I dread the possibility of your having to remain in Greenville all winter surrounded by the American citizens of African descent. The black picture is unrelieved by a single ray of light. You may, however, manage to get along better than I can imagine.—

The news is very encouraging from Genl. Bragg and we have some four thousand prisoners and thirty pieces of artillery. Bragg is reported to be vigorously pursuing Rosecrans' retreating columns, and driving everything before him. Making all due allowances, we have gained a signal victory and have convinced the Yankees that there is life in the "Old hulk" yet. Conjecture leads the way to a thousand distant prospects, and I find myself indulging again the hopes so often expressed that we will have peace on the reassembling of the Lincoln Congress. It is no use, however, to conjecture as to the future. The Democrats may not succeed in returning a majority to the House of Representatives and the Black Republicans will continue the war to an indefinite extent. The contractors are not yet satisfied with the blood that has been spilt and are thirsting for more. *Nous verrons,* as the Frenchman says: sufficient unto the day is the evil thereof.

Here I am snugly esconced in a comfortable room writing by the light of two candles; and yet at times I imagine I would prefer the active duties of the field. Accustomed to "roughing it in the Bush", I am not yet fully accomodated to my new mode of life. The General's Brigade is rapidly becoming drilled and disciplined and will make a good fight when the Yankees give it a fair chance. They have of late become rather timid about making raids down into the State and appear to be satisfied with a quiet possession of the Railroad. How long we will permit this is a question very difficult of solution. Major General Hurlbut has his Head Quarters at Memphis and makes every man woman & child who comes in take the oath of allegiance, before he will allow them to trade. We had up yesterday some half dozen trading wagons and a whole batch of women, whose goods had been confiscated. They begged hard, but the General was unmoved by their entreaties. Some of these women had traveled one hundred miles to trade, carrying a bale of cotton with them. They all brought back a full supply of *Scotch Snuff* and were as busy as bees with their rubbers. Think of a female with the dirty colored tobacco streak around her mouth & on her lips, squirting discolored spittle all around her, and you have a fair sample of the "Buncombe Gals"—You must, though, add to the pitiable picture, a *tousled* head, unwashed face, drabbled dress, (no corsets) heavy shoes, a guffaw laugh and a sidelong leer. A dirty baby, too, is no infrequent addition to the scene. These women will take up their line of march hence to Memphis, preceded by a small wagon drawn by a pair of mules in reference to whom there are several bills of foreclosure filed by the undisciplined flocks of buzzards hereabouts, with as much nonchalance as they would to go to the Cross-roads Meeting House. "Friends & feller citizen," we live in strange times and amid novel and stirring events. We have two of these women in the Guard House for practicing their tory principles and keeping our people in dread. The Yankees have unhinged things terribly here.

They made a pyrotechnic display in this little interior town. Some Dutch rascal wanted to warm his toes & set a house on fire to save himself the trouble of collecting a few faggots. The raw ingenuity displayed became catching and in a short time the town was in ashes. This was the result of Col. Phillips' orders and his muley Regiment are very good adepts at houseburning, I assure you. Insensible to pity and the finer sensibilities of human nature they would take the last morsel of bread from the hungry and then taunt them with being rebels and graciously invite them under the protecting folds of a flag, that just before waved over their burning houses. They believe this system of terrorism will force us back into the Union. Maybe so—we shall see what we shall see.

I long for the day when the Cavalry in Mississippi will be turned loose upon the vandal hordes who are infesting our borders and let slip the dogs of war upon them in all their resistless venom. I do hope we will continue to concentrate our forces and wipe one army completely out before we begin an attack elsewhere. In this way alone can we succeed. We may have to give up territory for awhile but it will be better for us in the long run. One army destroyed is worth a thousand successes, because it necessitates the complete organization of an entire corps; a thing which requires great labor, expense, & preparation—

My health is good, thank Providence, and promises to continue so during the winter. I am busy preparing an outfit for the winter but have no blankets. Is there no way in which I could manage to send you a calico dress or so?

Give my love to all; Kisses to the well remembered folks at home—and may God in his infinite goodness & mercy abundantly bless, comfort, and preserve you & yours is the ardent prayer

Of your devoted husband
W. L. Nugent

N.B, Write me a full long letter & let me know everything that is going on—
Direct to
Capt W. L. Nugent
A.A. General
Okolona, Miss
Care Post Commandant

Hd. Qrs. Ferguson's Brigade
In the Field, Oct. 11th, 1863

My darling wife,

My last letter to you was written, I think, from New Albany, Miss. Since then we have moved and are now stationed near South Florence Alabama, with something in value beyond my usually acute perception. I fear that the Yankees have been too much on the *qui vive* for us and that the original object we had in view has been somewhat defeated. At any rate we cannot afford to return without making the Yankees feel there is life in us yet. I had hoped to hear from you before I left Mississippi, but the fates or the mails were against me, and I have been compelled to go ahead uncertain of your present condition and health. The time for your great trial has now passed and I am desirous and extremely anxious to learn whether the best of your devotion to your unworthy husband has resulted disastrously or otherwise. I have almost settled down into the opinion that the end of the year will not witness the termination of our present struggle, unless something decisive occurs. The news from Chattanooga is still encouraging and if promptly & timely reinforced Bragg may be able to cope with and even defeat Rosecrans. If this can be accomplished we may somewhat confidently expect a reaction in the public sentiment North. This result is very vague and we will have to look a long ways ahead for the "Silver lining" to the cloud of war which encircles our whole horizon. We can, however afford to be patient a little while longer, and feed ourselves on hope, while events, big with the hopes of millions, are daily transpiring around us.

My health still continues good notwithstanding recent exposures. I have, I hope, at last become inured to the hardships of a soldier's life, and am better prepared to enjoy the sweets of home, when the privilege is once more extended to me.

I have very little hopes of this ever reaching you, and will close—May God bless, comfort, preserve & protect—Love & Kisses

Your devoted husband
W. L. Nugent

Direct to
Capt. W. L. Nugent
Ass't. Adjt. General
Okolona, Miss.
Care Post Commandant

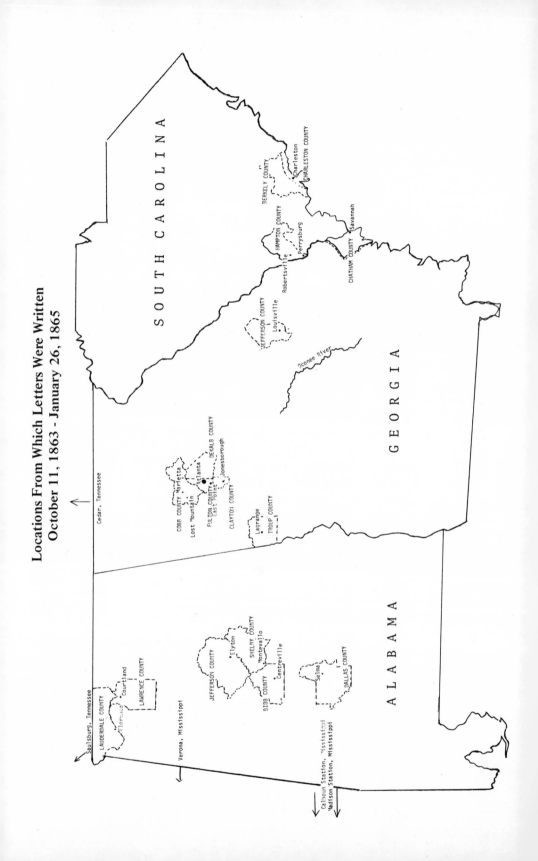

Locations From Which Letters Were Written
October 11, 1863 - January 26, 1865

SOUTH CAROLINA

Charleston
CHARLESTON COUNTY
BERKELY COUNTY
HAMPTON COUNTY
Perrysburg
Savannah
Robertsville
CHATHAM COUNTY

JEFFERSON COUNTY
Louisville

Oconee River

GEORGIA

Cedar, Tennessee

DEKALB COUNTY
COBB COUNTY Marietta
Atlanta
Jonesborough
Lost Mountain
FULTON COUNTY
East Point
CLAYTON COUNTY
Lagrange
TROUP COUNTY

Saulsburg, Tennessee

LAUDERDALE COUNTY
Courtland
Florence
LAWRENCE COUNTY

Verona, Mississippi

JEFFERSON COUNTY
Elyton
SHELBY COUNTY
Montevallo
BIBB COUNTY
Centreville
Selma
DALLAS COUNTY

ALABAMA

Calhoun Station, Mississippi
Madison Station, Mississippi

Head Quarters Ferguson's Brigade
Near Courtland, Ala. October 19, 1863
My darling wife,

The opportunity of forwarding you another brief letter presents itself tonight, and I hasten to avail myself of it. We are camped on ground that has already been rendered historic and affords a lively example of the destructive effects of war. In the wake of our own army as well as that of the enemy there is nothing hardly but pillage and destruction. The burden thus imposed upon the poor citizen is almost too grievous to be borne from the fact that the Federals leave but few "pickings" behind them; and our hungry soldiers will steal a few hogs & potatoes. What can possess people to live upon the border I cannot imagine; but I suppose "there is no place like home" even though a heap of ashes marks the spot. This must have been a delightful country before the inauguration of this terrible civil war. The landscapes are beautiful; limpid creeks; and gushing springs. I am continually reminded of Tennessee, although the scenery is not so varied and the careful hand of industry has not been so much employed in the ornamental or the useful. I have seen very few married women and only an occasional winsome lass as we were marching along the public highway. I have no inclination to visit at all and have "tea" with but one, a Mrs. McKeinan, whose hospitable board was loaded with the choicest comestibles. Hot coffee, hot rolls, hot battercakes, warm toast, elegant wafers, (reminding me of home), & choice beef steak:—and after supper a Simon pure *Havana* to console our wandering anxieties about the absent ones & promote digestion. This kind gentleman has invited me to leave the field for a day or so & make his house my home; and I would avail myself of his kind offer were it not that I feel my duty calls me elsewhere.

We are far away from any mail communication with the balance of the Confederacy, and are in consequence afflicted with a thousand rumors every day. Now we have it that Rosecrans has been again defeated with the loss of some ten thousand prisoners & then that his whole army has been captured. Of course, I am not silly enough to credit this story. It is too good to be true. I fear we will not be able to drive him away from Chattanooga. I was only surprised that he should have ventured beyond it and attacked Bragg. The possession of Chattanooga not only conquers all

Tennessee, but is the key to the possession of Mississippi, Alabama, Georgia, & South Carolina. Our voracious enemies know this and they are evidently preparing to hold it. Let me picture out their plans they will hold and fortify Chattanooga, rebuild the Memphis & Charleston Road as well as that from Nashville to Columbus & Decatur. A column will move from Vicksburg to Meridian building up the Southern R. Road. The possession of Meridian will give them possession of Mobile at which point their supplies may be collected. The Mobile & Ohio Rail Road will give them communication with Memphis via Corinth; and these roads can be protected by a comparatively small force. The Memphis and Charleston road will afford them sufficient supplies for the maintenance of Rosecrans' Army. If we had the supplies ready at hand we could defeat this movement in a manner different from that of attacking Chattanooga. I am in hopes, however, that there will arise some foreign & domestic complications which will prevent the carrying out of this gigantic scheme for our subjugation—

My health is very good at present. I am anxious to hear how you & your *babe,* shall I say it, are. Give my love & kisses to all at home—May God bless, comfort, protect & preserve you is the daily prayer of

Your devoted husband
W. L. Nugent

Direct to
Capt. W. L. Nugent
A.A. General
Okolona, Miss.
Care Post Commandant

Hd. Qrs. Ferguson's Brigade
Courtland, Ala. Nov 6th, 1863

My darling wife,[24]

Your letter of the 15th October is the first intimation I have received of the birth of our last child, the letter Ma wrote not having reached me as yet.[25] I have been weighed down and oppressed with anxiety for sometime

---

[24]The original of this letter is deposited in the Nellie Nugent Somerville–Lucy Somerville Howorth Collection, The Arthur and Elizabeth Schlesinger Library on the History of Women in America, Radcliffe College, Cambridge, Massachusetts. Hereinafter cited as the Schlesinger Library, Cambridge.

[25]The child was named Eleanor, but she was known throughout her life as Nellie or Nellie Nugent.

past knowing that the hour of your great trial had elapsed. The uncertainty that beclouded my mind was worse than any actual trial I could have been called upon to undergo, and now that I know all I am relieved, though sensibly saddened by the contents of your letter. If God, my darling, in his infinite mercy, see fit to take our babe away from us, we must bow with resignation to his afflicting hand and draw therefrom lessons of fortitude and usefulness. We must recognize the justice of his Providence and bow ourselves in humble supplication at the footstool of grace, that we may live better and walk uprightly. Our own wickedness has been great indeed and we are undeserving of any favor from the Giver of all good. If this great truth is properly appreciated by us, we may yet feel that the chastening hand of our Heavenly Father was not unadvisedly laid upon us. Of one thing we must be convinced, that this world is one of trouble and continued privation and that there is and can be no rest except in Heaven. But while we know this, we should yet learn that life, beset though it be, by so many sorrows and afflictions was given us for the wise purpose of preparing for Eternity, and that all its real joys are purchased by an humble submission to God's will and a diligent cultivation of that wisdom which comes from above. If it were not for the hope that religion inspires within us, this would be a dreary world indeed, and more especially so under present circumstances. These may be the approaching days of tribulation and it will be difficult for even the elect of God to remain steadfast in their faith. Oh! that I could persuade you, my darling, to fall in with the overtures of mercy and become an Israelite indeed in whom is no guile. You could then be comforted under all distressing conditions of life and be buoyed up with a hope that beyond this vale of tears there is rest for the weary. While here we have no continuing pleasures; but when the days of this life are past we have an eternity of bliss beyond the grave, in expectancy. Let us make sure of our title to this inestimable possession while time and opportunity are afforded us.

It is, of course, to be regretted that our babe has a deformed hand. She may have an exalted intellect and a pure heart that are far more essential than mere personal comeliness; and if God spare her, (which I hope & pray he may) she will doubtless prove a blessing to us both. Don't let this afflict you so as to injure your health but bear your sufferings patiently and bravely, and comfort yourself with the reflection that if our babe is taken away from us, it may be done in mercy to her and to us. We do not know what is yet in store for us and a tender babe could scarcely undergo the hardships we may be called upon to undergo. At any rate let us be patient and submissive.

If God still spare *you* to me I shall feel grateful indeed; and if after our troubles are over we are privileged to reunite once more as husband and wife, we will have ample cause for pouring out our souls in adoration to God. So far I have mercifully been spared notwithstanding the dangers to which I have been frequently exposed, and I believe I will survive the war and be restored again to the bosom of my family. This will be more than we could well hope for.

I presume your troubles and physical debility prevented your writing me fully about the members of the family and the people in the neighborhood & County. I hope tho' that the balance of the family with the exception of yourself and Alf are well. If you are not in a condition to write get Ma to write and let me know how you are getting along. Whether you have the comforts of life or not, and whether your servants have all deserted you.

It would be difficult now to get Alf a position, there are so many officers without any field of labor. I do not think, however, they will conscript him if he acts advisedly. His health is not restored sufficiently for him to take to active duty again; and if he reports at all, I presume they will put him in some Department where his labors will not be so heavy—If he is compelled to go into the army again I think he had better come up to me, and possibly I can put him in a position where he will be better enabled to take care of himself. By the way I can assign him to the command of my couriers or make him my clerk; and if necessary or he would like it, I can easily get him into the Q.M. or Commissary Department. At any rate, let him report to me as a clerk. I will protect him from Field Service until he is sufficiently recovered to stand the hardships. Who has been elected to the Legislature from our County? Say to Ma I think she had better get Jack out of the army. Possibly he can be of some service to her; at least he will be some protection against insult from every passer by, and I think will be a managing boy. I will interest myself in the matter and write to Genl. Cosby as soon as practicable.

My health is very good just now and I have a comparatively easy time of it here. We will move back to Mississippi soon I presume, and you can direct your letters to Okolona to care Capt. C. G. Fields. Dr. Talbott sends his respects to you all and to Mrs. Finlay's family. Please present my kindest regards to all my friends, and write as often as you can. And now, May God in his infinite mercy bless, comfort, preserve and sustain you & your babe is the ardent prayer of your devoted husband

W. L. Nugent

Hd. Qrs. Ferguson's Brigade
Okolona, Miss. Nov. 18th, 1863

My darling wife,[26]

Again, after a fatiguing raid of one month's duration extending over a large portion of No. Eastern Mississippi and North Alabama, I find myself seated in a chair in a comfortable room enjoying for a brief season the sunny side of a soldier's life. I have, also, been living excellently well for a day or two past despite the blues & a severe cold that troubled me not a little.

Our campaign in No. Ala. was a very active one indeed. We had skirmishes with the enemy every day from the 21st until the 28th day of October, when they were finally compelled to cross the Tennessee River and adopt a course for the march to Chattanooga different from that at first proposed, along the line of the Memphis & Charleston Rail Road. Genl. Lee is a fighting General and will keep the Cavalry busy for the winter.

After receiving your & Ma's letter I determined cost what it might to apply for a furlough and go to the Swamp; but upon broaching the matter to General Lee, he told me not to do so intimating that I might get home sooner than I expected. I have, in consequence, concluded to await for awhile the course of military movements in hopes of being *ordered* on duty near you so that I may see you and not be charged up with a furlough which I mean to strike after whenever I can do so with the best prospect of success. I earnestly hope our Brigade may be ordered into the Swamp to afford the people some protection & let them move out of the country, if they so desire. By the way I can get you all a tolerable comfortable home out here in a land abounding in corn and wheat, and a good hog raising region also; and if you desire or mean to flee the Swamp let me know. I will have everything prepared and will go and help to move you out. We might drive enough beef cattle out of the Swamp to live on until the calves from

---

[26]The original of this letter is deposited in the Schlesinger Library, Cambridge.

the milk cows could grow up and by clubbing could bring out a good many hogs. Should you determine to move out let me know it in time, so that I can go and help you on the way. Meat is quite scarce out here, & can only be bought at a high figure.

I hardly think old Ned & Frank have gone to the Yankees and with them and Milly & Lucy & Agnes & what few negroes we could hire, I imagine we could live tolerably well in an humble way until the war is over. There are plenty of places in this vicinity to rent, and the only trouble with me is, that you may have to leave again. There is a doubt and uncertainty hanging over our military operations that makes me very timid. I would, though, much prefer having you here to the Swamp—For while here you would have the advantages of Society & Church and would certainly now be much more protected from Yankee insolence & raids. I would like to know what you & Ma think of it as I am very much averse to parting you on any consideration.

But I must drop this for a more saddening theme. You failed to let me know in what way my babe's hand was deformed and my imagination has given wings to my anxiety until my sleep has been disturbed and my waking hours rendered gloomy in consequence of all kind of vague suppositions. Let me know the worst and I can be the better prepared to endure the affliction and love the innocent sufferer for perhaps her Father's sins. I was very sorry, my dear wife, to learn from Ma that you had detected a falling off in my sympathy and affection for you, because my letters were not as they used to be. This has troubled me more than anything else imaginable could and I have reflected over everything I ever wrote or said to discover the reason for your belief, but I must confess I am at a loss to know wherein I have failed to do my duty or act the part of an affectionate husband. So I have concluded your supposition was the result of your great sorrow and depression of spirits and in consequence I have been lifted up again. When you write, which you must do by every available opportunity, let me know how everything is going about home, how you live and upon what you live, how you spend the time, &c. &c. Give me news from everyone in the county and particularly Mrs. Finlay's family. I am glad to learn that Jack has at last got his discharge. He may be of some service to you all. Say to Alf. I have written to Richmond Va. & think I can manage his case so as to keep him out of the army. At any rate if he is compelled to report anywhere let him report to me. Give my love & kisses to all with

146

regards to all inquiring friends. Kiss the baby for me and May God, in his infinite mercy, preserve, bless, comfort, & cherish you & her is the prayer of

Yr. devoted husband
W. L. Nugent

Hd. Qrs. Cavalry
Okolona, Miss. Nov 22, 1863

My darling wife,

I have just heard that Jim Rucks will leave Columbus in a day or two for the Swamp and I will write a few lines by him, fearing my other letters may miscarry.[27]

After a fatiguing trip to North Alabama, we are here again preparing for another raid. I wrote you the other day that Genl. Lee told me not to make an application for a furlough yet, and I inferred therefrom that we might by chance be sent over to the Swamp with a view to operations against the enemy's transports. If this turns out to be correct, I will have an abundance of opportunity to see you, if not, I will make application for a leave of absence and go home for awhile. I hardly suppose the Yankees would permit me to remain at home, however, beyond a day or so. Still a day even would afford me infinite pleasure and would doubtless relieve you from a world of trouble. I think you had all better come out of the Swamp, though, and live in this neighborhood, where you could manage to live after a fashion. I can rent a small place for you and you can at least be comparatively comfortable. If you determine to move let me know at once so that I may be able to rent a place for you, and have some repairs made. The only difficulty in the way is that of transportation. I do not know what your facilities in this respect are, but fear they are entirely too limited to enable you to bring out what your actual necessities require. If you can manage it so as to provide wagons to haul your furniture etc. I will bring an ambulance over after you if informed as to when you will be ready to move. I notice the Yankees are pressing every man in Memphis, capable of bearing arms into the United States Service, and their operations in this respect may extend lower down along the River.

---

[27]James T. Rucks, son of Judge James Rucks, lived on Twin Oaks Plantation on Deer Creek, PWCHS, 251.

I also wrote you to say to Alf that he mustn't be too hasty in joining Blackburn's Company. I have written to the Secretary of War on the subject, and will write Col. Chambers. It might be well for him to see Judge Yerger and get a letter to Mr. Seddon, Sec. War, as these things have to be gotten through by outside influences purely. I think he will meet with no great difficulty in remaining at home; and if compelled to leave, he can report to me. I will put him in a way to save his health as much as possible and yet do the country a service. He must not go into the army again and leave you all unprotected. I could not be contented at all if this were so, and would try to resign at once and go home. A man cannot neglect his family to the extent of leaving them isolated and unprotected as you would be without Alfred.

It almost breaks my heart at times when busy cares leave my mind a vacant interval in which I am left to think, to feel that you are separated from me and suffering untold miseries and afflictions. And then to know the utter impossibility of my being near to comfort you adds poignancy to my bitter thoughts. The constant trouble with which we have been afflicted for the last year or so has made me a much soberer man than I ever was. I feel as if my present life was a disagreeable and painful dream, and not a reality. Cut off from the fond endearments of home and any communion with the partner of my bosom I hardly can realize the situation in which I am placed. A daily routine of the same duties without variation, poor fare, no comforts and cheerless, dreary isolation that chills the very life blood within me. God grant I may never see another war and never participate in one! Blood, butchery, death, desolation, robbery, rapine, selfishness, violence, wrong: a disregard for everything holy or divine, and a disposition to destroy constitute some of the incidents of war. Nothing good comes of it. It is an unmixed evil palliated only when waged in self defence. I am heartily sick of my present life, I assure you, and am sustained alone by a strong sense of duty that keeps me up.

My health is very good now, my cold being nearly well, God has blessed and mercifully preserved me so far, and how ungrateful have I been. I feel that I will be spared to reunite with you after the war is over, by the great mercy of God. Pray for your absent husband whose constant aspirations are after your welfare.

The mail messenger has just come in. Love and kisses to all and may

God in his infinite mercy bless, comfort, protect, and preserve you is the prayer of,

Yr. devoted husband
W. L. Nugent

Hd. Qrs. Brigade
New Albany, Nov. 29, 1863

My own darling Nellie:

I wrote you several days since from Okolona, and now much to my gratification have another opportunity to send a letter with some hopes of your getting the letter. Al Worthington is going home after a horse and promises to see your missive safely through.[28] The difficulty attendant upon sending letters and the few I get from you renders my situation in some respects very uncomfortable indeed. And yet were I to completely lay bare my feelings it would give a tone of sadness to my letters which could have only the effects to dispirit you at a time when all the energies of your mental and physical nature are necessary to enable (you) to bear your great misfortunes. God knows *my* heart, my own true Nellie, and if there is a single pulsation of it that does not beat in continual sympathy to your own, and if not burdened with sensations of the utmost affection and devotion for you, it is only when sleep has rendered it forgetful of its native instincts. I had rather its beatings were hushed in death and the warm life blood which it circulates frozen in its channels, than that one wayward thought of mine should wander from the idol of my younger days and what I hope and believe may prove the supporting ivy to the old grown oak. Oh! Nellie never think I love you less but always that I love you more. If the opportunity could now be afforded me I would give all I have to be with you and fold you in my arms once more. There are, however, duties and responsibilities resting upon me which if I did not properly discharge I should be unworthy of the wealth of love you have bestowed upon me and recreant to all that a man of honor considers noble—and yet at times it is certainly difficult for me to bear the idea of a longer separation from you. It

---

[28]Albert Worthington lived near Lake Lee. While home a Union raiding party discovered him, and he ran toward a field to escape. However, he was shot and he died within hours of his injury, PWCHS, 361.

entails a great deal of distress upon you and much want and suffering upon
you. Let me, though, my darling, carry along with me on the long and
tiresome march, through the dull routine of camps, and by the lonesome
camp fire often as it must be on the bleak hillside, the comfortable assurance of your unabated confidence and affection, and I can endure it all.
Hard is, and must be your lot: but remember my brave little wife mine is
no easy or agreeable one. Life is made up in the main of sorrows and your
future existence will more than demonstrate it. There are few real sunshiny
days and these are generally of our own making. Nothing could demonstrate as well as this, the necessity for calling in to our assistance the help of
Him who measures the days of our lives and is not unmindful of the wants
and necessities of the least of his creatures. Comfort yourself always, for the
Polar Star does not turn more constantly to its Northern home than turns
my heart and mind to you.

We are off on another raid and will be gone for several days. When we
return I shall apply for a leave of absence and go home if I possibly can. I
expect though you will have to go out to the creek so that I can with some
safety remain with you. To be on the River would be too dangerous,
because if taken I would have to go to Johnson's Island and spend the
balance of the war. The Yankees have ceased to exchange prisoners now
and when a man is captured now he is detained in prison and rigidly
dieted. I would not, therefore, relish the idea of being taken; and would
only risk it to see you or do my country some especial service.

My health is very good at present and promises to continue so by the
blessing of God. I much dislike the idea of taking the present trip as the
weather is cold and disagreeable, the roads muddy and no earthly chance of
our getting anything for ourselves or our horses to eat. I had Bally taken
back to Okolona with my grey horse where he will have a comfortable
house and be well taken care of. Tell Agnes he is well and seems to be
perfectly satisifed. Tell her, also, I hope she may not prove ungrateful and
desert you in your hour of need.

I wrote you fully about Alf. I have no doubt I can get him a position; but
if possible I want him detailed to remain at home with you. I hope Jack is
of some service to you all. The General would like to have him here but if
he can do any good at home I want him there. He can do much if he is
disposed and I have every confidence in him. Tell him I want him to write
to me whenever he has an opportunity.

Dr. Talbott requests to be kindly remembered to you all and the balance of his acquaintances.

I wrote to you all about moving, if you or the family decide to be moved out I can rent a place for you. Provisions are scarce and high. Kiss Ma, Evie, Kate and the baby for me and whisper in little Nellie's ear that her Pa will love her with his whole heart and support her with his strong arm and sympathy until she in turn can support him. And now may God Almighty bless, comfort and preserve you is the prayer of

Your devoted husband
Will

Love to all.

Hd. Qrs. Brigade
Verona, Miss. Dec. 15, 1863

My darling wife,[29]

I have been in camp again for several days and determined at first not to write awaiting in great anxiety my leave of absence, which Genl. Lee had the kindness to *approve.* and forward for me to General Johnston; but as these documents are often slow in taking the rounds, I have concluded to write to you for fear some anxiety may be superinduced in your mind by a knowledge of my going on a raid to the Rail Road.[30] During the whole trip I was exposed to nothing very dangerous except inclement weather. We had several skirmishes with the enemy, the advance guard being mainly engaged. Of course, the General & staff were behind the guard, and many a brawny arm would fall powerless to do violence, before their sacred persons could be touched. At times, however, I have heard the bullets of the enemy whistling in rather too close proximity to my head to be comfortable. We made a dash on the Rail Road at Saulsbury tore up the track for a mile or two and burned several important trestles between that point & Corinth on the East & Memphis on the West. The expedition started under the most unfavorable circumstances and the men all behaved extremely well, frequently having nothing to eat for several days at a time

---

[29]The original of this letter is deposited in the Schlesinger Library, Cambridge.

[30]Nugent's request for leave was approved by General S. D. Lee, December 11, 1863. In his request Nugent remarked that he had never received any leave since enlistment, and he desperately wished to make arrangements for his "Family in the Swamp." Confederate Archives, R.G. 109.

except what they could pick up along the Roads & bye-ways. The people in the Northern portion of the State who have been repeatedly despoiled by the Yankees and insulted by the insolent foe, notwithstanding the fact that they have repeatedly traded with the enemy, are in the main as true as steel to our cause. Everywhere we went the ladies ran out to welcome us with shouts and waving handkerchiefs. The demonstrations of the men were not so suggestive, I presume because they were afraid the Yankees might pay them a subsequent visit and to use a trite expression "tear them to pieces." I am happy to know that the most of the people are still loyal to us and opposed to the Yankee dynasty.

Both Congresses are now in session and what the result will be none of us can know. From all indications they will use all their exertions to increase their respective armies to the fullest extent, and to prepare for a protracted war. I am satisfied we have nothing to expect from foreign nations. Our *peculiar institution* places us in antagonism to the educated sentiments of the civilized world and we can expect no favors. If successful at all, it must result from our own persistent efforts with[out] any extraneous aid whatever. This may appear almost a hopeless job, but we can nevertheless accomplish it if we but persevere "to the end." The wide extent of our territory will prevent military occupation by the Yankees. Let politics & war have a little rest.

I haven't heard from you since the *15th October* directly, tho' several persons just out from the Swamp have reported you as being in good health. In the absence of bad news, I have buoyed up my almost fainting heart, with the belief that our darling babe was still alive and well. I shall, with you, love it all the more for its misfortune and be a shield for it, God willing, as long as she is spared to us. The cold charity of an unfeeling world is a dreary theme to descant upon, and we must expect the gleams of a happy sunshine tho' the morning sky may be overcast with clouds. Little Nell will, I believe, prove a blessing to us and draw us nearer to each other & the Great Giver of all good; and will have a heart & mind that will adorn her character. Wisdom & excellence of disposition are more priceless than mere outside physical beauty. The latter is ephemeral in its duration, but the former will continue long after this world shall have ceased to exist.

My health is good at present, thank Providence and indications are that it will so continue. The active life I lead is productive of robust health & tends to invigorate my constitution. Our soldiers are poor clad as a general thing & yet stand hardships remarkably well: generally without a murmur or complaint.

And now my darling Nellie, before I close let me invoke the choicest blessings of Providence upon you & our babe and His ever watchful care. Be cheerful, hopeful. Believe that you are ever present with me & lean upon me for comfort, consolation & support. Rely upon my constant affection; my unabated sympathy, my fixedness of purpose to bear all your burdens and brave all life's storms with you & for you alone; and may God Almighty in his abundant mercy throw the protecting aegis of his Providence around you & our babe & have you in his everlasting keeping until we are gathered together in his upper & better mansion not made with hands is the prayer of

Your devoted husband
Will

Love & Kisses.

Pikeville, Miss.
January 22, 1864

My darling little wife,

After a very fatiguing and disagreeable trip I arrived at Headquarters three days before the expiration of my leave of absence. I should have been delighted to spend a day or two more with you, but the hazard of capture was too great to justify the risk. And besides one is compelled, more or less, to calculate the effect of one's actions may have upon the moral sentiments of his fellow men. It is scarcely possible for Captain Blackburn to survive or outlive entirely his unfortunate capture.[31] People will condemn him and detractors find an unfavorable explanation for it. While I do not myself attribute his going home to anything wrong, I still think it was improper. In my heart I deeply sympathize with him, and hope for his sake he may soon be exchanged and returned for duty. I have always found him a gentleman and a steadfast friend; and shall palliate & excuse his conduct as far as possible. Our trip over was very monotonous and one night we were compelled to travel a long time in the night before we could get a

---

[31]Blackburn did survive his capture. Union troops generally controlled the Delta section by 1864, and local citizens were understanding when their furloughed soldiers were captured. Blackburn was prominent in the county after the war. PWCHS, 366.

stopping place. As I have often said a large portion of Mississippi territory is almost worthless. Rugged clay hills and boggy unproductive bottoms are quite a dreary prospect for a traveller wearied with a hard day's ride and anxiously looking for a "roost". Still I found the hill people as a general thing very hospitable. A great many of them are in such a deplorable state of destitution that it is utterly impossible for them to supply even a single person with a meal, without stinting themselves almost to the point of starvation. And then you know the days of the prophets and the widow's cruise of oil, have long since past. For an instance of this great destitution, I called at a little log cabin by the road side and counted *thirteen* children besides four or five grown persons. The house was rudely constructed at the base of a long and dreary looking hill, whose sides were covered with the withered sedge so common to old fields in this country and a few scattered pines. At a point where the hill flattened into a miry bottom there was a corn field of about ten acres, the stalks of maize resembling—to use a familiar phrase of my Father's—pipe stems. This was, as far as I could discern, the only source of supply for bread they had. A few peaked nose specimens of the swine tribe, lazily grunted around the door and about a dozen chickens were busily picking up the few crumbs that fell in their way. How these and other people in their circumstances manage to exist is an enigma to my mind. And yet they do live and *multiply* almost *ad infinitum.* It is, however, from such retreats as I have been describing that our soldiers have, to a great extent, been drawn.

I am, so far very well pleased with my horse Dixie. She stood the jaunt remarkabley well, and does not appear at all worsted. You must know, too, it is one hundred & seventy-five miles from this place to our home. Lieutenant Barker is quite a hero for a Charleston blade, and looks improved by his trip. Whether or not he would like to try it again I have not inquired.

As you anticipated when we were speaking of moving out to this section of Country, our Brigade is destined for another Field of operations, and will soon move near your relations below. I hope soon to have the pleasure of seeing the Jefferson County *Kin.* Let this matter not be publicly spoken of as yet, because when we go we hope to strike the Yankees a blow.

The news from all quarters is: The army is going into Winter quarters. But while this is the case, Genl. Sherman has reappeared at Corinth with his Corps D'Armee' and rumor has it that he purposes coming down the

Central Rail Road again. General S. seems to be an active, enterprising,
energetic man and will do us some harm unless we watch him closely.
Since October last he has been from Memphis to Knoxville, Tenn. & back
with his Command; and a portion of his march was conducted during the
last very cold weather. We hear that the enemy have evacuated Corinth &
settled down at Grand Junction; but dame Rumor is a very unreliable old
lady, and I scarcely imagine the Yankees will voluntarily surrender a post
they have so obstinately contended for so long. Still there is some probability in the report that Mobile is the next seaport to be assailed, and this with
a view to cooperate with Genl. Grant at Chattanooga. My own idea is that
Grant will find it an extremely difficult matter to operate from Chattanooga
as a base into Georgia, from the great difficulty of getting supplies; and a
flank movement in force from S.Western Virginia will jeopardize his whole
army. There are limits to human possibilities, and the larger the army at
Chattanooga, the greater is the difficulty of subsisting & clothing it. The
enterprise is now a very gigantic one. If Grant does invade Georgia and our
people will bear with patience a retreat of sixty miles, we will whip. He is
bound to do something for inaction will be destructive of the morale of his
army; yet what that something will be no one can as yet positively determine. I never did think he would move during the winter, and it will take
him sometime to accumulate sufficient supplies to advance in the spring.
Chattanooga is an important strategic point of defense but a very poor one
for offensive operations; and if we can so manage it as to compel the enemy
to attack our seaports and divide their armies, our plan would be to
concentrate in Southwestern Virginia and by a movement via Knoxville
force the Yankees back by threatening their communications for which
purpose Mississippi ought without hesitation be given and Alabama held.
Our Cavalry could keep back anything but a very large army, and this
could scarcely be collected here. This would, however, be strategy and we
are not accustomed to that in this Department owing to the continous
clamors of our Governor *et id omne genus*. The only strategy displayed
however was Bragg's invasion of Kentucky, and this was an idea borrowed
from General Beauregard and very inefficiently carried out. I am still
hopeful of the ultimate result, because the scheme of the Yankees is so
entirely contrary to reason and right, that I cannot think it will be successful. What more of suffering, distress, privations, wrong, violence and
rapine is in store for us God only knows. We must though "Suffer on our

three score years 'Till our deliverer comes."—feeling assured that we will in time reap the reward of our labors.

My health is good, and tho' somewhat blue on account of my absence from home, I keep up a tolerably lively flow of spirits. And now, my own darling, let me remind you again of my constant admonition to be cheerful & hopeful. Reconcile yourself to our separation for the time being, as an imperious necessity forced upon us by the exigencies in the affairs of our country, and rely upon the Giver of all Good for consolation and support. Be careful of your little self for your husband's sake, for without you he would be like the foundering ship at sea or the prematurely decayed oak whose trunk has lost its accustomed supports. I believe I am brave & strong, but I have an excessively tender heart as far as you are concerned and lean upon your affection more than you will ever believe. In contact with men I am philosophic, to a certain extent stoical and self possessed; with you I am swayed by an impulsive affection, and the simple story of love can always steal its way into my innermost feelings, rule dominant over them, and evoke the softest emotions, emotions that struggle for utterance and can only express themselves in the unsought tear and warm embrace. At time I have thought you must imagine me weak indeed, and doubtless with reason, for I can never speak of the tenderest feelings that lurk within me without giving vent to them by involuntary weeping. I have found it an extremely difficult matter to know myself aright, and no doubt you have found me rather mystical at times—The hour of greeting you upon the gallery a short time ago still follows and irradiates the tedious routine of my daily labors; while the long fervent embrace at parting diffuses its painful reminescences around. With all this I break through the clouds and am cheerful. Oh! What a blessing it is to possess an elastic nature; one which no suffering can subdue, when sustained by the favoring smile of Divine Providence. It buoys us up; sustains us amid the most dreadful passages of life; and points, as an inducement to patience, to the "Mansion not made with hands" beyond the surging billows of life's troubled sea. To that mansion may we all so live as happily to terminate our pilgrimage, when we shall have passed the Jordan of death. To that Mansion may our spiritual aspirations ever ascend and may we all feel that it is specially prepared for us.

I forgot to say that I wrote a note to Will Montgomery by Alf, & hope he succeeded in getting you two bales of cotton.[32] Frank Comezzo promised me he would let your Ma have some. Tell Ma she must not hesitate to make use of our means whenever she can make them serviceable. I shall esteem myself very unfortunate, if she refuses, in realizing the fact that I have lived so long with her in vain.

Kiss the baby a hundred times a day for me, and extend the same greeting to Ma & the girls—and say to my sweet sister Evie that she must be careful of her feelings and improve her mind as much as possible. I send her two stanzas I found in an old journal & hope they may prove edifying. Love to all; and may God Almighty bless, comfort, protect and preserve you is the prayer of your devoted husband

W. L. Nugent

Mrs. W. L. Nugent
Greenville, Miss.[33]

Hd. Qrs. Ferguson's Cavl. Division,
Madison Station, Miss.
March 8th, 1864

My darling wife,

Clarence has just come in and reports that Davis Buckner leaves day after tomorrow for the Swamp; and although I have written several letters recently, the opportunity of communication with you thus presented is too good to be lost. After nearly forty days of incessant riding and almost constant skirmishing we are now camped at this [place] to rest and recruit—as long as the movements of the enemy will allow. The people of Mississippi as usual were stupefied by Sherman's crazy movement to Meridian and in consequence a large number of our Mississippi troops have gone home, because they said their state was to be given up. Sherman has made an astonishing march, has plundered a great many of our citizens and has torn up the Railroad centering at Meridian for miles; beyond this he has accomplished very little. Our Railroads will soon be repaired, as far as

---

[32]Will Montgomery was a scout for the 1st Mississippi Cavalry. He resided on Locust Plantation. PWCHS, 174.

[33]The address of Greenville, Mississippi is unique in that the entire town had been destroyed.

we need them, and the Yankee soldiers will not be inclined to reenlist after their practical experiment at marching into the heart of our territory. Had we been as active as we might, Sherman would have been annihilated before leaving Meridian. As it was, Hardee got to Demopolis after the enemy had retired from Meridian. If this unprecedented movement will have the effect to drive all our Infantry out of the State to Genl. Johnston I will esteem it a great blessing.

As we moved back after the retreating enemy an amusing and somewhat dangerous incident occurred. We had thrown out an advance guard, which soon began skirmishing with the enemy and a Regiment was hurried up to reinforce it. Before the dust raised by this Regt. had subsided, a company of Yankees dashed in on a side road, just in front of the General & his escort and began firing upon us. The General whirled his horse to the right about, & galloped back to form a Regt. apprehending an attack on our flank, the balance of the staff followed, the escort wheeled about, and left me facing the audacious Yankees alone. They kept on until they got into the main road we were travelling and followed on behind our Advance Guard. I immediately ordered the escort to wheel about & we charged the Yankees, killing & capturing nearly the whole tea party. One blue coated fellow had the hardihood to gallop up to the rear of the Regt. in front and demand its surrender. A stray pistol shot however, soon stopped the beating of the Yankee's heart. I saw him stretched in the middle of the road; and a handsome looking fellow he was indeed. He was shot directly through the heart. From my experience on this expedition I would rather see you in the enemy's lines than exposed to raids like the people are here. We have a hard time of it. Our wagons were sent back to Demopolis, Alabama, and I haven't had a change of clothing for more than a month. I have my underclothes washed at night & have managed to get along very well considering. I am almost without a shirt; bought a homespun shirt the other day for twelve dollars, and rely upon it altogether. I have to get another soon, but if I cannot succeed it makes very little difference. I think we will whip the Yankees this year anyhow and I can afford to transport a scanty wardrobe until then.

General Sherman complimented our Cavalry very much on their fighting; and if we could have drawn his cavalry out by itself, there would have been very little of it left. As it was we didn't care to exhaust our horses &

kill our men in vain efforts to stop the march of the infantry column opposed to us. Had Sherman gone to Demopolis he would have never reached Vicksburg again with a thousand men; this we know, & I suppose he found out in ample time to travel back.

I hear various rumors partially true. Banks has been defeated in Texas, Grant at Chattanooga; Smith at Okolona, Meade in Virginia; and things generally are looking somewhat brighter. I heard today that Longstreet had taken Cumberland Gap. You may tell your friends that I say we are not near whipped; and the Yankees will find it out this spring, God helping us.

I saw Judge Cocks & Phil's family the other day.[34] They are living about ten miles East of Carthage, Miss. and inquired very particularly after you all. Mrs. Cocks has lost one of her children—a little boy I think, Uncle Jack has changed very much. His beard is long & grey, wig gone & fancy clothes doffed. He was wearing, when I saw him a common soldier's shirt. Phil is in for the war. The repeal of the Substitution Law puts him in. I saw his outfit, but don't think it suitable to the life of a tentless cavalry soldier. The Yankees passed all around without injuring them. The judge was in a perfect stew for fear his negroes would be taken.

I was in hopes we would be sent below to Jefferson County where your kin folks reside. My present impression is that we will not be granted that privilege but will be on the road elsewhere soon. May be to attack Grierson in his lair at or near La Grange, Tennessee, but off as I am from communication with you I am indifferent where the chess players place me, so it will have the effect to bring about a speedy *mate.* Excuse the play upon words.

My health continues excellent thank Providence, despite the hard service to which I have been subjected and I think I am gradually fattening. Tell Agnes Bally has been to Demopolis, Ala; is well & sends his love. Kiss Ma, Evie, Kate & the baby for me; and be sure to teach Nellie to call me Father and to know my likeness. Write to me as often as you can, because I miss your society oh! how much, and would feel dreadfully blue if I was [not] hourly sustained by the hope of soon meeting you again. I do long for the day to come, when I shall unbuckle my saber and return to the genial sunshine of home without which and the presence of my precious little wife the world would be a weary waste.

---

[34]John and Philip Cocks were brothers of S. Myra (Cox) Smith. They resided in Yazoo City but had moved for safety. Cox Bible.

And now may God Almighty, in his infinite goodness; bless, comfort, protect, & preserve you is the prayer of

Your devoted husband
W. L. Nugent.

Hd. Qrs. Ferguson's Div. Cavalry
Madison Station, Miss. Mch. 13, '64

My darling wife,

Mr. Pinckney Montgomery is going to the Swamp and has promised to call by & get a letter for you. The opportunity thus afforded I cannot possibly overlook. A few days [since] I wrote you a letter giving all the news, which will, I hope, be delivered to you by Davis Buckner who is going home on leave of absence; but for fear it may miscarry I will give you a short resumé of the rumors, most of which have an air of plausibility attached to them and some truth. Gen. Johnston had a skirmish with the enemy at Tunnel Hill, Ga., and drove them, Genl. Forrest has defeated the enemy at or near Okolona, Finnegan in Florida, Jones in East Tennessee & Magruder in Texas. Sherman has recrossed the Big Black and is now in Vicksburg, unless, as the papers say, he has gone to New Orleans to confer with Genl. Banks as to the best mode of attacking Mobile or invading Texas. The grand scheme of the enemy so far has terminated in nothing very material.

My health continues to be excellent, spirits equable, temper good and appetite for the substantial, we have nothing else, splendid. The long, tiresome, harassing march to which we were subjected, when the Yankee Army was on its way to Meridian, has not, in the least, diminished my size or weight; and I find that now, after a few days rest, I am ready for the field again no matter where I may be called to go. When I last wrote my impression was, we were going to Tennessee. I now think we are going to stay in Mississippi and operate in Jefferson and Copiah Counties and perhaps along the Mississippi River below Vicksburg and above Natchez. In which event, I may have frequent opportunities of writing to you and maybe a chance to drop in on you unawares as I have done on several occasions heretofore.

This country is a dreary spectacle indeed. The largest plantations are thinning out, grown up in weeds & pastured upon by a few scattering cattle; fences are pulled down & destroyed; houses burned; negroes run off. A general gloom pervades everything and the people appear to be in a listless spirit, perfectly impassable, subjugated, in some instances, by prospective want and suffering, and utterly devoid of any disposition to continue longer the struggle for Independence. In the glow & hurrah of excitement that ushered in the war, they doubtless freely participated. Flag presentations and gay parties have however given place to a serious war and the end is not yet. What the poor people here as elsewhere will do I know not. The prospects are gloomy enough and may be worse. I think the present year will wind it up and next December, by the blessing of Providence see me at home again. I must confess, though, that we need better management in this Department to keep our Cavalry in some proper state of discipline.[35] The major portion of it remains at home nearly all the time and can't be brought into the field.

I must confess to considerable uneasiness on your account, not having heard a word from you since I left home. Do write to me at every opportunity and write fully. Give me minute information of your *inner* & *outer* life. I like to read your letters always & particularly when they speak of you and the baby. You are my treasure; the repository of all my earthly affection. How I long to be with you pen cannot describe or imagination properly conceive. From all the stirring scenes of war, I turn my thoughts homeward as the caged bird to the heavens above it, when freed from confinement.

March 20th, 1864

P.S.

Darling Nellie,

The enclosed letter was written to be forwarded by Mr. Montgomery. He couldn't get across to V. Burg and returned. He now proposes to go thru' the Swamp and I have concluded to add a post-script, tho' it is now 11 o'clock at night. I have been very busy all day long, and until this unreasonable hour of the night making out reports of one kind and another to satisfy the curiosity of the General Commanding and the result will be nothing; for I am satisfied no one besides myself will ever read them. Still it does to call for them occasionally as it stirs us out of our sloth.

---

[35]In a letter to General S. W. Ferguson, dated March 22, 1864, Nugent reported an apparent plot to pull troops from General Ferguson and join them with General James Clanton's Alabama unit. Nugent stated that political considerations and personal ambitions undergirded the movement. He urged Ferguson to return to his unit to prevent such actions. Confederate Archives, R. G. 109.

It is quite a noisy & disagreeable night without. The Artillery of Heaven is resounding in sharp & continous peals and the rain is pattering on the poorly clad tentless soldier—Ah! my precious little wife never turn a hungry soldier off as long as you have a morsel to divide or fail to minister to his wants when he needs a garment to protect him from the weather or a blanket from the dreary winter wind, if God gives you "enough & to spare." I know the story of his hardships & suffering by heart. I have seen him, sustained alone by unadulterated love of freedom, with no rights of property to protect, go forth, exultant in the pride and strength of his manhood, to the fray and return pierced by the relentless bullet, and meekly, as the warm blood ebbed from his veins, breathe his last. I have seen him, too, on the long weary march, patiently bear up against hunger & fatigue. I have watched him, with his tattered garments & thin jacket, when the pelting rain drove against him, & froze as it fell; and listened to his cheerful laugh when he drew close to the camp fire & thawed his stiffened limbs. And with all this fail to receive the bare pittance necessary to satisfy the cravings of an appetite rendered morbid by continual fasting. Few officers ever sympathize properly with them, or if they do, venture to express it. You know, my darling, that the gentle look or tender word, in such cases, is powerful for good. I can hardly think of the subject without giving vent to my feelings and if your sympathetic tears have blotched this sheet, God bless you for it. I would not be without this woman's weakness for all the wealth of Croesus.

Startling rumors have reached us recently enlivening our hopes and brightening our prospects. It is said that France has recognized us, and Spain and Mexico & Austria. Gold has advanced in the North and declined with us. If ever the money pulse in the United States becomes excited to fever heat, Greenbacks won't be worth a copper and the fighting is over. Already large amounts of specie have been sent from Northern ports to Europe and as soon as the people begin to secrete their coin, the Yankee despots will be forced to forego their labors at our subjugation and let us "go in peace." At any rate their thoughts will soon reach beyond the point of conquest and they will begin to inquire what they can or will do with us. There is no half way ground. They must extirpate or let us alone. If they succeed in breaking up our armies they must fight us in squads along the highways & byways of the land. Thousands of our soldiers have come to the conclusion to die before they will give up and the whole country will be alive with guerilla bands. We have now an accredited Minister at Havana awaiting the arrival of Maximilian, Emperor of Mexico.

I think our Railroads will soon be repaired, and when the Yankees try to march to Meridian again, they will find force enough to whip them. Sherman just got away in time. If he had waited a week he would have been crushed to atoms. His wild hair-brained enterprise would have cost the Government a fine army. Hardee didn't move out in time & when Sherman comes again, he will find a worse than Hardee to meet him. We may, possibly, have one more grand fight in Georgia; after that we may expect nothing more than raids.

You cannot imagine how much pleasure your last letter afforded me. It was just the kind of letter I relish. Do let me know how you are all off for clothing & whether Alf got you any cotton or not?—Give my love to all. Kiss Ma, Evie & the baby & Kate for me. And may God Almighty bless, comfort, direct & preserve you is the prayer of

Yr. devoted husband
W. L. Nugent

Tell Ma to write to me—

Hd. Qrs. Cavalry Brigade
Calhoun Station, Mch. 27, '64

My darling Nellie,

You cannot imagine what a pleasant surprise it was to me when Alf came into my office with his joyous hearty laugh and his exuberance of good humor, and the surprise was heightened when he presented me with a magnificent pair of Cavalry boots, a nice woollen shirt, a handkerchief and a check shirt.[36] I had managed to get three or four pairs of drawers, but have only one undershirt, and my hat is a miserable one indeed. Still I can manage to get along very well as it is, and will rest satisfied if the war will only terminate this winter. I am very well off at the present in the way of clothing having two pair of pantaloons, a coat & a jacket, with a moderate supply of underclothing.

I wrote you a few days since by Mr. Montgomery a long long letter in

---

[36]Alfred Cox Smith had recovered and joined Evans' Scouts. The fine equipment presented to his brother-in-law came from his raiding. Notwithstanding the loss of his father and home, Alf continued active in the war effort. PWCHS, 377.

which I gave you all the news prevalent in any shape and hope you have received it, and the one sent by Davis Buckner, who went up to the Swamp several days ago. The present supply of news is pretty much to the same effect, and I believe it is now generally conceded by the Yankees that in all their recent operations of the Spring Campaign they have been eminently unsuccessful. Defeated in Florida, whipped at Dalton and pushed back from Meridian, they are even now at a standstill, and do not know where to begin their operations. Lieut. General Grant is now in Command of the whole United States Military force, and has his Headquarters in the Field with the Army of the Potomac. He will, I suppose, make another "on to Richmond" and will move forward until he finds Genl. Lee's army, after which he will change his base. The report in camp today is, that there is an Armistice for ninety days. In view of which *rumor* there are various propositions to bet that there will be speedy termination to the war. So mote it be! I cannot think, however, that it will close before next Christmas. And I do hope then to eat a turkey with the "loved ones at home."

Alf tells me Evie has gone to Memphis & returned. If Sis will allow me to play mentor awhile I would strongly dissuade her from making any unnecessary trips of the kind. It is very "demoralizing" for gentle girls to be brought into contact with the traffickers in Memphis & elsewhere in such times as these; and while I have every confidence in Evie's purity and modesty, I should dislike to see her thrown among them too much. Southern ladies are not regarded very highly by the miserable stuff that now, as a general thing, floats up and down the Mississippi; and it is strange but true, that numbers of our best & most polished girls have been gradually driven from the high ground of modest demeanor. I have know[n] nice ladies to travel in a two horse wagon over a hundred miles to Memphis without a male attendant and with no one in the city to whom they could confidently look for protection. Thrust a modest, unprotected woman among a rude, & bestial soldiery and I shudder for her safety. Already there have occurred instances of nice young girls marrying Yankee officers to be thrust aside, rudely & contemptuously, when the real wives made their appearances; and in N.E. Miss. there are numerous cases of illegitimacy among the wives too of soldiers who have been gallantly fighting in Virginia for two years. This is not by any means a necessary result; but it shows the extent of the demoralizing influence of traffic in an underhand way and against orders. You know the old stanza:

Vice is a monster of such hideous mien,
That to be dreaded, needs but to be seen;
Yet seen too oft, familiar with its face,
We first endure, then pity, then embrace.

Don't think I'm a croaker, but bid my gently sister be very careful. Everything now is turned topsy-turvy. Men have forgotten the old landmarks of honor, rectitude & propriety; and I grieve today, the ladies have become in your section of our frontier country, partially deranged. Even, however, if the former state of things existed young womanhood is a period of life fraught with responsibilities. It is the season in which habits for good or evil are formed, and paves the way for a useful existence or a wretched & unhappy life. It will require all her careful watchfulness to steer clear of the "shoals & breakers" which will beset her.

I have now quite a pleasant time. Have enough work to keep me busy during the day and a tolerably comfortable pallet at night. Two small cotton mattresses, which make all the difference in the world. I do not "fare" very well, being limited to ham & cornbread with butter & sweet potatoes occasionally. Still, I have learned to be content if I have "food & raiment," because I know there are large families in our country destitute of either.

My health is very good now; was never better. I would be horribly bored if I was not kept tolerably busy. Clarence has his head "set" on going to the Swamp. I have endeavored to throw cold water on the enterprise; but I think he will certainly go. He came over to borrow one of my horses to go home [Swamp] and I refused to let him have the horse. I don't know whether he will succeed in procuring a means of conveyance elsewhere. He pretends to want to go after clothing and a horse. I can provide him with clothing here of an ordinary kind; he thinks, however, he can get it in the Swamp. I suspect the real secret of his trip is to see Evie, and he will doubtless propose to her. What the result will be I do not know. I presume, though, she will refuse him flatly. He is a boy in education, experience & ability to provide for himself alone, and it would be, altogether useless for him to seek an engagement of the kind, with every probability of success. He is a good & worthy young man personally and if the war had not supervened would have been I think, an acceptable match.

165

As it is, there will be too much delay in a thing of the sort. I may be giving myself unnecessary alarm, though.

It is the Holy Sabbath day—Alas in the army how little regarded. We have all been busy almost the entire day.—

Give my love & kisses to Ma, Evie & the baby. Say to Ma I would like exceedingly to receive a long letter from her—and make the same request of Evie. Kiss little Nell over and over again for me. Teach her to recognize my picture so that she will know me when I come.

Don't forget but think of me often and write at every opportunity such letters as your last. Commune with me as you would in social converse & give me a picture of your "inner & outer life." And now may God bless, comfort, protect & preserve your is the prayer of

Your devoted husband

W. L. Nugent

Hd. Qrs. Ferguson's Brigade

Calhoun Station, April 3rd, 1864

My darling wife,

I wrote you a letter by Alf the other day and learned last night that he had not yet left for the Swamp. Today we are in receipt of orders to move to *Macon*, Mississippi on the M. & O. R.R. for what purpose I do not know, but presume to meet and repel an anticipated raid on the part of the Yankee cavalry. Foiled in their last efforts to subjugate us, the Yankees are now preparing a grand concentrated movement upon the heart of our country consisting of different armies, starting, as it were from the circumference of a great circle and converging at some common point; a favorite movement of theirs inaugurated by old Scott and persevered in by his successors. I feel confident of the result, tho' I may unfortunately be disappointed in my calculations. Meantime let us be still hopeful for, in due season, "we shall reap if we faint not." I regret the movement to the East so far as it carries me away from the idol of my heart, and almost altogether cuts us off from communication. Still with the fortitude & stoicism, of a soldier, I must to horse and away. I have one satisfaction, gratifying even in the "perilous edge of battle," that the end draws near, and that I will in a few months be at home again. And I tell you, my darling, that not all the enjoyments of earth beside, can compare to the pleasures evolved by a long, deep, study of the sunlit hereafter in our happy home. Happy it must and will be, if the even and delightsome experiences of the past give any indications of the future. Our round of marital experiences have had no interruptions of a disagreeable nature: and it is, now, much as my old fashioned ways have been unkindly judged by some, a source of intense gratification to me. The outerworld, that beyond the immediate atmosphere of your presence and the circle of your movements,—to me is but the theater in which laurels are to [be] gathered and trophies won—to be laid at your feet. If in the pursuit of these, vain & empty as they are, your smiles, & approbation & love are won, to me the result would be all that I could wish. Do you know, my precious little wife, my heart is full whenever I write and the warm & melting words of tenderness well up for expression and utterance, but are forced back at times for fear your few happy moments may be darkened by the shadow of my absence. If in the vocabulary of our tongue, the feelings could be conveyed in such a manner that the torrent of tears would give place to the sparkling eye & animated expression of countenance, as the sun after the April shower, instead of a saddenéd, troubled heart, I would covet the knowledge above all other things. And while I made you cry a little, with a few words would lighten your countenance and bless your days with the crowning joys of an almost perpetual sunshine.

I never like the expression: "Love me little, love me long." I never could be content with that sort of feeling which prompts a man to grasp your hand and let it drop without the warm pressure. I never admired the studied formal courtesy with which you are met in handsome parlors and beneath the blaze of chandeliers. But I do love & almost adore the firm, gentle, eager & warm embrace of my little wife, and the welcome grasp of her mother's hand. I shall not longer talk on a subject which tho' often spoken of never becomes threadbare to the parties interested. To me it is nearly a consuming fire.

Thank Providence for continued health and the numerous blessings which I enjoy from day to day. I was rejoiced to hear thru' Alf that you were all well and that the baby was in fine health. Write whenever you have an opportunity to send out: by directing your letters to care Brig. Genl. F. C. Armstrong, they will be forwarded to me wherever I go. I will find opportunities to write you. You know where there's a will there's a way. If Alf & yr. Ma could get some of Jack's & Katie's negroes & put them to work on the plantation it would be advisable to do so. Tell Alf to remain at home until he can learn definitely about his detail of which I wrote. Love & kisses. Teach the baby to love me & to know my picture. May God bless, comfort, protect & preserve you is the prayer of

Yr. devoted husband
W. L. Nugent

Hd. Qrs. Brigade
Elyton, Ala. April 20, 1864

My precious Nellie,

I wrote to you when we left Mississippi and endeavored to put my letter on the way homewards; with what result I do not know. A kind gentleman promised to forward it to Brig. Genl. Adams Hd.Qrs. so that it might be sent by first opportunity through to you. Like all our fond anticipations this may meet with a partial or complete want of success. I had repeatedly written to you before that and can only hope you have received some of my letters. If you *have not*, I shall have to endure the mortifying reflection that however much I may endeavor to communicate with you, I can never again hear from you, no matter how frequent your opportunities for writing may be. I have kept the last letter you wrote and have read the short random postscript at least twenty times. I had thought I deserved better at your hands and that the want of mail facilities and other means of frequent correspondence would be a sufficient excuse for any apparent neglect on my part. In consequence of your notification that I would not again hear from you unless you received a letter from me, I have at times been subjected to the most painful reflections: and nothing but my sterling common sense and a charitable construction of your remark could have afforded me relief. I scarcely think I could have ever given you a sufficient cause for doubting my affection, devotion or fidelity, and do not like to be made responsible for things entirely beyond my control. If I had my wish I would be always with or near you, to comfort, protect & cherish you. Circumstanced as we are and may be for sometime this is utterly impossible. If I resigned and went home I couldn't remain there without being everlastingly dishonored and disgraced: thus involving you & my innocent little babe in my own personal ruin. This I could not, for anything, under the sun, do. I have endeavored ever since I entered the army to write to

you as frequently as I could, regardless of the number of letters received
from you, and *shall continue to* do so to the end of the war, or the end of
my earthly pilgrimages. The uncertainty of life in the army continually
reminds me of the solemn obligations and vows I cheerfully assumed &
made on the night of our marriage, and I would not for worlds do anything
that would add to your already aggravated sorrows. I have protested this
repeatedly and have given you every possible proof of my undiminished
affection. To do this continually would make you disbelieve me at length
and hence I have occasionally written without reference to it. It appears to
me, however, Nell, that you ought not to suspect me of neglect. Consider
the distance between us, consider the almost utter impossibility of my
forwarding letters to you, consider the press of business that always engrosses
my attention, and if, I have ever appeared neglectful of my duty to you
I am ignorant of it. I have opened & bared my heart to your examination;
what I have told you in the private intercourse of our own chamber, I have
told partially abroad & practiced in camp and on the march. And while I
am continually endeavoring to keep up under the harassing toils, difficulties, and troubles of my position, deprived of the comforts and enjoyments
of home, it needed but such a postscript as followed yr. last letter to make
the cup of trouble run over. I have, however, after mature & painful
reflection, come to the conclusion that you wrote simply to stir me up a
little and with no idea of giving me pain. Seriously, my little wife, jesting
between husband & wife is a very serious matter; and when not properly
met is productive of the most disastrous results. If either is disposed to
doubt or misconstrue a sporting or random remark, the most promising
marriage may be productive of much suffering in after life. The relation
sanctified by the Bible is the most holy and affectionate that could exist
between man & woman. It should be cherished and tenderly handled. I am
not one of those who think a little occasional quarrel accomplishes good.
The waters of marital affection should never be troubled; their healing
properties appear to more advantage when in a state of placid repose. Some
may prefer the brawling brook interrupted in its flow by craggy rocks and
yawning precipices. The smooth and gentle flowing River has more attrac-
tion as a simile to me. Its graceful swell has power and beauty, and grace,
and equanimity about it. You are borne along on its current with a sense of
quiet enjoyment that continually increases—oblivious of the hurried, rough
& rattling tributaries that contribute to its waters and lose their individual-

ity in the waves on which you float. It may appear paradoxical for one of my ardent temperament so to think. I have buffeted with the world long enough to know the value of peace and quiet, and if God spares me through the war, I shall cultivate them with a hearty zest.

If you glance on the map of Alabama and run your eye along the road that leads from Tuscaloosa to Huntsville you will see Elyton, County site of Jefferson County, laid down. It is near this place that we are at present encamped. Jones Valley is quite productive, tho' now everything seems to have been consumed. Our horses are only partially fed, and in a day or two, we will have to move elsewhere for forage. My impression is we will soon have to go back to Mississippi for something to eat. There is hardly anything up here but iron. The mountains that hem in the valley are almost entirely composed of iron ore and several manufacturies have been erected in this neighborhood to blast the rock & manufacture the iron into different articles of utility to the Government.

The hourly expected battles in Georgia & Virginia seem to be deferred for sometime and will not, I think, be fought before the last of May. Our leaders seem to be confident of the result when it comes. God grant we may be successful. I tremble for the country if we fail. And now my own precious darling don't forget me or think I am indifferent to you. As God is my judge I am more fondly attached to you now than the day I married; I have been and shall ever be faithful to you. To tax me with neglect would be to say I was not only untrue to you but to myself. Love & kisses to Ma, Evie, Kate, Abe & the *baby*. May God Almighty bless, comfort, protect & preserve you is the prayer of

Yr. devoted husband
Will

Am in fine health.

Hd. Qrs. Brigade
Centreville, Bibb Co. Ala.
April 27th, 1864

My precious little wife,[37]

I wrote to you a few days since, and write, hoping (almost against hope), that my letters may reach you. In the expressive language of the camp,

---

[37]The original of this letter is deposited in the Schlesinger Library, Cambridge.

mails have nearly played out in Mississippi. A chance traveller may, however, pick this letter up, and out of sympathy for a weather beaten soldier,
may have it conveyed to you. If such should be the happy result, I will
never cease to congratulate myself; for as the Brigade moves farther to the
East my spirits slowly sink, and I greatly fear, if we go much farther
towards Georgia, I shall become completely crest-fallen. To feel that with a
home I am homeless, a wanderer over the face of the land, exposed to
every imaginable hardship and danger;—and with the best of wives, I am
alone in the worst sense of the terms is maddening in the extreme. I have
thought I suffered in the days of yore, but that incident to a continuous
absence from her to whom I am devoted and in whose smiles & happiness
my life finds its supreme enjoyment far surpasses anything I have heretofore experienced. I am alone though in a crowd; and notwithstanding the
effect of so many men around me and the busy labors of each revolving
day, the depressing influence of our separation haunts me at every leisure
moment losing its effect, when tired nature's sweet restorer "closes my
routine of duties at night," only to "wake to life again" as the coruscations
of light from the rising sun guild the orient sky in the morning. How you
can endure it, I am unable to conjecture, unless it be that our sweet little
babe gives you employment. How I long to see you now with your nursling
prateling around your knees and with you watch the scintillations of a living
mind manifest themselves in Nellie's sparkling eyes and animated countenance. Teach her, my darling, to know her Father and to love him. It may
be sometime before I shall have the gratification to see you & her; and I
want her to know me so well that I may at once clasp her in my arms with
all the warmth of a Father's love when I go home. I shall not want her to
show me any preference, because I think a child ought to love its Mother
more than its Father. She it is who has borne her, who has watched her
infant footsteps and nursed her through the perilous period of her tender
life. Yet if her heart overrun in love for you I desire to catch and appro-
priate the outpourings. This I know you cannot object to.

I saw Judge Cocks on our way out here. He looks well and so does the
family. He said he was going up to see you all this summer. I saw Frank
Comeggs on my way out of the Swamp, and he promised to let you all have
as much cotton as would keep you from suffering for any of the comforts of
life. Please say to Ma that I want her to keep an account of the number and
weights of the bales she gets from him, so that it may hereafter be

returned. I am sorry Alf took it into his head to join the army as I wanted him to remain at home and take care of you all. I think his conduct very precipitate though it may be patriotic in the extreme. I think it would have been better for him to go out to Texas and take direct charge of the negroes. If he becomes hampered by enlistment, he is entirely subject to the control of superior officers and can do you no good at all. I wrote to Col. Chambers on the subject & his advice is, for Alf to remain at home. He cannot now safely do so, and will either be compelled to go to Texas or join some military organization. The former would much more redound to the interest of the family. Still it is hard for a young man of pride & intelligence, when his country needs the help of every strong arm, to remain at home and leave his fellows to fight the battles of his country for him. And sooner than see Alf lower himself and lose his self-respect I would greatly prefer to see him in the army.

We have taken a considerable tramp since we left Mississippi. You will readily discern the route by looking over the map. From Canton to Macon via Philadelphia & from Macon to Elyton & Centreville, Bibb County Ala. via Pickensville, Pickens Co. on Tombigbee. A long, rough jaunt and for a considerable distance over terrible roads. Since we crossed over into Alabama we have had a fine time. I discovered some kin folks, distant, in Tuscaloosa, who entertained me in the most refreshing & hospitable manner possible. Mrs. Cochran is a lady of wealth, pleasant manners, elegant address and a thorough going Episcopalian. She is kin to you and me both. To you on the Gilbert side of the house. When Ma writes, if she ever will, tell her to give me the history of the *Gilberts* & Coxes. Mrs. Cochran delights in tracing genealogies and I desire to post her. She is quite clannish and I like her very much. She knows the Princes' very well, and her acquaintance may be very essential to me if anything unfortunate should happen. "Take to yourselves friends of the mammon of unrighteousness" figuratively applied is a good maxim at times. I found several kin folks in Tuscaloosa and almost became demoralized sleeping in nice beds.

There is now somewhat of a lull in army movements. Grant, having inspected the Army of the Potomac, is coming out to put that of the Cumberland in a fighting condition. As soon as his labors are accomplished here, he will return to Virginia and precipitate his horde of outlaws upon us in every direction. We all, however, feel confident of the result and when the crash does come will be in a condition I hope, to destroy his well-laid schemes for our subjugation. No well-informed person seems to think we will have a serious engagement prior to the last of May. Our forces are moving from pillar to post, evidently under orders looking to a grand tournament of Death, and will be concentrated at points from which the enemy will be driven back with the assistance of a beneficent Providence. Rest contented, my precious Nellie, that the army is in fine spirits and feels able to cope with any force the enemy can send against us. We have gotten rid of almost all our cowards & skulkers and have now a splendid body of troops to put into the field. Men who know no dangers, go where & when ordered, and never leave their post until ordered. These men will do to throw to the front when the battle cry for freedom is raised. Their lives, their fortunes & their sacred honors are pledged to the cause of their country; and sooner than fail they will lose all in the sacred attempt to breast the billows whose furious roaring may now be heard along the borders where armed hosts have been collected and the busy preparations for bloody strife are going on. Let us watch & pray and steady ourselves for the conflict. If the all seeing eye of that Jehovah, who rules the whirlwind and directs the storm, be favorably inclined towards [us], we have nothing to fear. We have been afflicted as no people heretofore have been. "Persecuted on every side yet not perplexed," and with the bold fronts of freemen, God willing, we intend to conquer. Life is not so sweet as to be purchased upon the terms Lincoln proffers. We will cling to our standards until the tide of revolution is rolled back upon our enemies. We are patient feeling that in a few short fleeting months "we will reap the reward of our labors."

I presume you have heard of Forrest's successes, the utter defeat of Banks, the capture of a Yankee Brigade at Plymouth and the disaffection growing up among the people of our North.

If we move further east I will let you know. Meantime address your letters to me—thus

Capt. W. L. Nugent
A.A.G. Ferguson's Brigade
Lee's Cavalry
Montevallo
Ala.
care Brig. Genl. Wirt Adams
Canton, Miss.

My health is excellent. Love & kisses especially to the baby. Bally is well and sends love to his Mother. May God Almighty out of his bounteous mercy, bless comfort & preserve you & vouchsafe to us a speedy reunion is my prayer

Yr. devoted husband
W. L. Nugent

Hd. Qrs. Ferguson's Brigade
Montevallo, Ala. May 5/64

My darling Nellie,

I have written you two or three letters since I left Tuscaloosa, and long ones too, which were sent to Brig. Genl. Adams' Hd. Qrs. to be forwarded by first opportunity to Washington County, and I hope have ere this come to hand. I got a letter of the 10th April by Ind. Leo and it came like a refreshing shower in a warm summer's day. I had begun to be very homesick, and a depressing loneliness of feeling was fast taking possession of me, when the perusal of your very welcome letter completely annihilated my ungracious mood and thoroughly rejuvenated me. The "harp that once through Tara's Halls—The soul of music shed"—was again taken from its hanging on the walls and strung again; and as I lay on my rough couch, lost in a fit of pleasing meditation, its music sounded along the chords of my heart with all its wonted melody. But then the finale was not so agreeable. The realization of the fact that I was still a soldier, went far to dissipate my momentary enjoyment and to make me feel that utter inadequacy of the means at hand to compensate in the least for all the pleasures of my byegone days. With this meditation the recollections of all the joys of our married life came thronging over me, until, at the bare thought, my whole being became convulsed as it were and my manhood dared not rebel against the falling of a tear: my surcharged heart could find relief only in that way.

We have been kept moving about so much recently that it is almost impossible to tell you where we will be two days hence. We will move from this place to Carthage, Alabama tomorrow. Your letters, if not sent by a carrier though, had better be sent to Genl. Lee's Hd. Qrs. at Columbus.

I am happy to be able to inform you that Capt. Evans' scouts are ordered back to the Swamp and will soon be with you. I had a conversation with

Genl. Lee myself on the subject and he said he would keep them in the Swamp. I am satisfied they were ordered out without the Genl.'s orders or knowledge, by Brig. Genl. Ross.

From all accounts the two great battles of the war will be fought about the close of this month. One in front of Dalton and the other in Virginia. We are all hopeful of the result, and confidently expect to win decided victories, God helping us. There are a number of soldiers here who in my opinion ought to be sent at once to reinforce Genl. Johnston and from all appearances will start for the scene of the war. They are doing nothing here but drilling & eating out the substance of the country. There will soon, I shudder to think of it, be a grand gathering of the hostile factions for battle, and the carnival of death, in all its hideousness, will reign supreme for a time. What will become of us if defeated? Renewed trials, greater difficulties, and almost complete destitution; and withal slavery in its worst forms. We feel determined to "strike till the last armed foe expires" if need be, and are confident. The news from the Tennessee Army is very cheering. The soldiers are well fed, well clad, well shod, and in excellent discipline. Old Grant will give us trouble and once defeated, the North will become dispirited and lose all interest in or care for the war. There are even now symptoms of despondency manifested, and a restlessness in Congress very gratifying. If kept up and the Yankee army is unsuccessful, Gold will bounce up to an exhorbitantly highness, Greenbacks will tumble down, and a heavy financial crash startle the Yankees from their present prosperity. When once they cease to make money out of the war, they will quit, and the inevitable result will be a split among themselves. The West will secede and the road cleared for Independence. There is an old prophecy, about this war which so far has literally been fulfilled. It predicts, however, that both sides will become exhausted and that peace will be declared in 1865, the two sides *reuniting*. This remains to be seen. How we can be brought together again except by a *forced* submission I cannot for the life of me see, and a forced union is worthless and merely temporary.

My health continues to be very good, notwithstanding the sameness of my diet, biscuits & ham, and my daily routine of duties keeps me constantly employed.

The news has just reached me that Grant & Johnston have commenced fighting and that our forces are hard pressed. I hope for the result.

My business calls me off and I must close. Love & kisses to Ma, Evie,

Kate & the baby. And may God in his infinite mercy bless, comfort, protect
& preserve you always is the prayer of

Your devoted husband
W. L. Nugent

Hd.Qrs. Brigade
Montevallo, Ala.
May 6th, 1864

My darling,

I wrote a letter to you yesterday which was forwarded to Dr. Talbott who
contemplates going to the Swamp. Maj. Lee is here now and intends
leaving in a day or so; and to take advantage of every opportunity, I have
determined to write again. The movements of our Brigade are fitful in the
extreme. We are hurried about from pillar to post without any ostensible
reason and it is impossible to tell where we will come to a stand. My
impression is we will lounge for a month or so about Carthage to recruit
our horses and prepare for an active cavalry campaign into Tennessee or
Kentucky during the summer. We are, however, kept so constantly moving
that we might just as well go at once to the front where fighting is to be
done. The news is not very encouraging from Dalton, tho' there has been
no defeat of our forces at that point up to this time. Our Cavalry had been
hard pressed and was falling slowly back upon the infantry. Hence the
rumors of a general engagement. This may have been a feint on the
enemy's part to draw all our forces to the right of Dalton. I am inclined to
think Grant will endeavor to turn Johnston's right and thus prevent our
reinforcing the Virginia Army, while he divides the Confederacy once
more. Hurling Johnston back into Alabama he will move on & take Charleston in the rear. This will doubtless be a hazardous game; but the old
Yankee is fond of such sport & has, in truth, been very successful at it.
Johnston, we all think, is equal to the task before and will be a match for
his gigantic rival. If Grant should move on towards Charleston instead of
Richmond, he will expose himself very much and may be easily annihilated. He will require a heavy depot of supplies at Knoxville if he goes to
Richmond and his transportation will be too limited to accomplish anything. And even if he reaches Richmond, it may prove a Moscow to his
wearied army. I am anxious for his plans to be developed so that we may

soon learn the worst, and have the matter definitely settled. Our Department Infantry will, I hope, have a hand in the fray and help to settle the controversy at once. This lingering along & keeping up a ruinous war is eating the vitals out of our country. The question of supplies is just now becoming very perplexing. Our soldiers get 1/3 lb. bacon & a pound of flour daily, and nothing more. They cannot well live on this long and it is, in the absence of any other food, too little.

The weather is generally warm up here in this mountain valley and tho' my tent is stretched in an open field the papers can hardly be kept on my table. The walls are tucked up and a delightful breeze is playing all around me. How much you would like a country like this in summer. The spring water is very cool, tho' of a somewhat brackish taste and the wind is constantly kept in motion up and down the valley. The country is poor: nothing but iron and coal. A few small fields on the hillsides yield a scanty return to the indefatigable husbandman, but the land looks miserably "lean" to one familiar with the rich alluvial deposits of the Mississippi bottoms. I could never reconcile myself to the idea of living here; but as a summer resort it would be pleasant. I presume, too, the war has blighted everything here as elsewhere.

I am just up from the perusal of a new novel "Marcaria" by the authoress of Beulah. I don't like the denoument. The lovers don't get married. The hero is a colonel in the army and is killed at the Battle of Malvern Hill. The heroine, altho' of aristocratic birth, great beauty and very rich, becomes the patron of an orphan asylum and a nurse in the Hospital at Richmond. How unromantic. You know I never could like a love story without weddings and children. It is unnatural and unpleasant. How a woman could really love a worthy man and not marry him when he asked her, while she makes no bones of admitting her love and permitting his caresses, I cannot understand. It is a species of refined sentimentality to which, I must confess, I am a stranger. Added to this, the heroine after discarding her lover sends for him, just before he leaves for the war and tells him flatly she loves him & has loved him for a long time. Miss Evans must be an *old maid* or she would be truer to nature than this.

How long, Nellie, will we be separated and this cruel war continue? I shudder to think that many weary month will drag its slow length along before I shall have the supreme happiness of seeing you and my only child. Sweet little Nell! Thy infant lips will hardly learn to lisp thy Father's name at all away off as he is, his country's soldier in the outer field. Don't forget me, my darling wife, or think hard of me. You are my better self, the polar star of my existence, the object of my undivided love and the comfort and stay of my existence. Don't think I am remiss in my duties. It grieves me to imagine you doubt me. Love & kisses to Ma, Evie, Kate & the baby—& Abe. Hug the boy for me. May God bless, comfort, protect and preserve you is the prayer of your devoted husband

W. L. Nugent

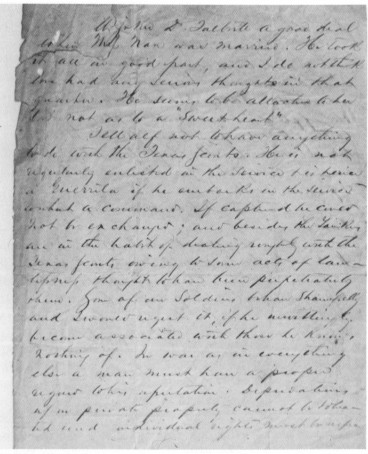

Facsimile of a letter, William L. Nugent to his wife.

CHAPTER VI

Sustained Alone by Patriotism

June 9, 1864–January 26, 1865

Hd. Qrs. Ferguson's Brigade
N.Lost Mountain, Ga. June 9th, 1864

My precious Nellie,

Another day of rest from the fatiguing duties on *Outpost* has nearly elapsed and I hasten to consume the little remnant left by writing to you. I had off my coat and was sitting out in the sun fixing up my papers and reports when your last letter reached me, in company with one from Ma. Instantly my spirits went up like a shot and I felt as if the war was really over. The whole atmosphere seemed changed, and I was far away in dreamland busying about the garden at our once loved home and listening again to the plashing of the Mississippi's waves. I could not help indulging the refreshing train of thought and dropping my head, gave free scope to my imaginings. Ah! little do those, who live in peace provided with everything that heart could desire, know what a torrent of feeling the bowed head of a Southern Soldier indicates. Sustained alone by a patriotism that has been purified by fire, in camp he often dreams of loved ones at home and wakes to the dread reality that encompasses him with a firm trust in the God of battles and a fixed purpose to abide his holy will. On the lonely picket post, in the damp & noisome trenches, sweeping over the open plain in a charge, or covertly seeking a tree to pick off & destroy the Yankee sharp shooters who continually annoy him in a fight, he is actuated by one moving impulse continually and that is to do and dare everything for the independence of his country. A soldier's life is very tame except when on a *raid* or in a skirmish and then the danger of being killed by any stray bullet that comes along is not very encouraging. It is absolutely shocking to witness the horrors of war; to see the number of the dead and dying scattered all around; to inhale the sickening stench of bodies in every state of decomposition; and listen to the obscenity & blasphemies that are being continually uttered all around. I have, however, been greatly pleased since I came to the Army of Tenn. There is a better moral tone exhibited here than I have ever seen among soldiers. Thousands have been converted and are happy Christians. Nearly all our first Generals have joined the Church and the army is fast becoming literally a God-fearing soldiery. This I regard as a very favorable omen and as strongly indicative of our success. In fact our men look upon success as certain whenever we get old Sherman to fight us squarely and quit his everlasting flanking. Genl. Johnston fell back from Resaca to enable his reinforcements to come up and no one at all familiar with affairs esteems the movement as anything but reasonable and right. His troops are now nearly all up and when the proper moment arrives, you may expect to hear of good news from this army. In fact we have so crippled Sherman that he has become excessively cautious in all his movements and for two weeks has been manoeuvering his army within sound of our guns. Had the country been as open as that in Virginia we would have long since, I think for I believe God is on our side, sadly defeated him. You can see nothing here from the top of the highest hill. The slopes of the mountains and the valleys are covered with a thick growth of timber hid away in tangled bushes and you can discover nothing. We have had numerous skirmishes with the enemy and several pretty severe fights along the line. In all of these we have, so far, by the mercy of God, been successful losing few men and inflicting heavy damage upon the enemy. Whole corps have charged Divisions of our army and have always been repulsed with great loss. I can give you no idea of the line of battle because we are on the left flank to protect the Infantry against any movements to turn it. It extends, however, for miles. General Lee has been unusally successful in Virginia, tho' now he is sick and General Beauregard has his old command again; the Army of No. Virginia. If he retains command any length of time Grant must look sharp for his laurels. I send you a description of the last fight near Spotsylvania Court House. I with you am of the opinion that we are beginning to see the end.

You don't know how I long to see you & our darling *Nellie*. How I fervently wish to pet her, dandle her on my knee, and witness her playful humors. I hope she resembles her Mother more than me, tho' I am perfectly willing for her to wear my smile if it pleases you. Teach her to know my picture and call my name as soon as she begins to talk. I hope our baby is beautiful, but I do want her, above all things else, to be good and intelligent. Purity of heart and an active acquisitive mind are preferable to mere beauty of person. I am afraid if I was at home I should help you spoil her. While I am on the subject I think you had better wean Nellie, if the Dr. thinks she can get along without nursing. If your system becomes enfeebled your milk may be an injury to her.

My health is quite good now, tho' I am by no means fat. The present active campaign has reduced me very much. My hair began to fall out again and I have had it closely cut. You must not think I sit in solemn judgement on your letters. Anything you write is a source of pleasure to me and I beg you will write just what you feel and as you feel. When the current of a strong man's love runs impetuously in one direction & to one object, he cannot, if he would, be critical. I promise if I am ever permitted to see you again, that I will pet you till you tire. I have not forgotten and never can forget how to kiss. It is one of my *fortes*, especially when you are concerned. I want you to take care of yourself both for my sake & your child's. Soon the war, I hope, will be over and we must be prepared to be a happy family together in our ideal home.

I am recommended for promotion to a Majority and hope to have a star on my collar when next you see me: and maybe ere long I will have two or even three.[1] Stranger things have happened and may happen again. Tell Sis to write to me. I will answer her letters with interest and presume the correspondence may be of some service to her. It will at least improve her chirography. Love & kisses to Ma, Evie, Abe, Kate & the baby and may God abundantly bless comfort, protect and preserve you is the prayer of

Your devoted husband
W.L. Nugent

At the Glen Camp
Near Marietta, Georgia
June 20th, 1864

My precious Nellie,

I have written you a good many letters recently and have so forwarded them that I think you will certainly get one; tho' from the length of each and your great desire to hear from me, I hope you have got them all and read them twice. I am now convalescing from a slight attack of bilious fever

---

[1]The Service Record of Nugent reflects the recommendation of Gneral Ferguson that was made June 1, 1864. Confederate Archives, R.G. 109.

and intend to take good care of myself I assure you. If injured at all I think it will not be by camp disease. We have had dreadful weather for the last twenty days. It has been raining nearly the entire time and the roads have become almost impassable in consequence. There is a terrible exhalation of odors from the ground near the trenches and in the vicinity of the camps: so much so, as almost to sicken a hearty man. From all I can learn a great many of our soldiers are becoming sick and going to the Hospitals in the rear. So far, however, we have lost comparatively few killed and wounded, by the blessing of Providence. It seems utterly impossible to get Sherman to fight. He makes gradual approaches to our positions and occupies his time by cannonading & skirmishing. His charges upon our breastworks have all been signally repulsed up to this time, with terrible loss, and he hopes to worry us out. Genl. Johnston has once or twice left the trenches and offered battle upon even terms and in open ground, but the Yankee General does not seem inclined to accept the wager of battle. He may, however, be waiting for better weather to make his advances, or to know definitely the exact position of General Grant in Virginia so that he can act in conjunction with him. I for one cannot fathom his plans and I do not believe any one else has yet done so, not excepting General Johnston himself. For two or three days we were expecting a general engagement, but the excitement died away and things remain in *statu quo.*

I had expected ere this to get a letter from you by Clarence. As he has not yet reached us I am beginning to suspect that Lt. Johnson has wisely determined to keep out of the big fights that are coming off around here and to occupy his time with light warfare in the Swamp; where he can have Yankee coffee and sundry parties to attend. "Odds fish" how I would like to be five thousand miles from here now. Mud, filth, rain; every imaginable species of vermin crawling all around you; little sleep, hard work & fed like a race horse; constantly annoyed with stray bullets, whizzing shells & pattering grape; dirty clothes and not a change along; little or no time to wash your face and hands and very little soap when the opportunity offers; no comb for your hair & no hair for your comb as mine is now—I got tired of having my head uncombed for several days and had my hair shingled down beautifully. Now, after it is dampened a few strokes of my hand is all it needs. Some scapegrace *stole* my comb & brush. I am tolerably bad off for shirts & drawers, but hope to do better "when this cruel war is over." I have three pair of drawers purchased from Government which have become all unsewed and hang very loosely about my person. They are about 2 sizes too large and are *perfectly* loose. I have remedied this defect by sewing a button right under my arm on the waistband; tho' I cannot even then fancy they fit. If I ever have another opportunity I will have my drawers made over again. I have two check shirts and the nice woolen shirt Alf brought me. One of the checks is nearly worn out and I do not think I will be able to replace it. Before leaving Miss. I had sent an order inside the lines for some clothes and would have gotten them had our Brigade not been ordered away from our Department to the Army of Tennessee. I did not want you to complicate yourself by buying anything for me. Say to Alf, however, that I wish he would get me some check shirting and some handkerchiefs, with three or four net undershirts, and a comb & brush— He will have a chance to forward these things to me by someone coming out.

I suppose you have heard of the death of Lt. Genl. Polk. He was killed by a Yankee shell while making observations from the top of Pine Mountain. Our army has sustained a great loss in him and we all feel it very sensibly. Still some new man always rises to the surface ready to step in a fallen hero's shoes. Such is war! Every day but enhances my utter disgust for it and all its vain trophies and glories. Nothing but an imperious necessity keeps me in it, and just as soon as that necessity ceases I shall incontinently withdraw and go home if God spares me.

I said before I was convalescing. Unless I am very careful I will have my old spells of bilious fever and I intend to be quite prudent I assure you. I am now in a position to do so and the Genl. is very indulgent to me. When you read the description of Forrest's fight at Tishomingo Creek I reckon you will think that Mississippians, Tennesseans & Kentuckians can fight too. With *4,000* cavalry—he whipped 7,500 Yankee Infantry & 2,500 cavalry—routed the whole force capturing, killing, wounding 5,000—taking all their Artillery & 250 loaded wagons. Love & Kisses to Ma, Abe, Sis, Kate & the baby, respects to all inquiring friends. May God bless, comfort, protect & preserve you & yours is the prayer of your devoted husband

W. L. Nugent

Bally sends love to Agnes.

At Infirmary Mt. Marietta
June 25th, 1864

My precious Nellie,

I wrote to you the other day giving information of my sickness and convalescence. The attack of fever was not very aggravated in its character and has yielded very readily to treatment. I am still taking quinine & hope to leave for the command in a day or two, when, with hard service, I will soon become restored to my accustomed vigor of constitution & elascity of spirits. Our army is still fighting in this vicinity and from all appearances, it will take Sherman a month to reach Atlanta. He always finds our army confronting him at every turn he takes contesting every inch of ground and inflicting heavy losses upon him. From all I can learn he has already lost some ten or fifteen thousand men. Between eight or ten thousand more men will leave in a few days, their term of service having expired. A few more such losses and several experiments at a charge upon our breastworks will so far cripple him, that we will be able to initiate the offensive. When this does occur you may look out for rapid movements, startling combinations, heavy fighting and a crushing defeat to the Yankee army by the blessing of a Good Providence. Genl. Johnston is a close able commander and will do everything for the best. The troops have every confidence in him and all say they can whip the Yankees whenever they are lead against them. It is significant fact that we have heretofore repulsed the enemy in every charge and have foiled him in every movement he has attempted yet. As I before wrote you General Johnston was compelled to fall back as so to effect a junction with his reinforcements and I very much question whether his large army could be supplied at any point north of Marietta. At any rate the reinforcements were withheld him for sometime after they should have been forwarded. If he had secured them north of the Oustenella River the decisive battle of the campaign would have been fought at or near Resaca, and a great triumph achieved I firmly believe. At Resaca the Yankees detached a whole army corps and sent it to Rome beyond supporting distance. If Johnston, at this opportune moment, could have had Polk's army and all the troops he now has, Sherman would have been crushed. As it was, however, he was compelled to fall back to secure his left flank & protect the communications. All the troops did not get up until some time after we reached Marietta. I do not know who is to blame for all this, nor that any one is censurable. You know, Nell, I always would have my own opinion and "out of the abundance of the heart the mouth speaketh." Everything looks encouraging here and in Virginia also. We have nothing to fear if we have the approving smiles of Heaven and are true to ourselves. This army is well fed & as far as I can discover well clad. There are a great many men in so large an army who neglect themselves and throw away their clothing. These necessarily look shabby. Let me tell you, though, the large proportion of prisoners from the Yankee army are wretchedly uniformed, miserable specimens of humanity. They look more like cut-throat mercenaries than Union soldiers they vaunt themselves as being. Their clothes are filthy, torn & greasy and their persons are very offensive. In fact the whole Yankee camp is filled with vermin of every description. Our infantry camps, it is true, are obnoxious to the same objection to a certain extent: but they are not near as bad as the Yankees. We have been compelled to occupy their camps and the consequence is, we have all been visited by these "grey backs." Cleanliness and a careful attention to one's person soon corrects the evil. I am extremely anxious, however, to get away from this big army and breathe a little fresh air. The great number of dead horses, mules and human beings, make the air extremely offensive in the vicinity of the trenches, I am very nearly worn out under it and greatly fear I can never become accustomed to it. I forget though, that I am unnecessarily drawing an unpleasant picture; for I know that the bare recital of a reality which shocks me, is sufficient to unstring your nerves. Let me then draw the veil over the sickening theme, and wandering over the weary waste of miles that separate us neither in imagination & heart close to the side of my precious Nellie and wake to cheerful smiles her troubled, well-remembered face. Often by the bivouac fires, listening to the measured booming of artillery, & the frequent & irregular patter of the sharpshooter's bullets have I lost myself in dreamy thoughts of home, wife & baby until overpowered by the wild rush of surging emotions I have laid my head upon my pistol for a pillow and gently fallen into a quiet sleep while the fresh tear drop was glistening on the brink of its native spring. The days pass by and are scarcely remembered, the routine of duties being almost invariably the same. You have frequently heard of the wild excitement of battle. I experience no such feelings. There is a sense of depression continually working away at my heart, caused by a knowledge of the great suffering in store for large numbers of my fellow men, that is entirely antagonistic to any other emotions. It is doubtless true that I feel exhilarated when the enemy is driven back and our troops are cheering and advancing. Still I cannot be happy as some men are in a fight. I believe the whole machinery of war is indefensible on moral grounds, as a general proposition, and nothing but a sense of duty and the sacredness of our cause, could at all buoy me up. I frequently wonder what you are doing at home; how you spend the long hours of a summer's day; and what your thoughts are. You know I like to know what you think & how you feel upon every subject; and I never enjoyed your letters more than I do when you throw off all your reserve and unbosom yourself. That I consider a valid plea for my sympathy and grave affections; and, like most men, I suppose I am somewhat vain of being the husband of so precious a wife. And then the current of feeling should flow uninterruptedly & constantly from husband to wife & wife to husband. You know, Nellie, that the mountain rivulets, though broken occasionally by huge ledges of rock in their beds, flow on until their bold identity is lost in some majestic river, the temporary obstruction only giving a merrier dash & madder rush to the current. And yet, if across those streams the avaricious hand of man constructs a dam, their individuality is lost; and the thirsty traveller can scarcely find sufficient water below to attract his eager appetite. This is a simile of my own making. I leave you to draw the moral. And now my precious Nellie let me invoke you to be hopeful, prayerful, faithful & we will soon meet again. Love & kisses to Ma, Abe, Sis, Kate & baby, and may the Giver of all Good ever bless, comfort, protect & preserve you is the daily prayer of

Yr. devoted husband
W.L. Nugent

Hd. Qrs. Ferguson's Brigade
Near Atlanta, Ga. July 6th, 1864

My darling Nellie,[2]

I have repeatedly written to you of late, at times twice a week and long letters, in hopes that a good gale of wind might blow one or two across the forsaken and almost forgotten space that separates you from "Dixie." These

---

[2]The original of this letter is deposited in the Schlesinger Library, Cambridge.

letters have been sent in every imaginable way, some by hand and others to care Capt. Evans at Canton. I hope those sent to Capt. Evans' care may eventually reach you. I will send this to the care of Genl. S. D. Lee at Meridian and ask him to forward it if any opportunity offers. If, therefore, you do not regularly receive information from me, do not believe I either forget or do not write to you. Bad news travels fast and if I am injured at all you will be certain to hear of it.

Your welcome letter of the 27th May was handed to me today by our Post Master and afforded me that peculiar pleasure and inspiration which the missives of my darling little wife can alone afford. As soon as they are opened, the familiar handwriting wakes to "light and life again" the memories of many a happy bye-gone hour—full of happiness as they were flitting away and doubly treasured because they cannot recur again for many a weary day to come. If I could be otherwise than kind in my letters I would be untrue to myself, to you and the devoted, gentle Mother who fashioned my native impulses after her own generous nature. I hope the time is far distant and may never come when you may have cause to complain of me. My daily experiences are not such as to encourage the finer feelings of my heart, but I will never let them provoke anything that will in the least mar the recollection of the supreme pleasure that has hitherto characterized our married life. I have no doubt, Nellie, that you grow better every day and that I shall find you at the close of this war, much improved every way as my imagination frequently pictures you. I never have believed a woman's entire character and individuality could be developed until she became a mother. This event draws her into a closer relation with the man of her choice. They were husband and wife before; they are Father and Mother then. And then, too, there is a common object upon which they can lavish their affection; a daily, living exemplification of that spiritual unity which cannot be realized when the vows of marriage are taken and they are pronounced one. It is only when the innocent child is prattling around their knees that they feel that oneness so indeterminate before.

You know, Nellie, I am much addicted to discoursing of life. I have always endeavored to enshrine love as our household God. I had no other and wanted none. I knew the jewel of happiness could only thus be found, and I gladly close in with your proposition. While this household God is enshrined there can be no feeling or thought, or jest, or action that would militate against the happiness that should reign supreme in every family. Still I do not think we can be really happy, in the truest sense of the term, unless we are lifted up and sustained by the Great Giver of all good. There are so many sorrows in this world, so many difficulties, so many trials, that we need and must have encouragement and support from a higher source. It is impossible to be reconciled to everything of change that happens in our life unless we recognize a Divine Ruler and are propped by the stays of a religion that purifies, refines and enlivens the heart. We have a household, a treasured household, and when the war is over we will have a house; and our household God will be enshrined with all due solemnity. You will never find me tardy or unwilling about making or keeping any compact that will increase our happiness. How it cheers me when you speak of our precious treasure, our only child, may God spare her to us! How I would delight to see her, to hear her innocent chatterings, mark the winsome gladness of her smiles. Does she know my photograph yet? Or does she look upon it as a toy? You don't say enough about her. Do let me know what she does, how she looks, and how she laughs. Everything from home is pleasant, and the thousand little things, that daily transpire, tho' regarded almost as nonentities, afford me the greatest amount of gratification. You must all keep a long letter to me on hand to be forwarded by the first opportunity, a P.S. stating that all is well could answer when the letter is finished. Tell Sis she must write. She has plenty of time and I am an excellent subject for her practice. I will be charitable if necessary and will keep closely all her secrets.

I am in fine health now. Our army is only about eight miles north of Atlanta. The soldiers are all in fine spirits and tho' greatly outnumbered will give Mr. Sherman a sound drubbing at the proper time. My brother John who lost his leg is doing well but is in the rear of the Yankee army.[3] He is treated kindly and furnished with everything necessary for his comfort. I had hoped to hear from him within the last few days, but have not been so fortunate. Clarence, I hope, will not come up here. We have hard times and a great deal of fighting. Kiss Ma, Evie, Kate, Abe and the darling baby for me. Regards to Tom Hinds & all inquiring friends. May God

---

[3]John Pratt Nugent, Jr. lost his leg in the Battle of New Hope Church. He later lived on William's Arcadia and Reveille Plantations in Bolivar County. Edmonds, Nugent Family Papers.

bless, comfort, protect and preserve you all is the prayer of your devoted
husband

W. L. Nugent.

Hd. Qrs. Ferguson's Brigade
East Point, Ga. July 26th, 1864

My darling Nellie,

I was surprised, delighted, and transported today, beyond all my powers
of description, when a stranger stepped up and politely handed me your
letter of the 3d July. Only think I hadn't heard from you for three months,
and of course had become very uneasy. Shut up in this large army from all
intercourse with society, and restrained by rigid laws and orders, from all
freedom of locomotion, I can find no pleasure in anything unless it is when
I get one of your letters. Before I forget it, please say to Ma that I have
written her one or two long letters and regret very much she didn't get it.
Please say to her that I haven't changed at all in my attachment to her and
am determined never to be derelict in any duty, more especially when she
is concerned.

Since I last wrote to you I have passed through stirring scenes, fighting
nearly every day of the week and scarcely able to take any rest at all at
night. God has wonderfully manifested his love and mercy in my behalf
recently. The other day in front of Decatur I was reclining on an old
bedstead under a pear tree preparatory to taking a nap, not suspecting the
Yankees or their invariable precursor's shell, when a shrapnel shot struck
the tree under which I was lying and killed Capt. McGill who was standing
by my side and quite touching me. We had just before been remarking
upon the probability of our being disturbed by the enemy. The poor fellow
was hurried out of the world almost without any notice whatever, and his
words had scarcely died upon his lips before he fell striking my left arm and
falling between me and the bedstead. Such is life and at such prices are our
liberties to be purchased. How great the cost.

We attacked Decatur on the 22d and took the town driving out a Brigade
of Infantry and a good deal of Dismounted Cavalry. Our Brigade really took
the town, tho' it was supported on both flanks by a Brigade of Cavalry
dismounted. The fight lasted about two hours and was very hot for awhile.

The Yankees had the hills and houses on us and fought very well for a time. Our dash was made to distract attention while Hardee made the real attack on the enemy's flank. We captured over a hundred prisoners and killed and wounded about one hundred and fifty. Our loss about seventy killed and wounded. We have now a new General—Hood from Texas and he is for fighting all the time. He has so far done very well and gives evidence of some ability—but at what fearful cost. We have lost about *8,000* killed and wounded in the last two or three days. This sort of fighting, unless we meet with some more decided success will dissipate our army very soon. Eight more such fights and we will have no army at all. The Yankees have become more cautious since, though and have quit their everlasting flanking. There is some movement on the carpet now, but I am wholly unacquainted with the nature or character of it. We have captured some four-thousand prisoners, taken twenty-two pieces of artillery and driven the enemy's flank back, Atlanta is safe for awhile yet, tho' I fear we will have to abandon it unless reinforcements are sent us. Hood is taking all the dismounted Cavalry to the front and will make them count. We sent him for duty today three hundred and forty able bodied soldiers and he will get in my opinion some four or five thousand from the different Brigades attached to this army. This will nearly make up our losses. The Cavalry here is abundantly able to cope with that of the enemy without this depletion and I am surprised that the matter has not sooner been attended to. Up to this time we have had almost incessant fighting and no manoeuvring. The Cavalry has been dismounted and put to fight the Yankee infantry from behind rail piles and breastworks. In this way we have damaged the enemy a great deal more than we have suffered. Our army would, when outflanked, fall back four or five miles, be formed in line of battle, stack arms throw up breastworks, in one or two hours and prepare to fight the Yankees. The enemy would advance, from his line, throw out skirmishers to feel our position, build his breastworks, and make gradual approaches until he had discovered our position; when the flank movement would begin again. The Yankees made very slow work of it, advancing, having become very cautious from repeated repulses and severe losses. Their skirmishers are almost afraid of shadows and step as lightly as Indians through the woods. The Yankee Cavalry appears to be heartily afraid of ours and hunts cover whenever attacked. Ferguson's Brigade has done some good fighting recently and has successfully given the lie to the imputations heaped upon it by reason of Genl. Jackson'[s] infamous order; for which, by the way, he has apologized I learned. At any rate, neither he nor any other man can traduce the General or his Brigade and go unpunished. The Yankees are making raids in every direction and are endeavoring in every possible way to drive us from Atlanta. Hood will not leave, I am satisfied, without a big fight; and even as I write movements may be on hand that will wind up Sherman's career by the blessing of Providence. May he who rules the world and holds in his hands the destinies of nations take us safely through all our troubles, and speedily give us peace!

I can hear absolutely nothing from Virginia. The telegraphic or Railroad communications must have been cut. I have no fear of the results in that noble old state. Robert E. Lee is a tower of strength and under him and the gallant Beauregard all will work for the grand result for which we so ardently wish and so devoutly pray. The symptoms of approaching disintegration at the North are very favorable at this time; and if we can keep the Yankees back until the Democratic Convention assembles, the Peace candidate will be nominated and elected. It almost looks childish to speculate, but when the ordeal through which we are passing is so terrible and everything like even momentary pleasure has disappeared, it is some gratification to peer into the future colored with the highly wrought pictures of our imagination, and conjure up scenes of happiness. I take no delight in parties. They are great bores to me; don't suit my nature or disposition. The surface enjoyment that predominates at such occasions is absolutely painful to me. I wouldn't give a quiet hour's cozy chat with my darling little wife for ten thousand of them gotten up in the most approved style. Say to Ma should she not get my letter, that I am not unmindful of my allegiance to the Great God, who has so mercifully protected me, and with His help, I purpose remaining steadfast in my purpose to love, honor, and obey Him. While I do not enjoy religion as I would like in the army, there are times when the little I have is a great comfort to me indeed.

My health continues to be good tho' I have been compelled to take "Fowler's Solution of Arsenic." We are now resting for a day or two preparatory to a trip of some kind: I hope to go to the rear of the army.

Dr. Talbott hasn't come up and Ben Johnson is hanging back in Mississippi.

Love to all, Kiss Ma, Abe, Evie, Kate for me and little Nell a thousand times. May God bless, comfort protect and preserve you is the prayer of

Your devoted husband

W. L. Nugent

Direct

Capt W. L. Nugent

A.A.G. Ferguson's Cavalry Brigade

Army of Tennessee

Hd. Qrs. Ferguson's Brigade

Near Atlanta, Ga.

August 2nd, 1864

My darling Nellie,[4]

Three letters this evening running back in point of date to the 8th June! This was a great treat I assure you, and one which afforded me infinite pleasure. I am aware of the almost insuperable difficulties attendant upon forwarding letters to the Swamp and receiving them from that section of [the] country, and hence never grumble at my fate, if your dearly prized missives fail in reaching me at the proper times. All my letters are sent to the care of Captain Evans at Canton, and I hope they will reach you from that point. I presume Captain Evans sends couriers out to Canton regularly, or at any rate that they would call by that place. If you know of any point more accessible, please let me know and I will direct my letters accordingly.

We are still near this place and holding the enemy in check. For eight or ten days Sherman has been fighting and flanking with a view to gain possession of Atlanta; but having been tolerably well used up in two pitched battles and been driven, with great slaughter, from his flanking breastworks he appears now to entertain no other disposition than to fortify and skirmish in front of his breastworks. Now and then he will make a bold attempt to drive our pickets in and advance his lines; these attempts, though, have generally proven unsuccessful, and his "blue coats" have the mortification of being driven back in disorder to their ditches. The same policy is being pursued by Genl. Grant in Richmond; *Virginia,* I should

---

[4]The original of this letter is deposited in the Schlesinger Library, Cambridge.

have said. You need not believe one half the Yankee papers say. For instance Sherman reported a loss of 2,000 in the fight of 22 July, when we had in our hands about 2,000 prisoners. Atlanta has been reported as in the possession of the enemy, while they are at least three miles distant with a Confederate army in their front, and have a hard time of it. Their raiding Cavalry has been defeated leaving in our hands between 1,500 and 2,000 prisoners, a large number of horses, equipment etc. We do not now anticipate much further trouble from the Raiders, and I hope we soon make an attempt to get into Sherman's rear and destroy his communications with Chattanooga. If this could be done we would soon be rid of the mortifying presence of an invading army so far into the heart of our country. Few of our leaders supposed that Sherman would have the hardihood to march so far south; but he has done it, has few or no guards along the Rail Road, and still no attempt is made to cut the Rail Road. Our losses have been tolerably heavy owing to the recent fights in which we have been com-pelled to charge the Yankee breastworks. Behind such works as they construct a man is almost perfectly secure. They are as high as a man's head, and have a large log laid on the top, with skids under each end, thus leaving room enough for the rifles between the log and dirt. With all this protection, however, the soldiers out of mere curiosity will now and then poke their heads above the logs to make observation; at which times they are frequently picked off by our sharpshooters. There is a constant patter-ing along the skirmish lines from sun to sun, and only occasionally anyone is hurt. Our Brigade now occupies the trenches just behind where the big fight occurred and at times the stench from decaying corpses and carcasses is terrific. Petersburg was not taken at last accounts from Virginia. Grant was making regular siege approaches and would soon attempt to storm the place. If he has the temerity to attempt it, he will be whipped terribly. As soon as a general engagement comes off either near Petersburg or Atlanta, in an open field, we will whip the Yankees terribly, by the blessing of God. The caution with which the Yankees advance convinces me that they are anxious, for political effect, to take Richmond and Atlanta without a deci-sive effect. If they can bring this about, it is supposed Lincoln will be reelected, and the abolitionists will build up a strong, centralized Govern-ment, they think, capable of coercing the States into abject submission to Federal Rule. The war will then be continued to the bitter end regardless of loss or expense. I believe the war will be concluded this year, though

there will be irregular fighting for some time to come. At any rate I will go
home this winter if it can possibly be done. I certainly will leave no stone
unturned to accomplish this end.

I regret excessively that we were compelled to leave Mississippi as I
intended to bring you out of the Swamp and if I can provide a home for you
will bring you out anyhow. "Uncle Jack" might have offered you a home:
but as he did not do so, I do not like to make application to him.[5] I will
write today to Tuscaloosa, Alabama to see if I can get you a good boarding
house at that place, where you will have some very agreeable kinfolks, and
pleasant society. I think myself your health would be better out of the
Swamp and away from the everlasting Yankee. You need some *rest* as much
as anything else and will have to wean Nellie. I cannot form any opinion in
reference to her hand at this distance. If it is practicable to separate her
fingers and make her hand more useful to her, it should by all means be
done and as soon as possible. I do not know whether you could visit New
Orleans or not, nor who could go with you. Some good physician ought to
be consulted before the operation is performed. We have a surgeon in our
Brigade who has the ability and skill necessary, but he is further off than
Dr. Stone. It is extremely difficult to say what Ma ought to do. My opinion
is that it would be much better for her to go to Texas and rely upon the
negroes to support her, and it was, in view of the possibility of such a thing
that I wanted Alf to remain out of the army so that he might be in a
condition to support and care for her. The negroes will certainly desert her
if she brings them back to the Swamp. Possibly John and one or two others
might not. The most would, though, to a certainty.

I am glad you did not suffer Talbott's nonsense to have any effect upon
you. The simple fact is that I attended an evening party at a Kinswoman's;
made the acquaintance of several married and unmarried ladies; sat down
in the parlor (not dancing room) conversed with them very pleasantly for an
hour or two, principally about "my little wife and baby"; and enjoyed
myself in a quiet, dignified way. My principal entertainer was Mrs. Lewis,
the wife of a Lieutenant in one of our Regiments who accompanied her.
She is a good Methodist. When we went into supper I discovered a nice,
timid young girl without escort and at once sought an introduction to her,
that I might relieve her from her embarrassment. I paid her the proper

---

[5]John and Philip Cocks did later assist their sister, Mrs. Smith, in building a Greenville
residence.

respect and attention as a matter of course, but let even her know I was a married man. In fact, I feared lest some persons might think my vanity was excessive as I appeared to take such pains on the subject. As I told the ladies, I am too proud of my wife to conceal or ignore her existence at any time or in any place. And now, my own cherished Nellie, I hope you will not suffer yourself to be afflicted with the idea that you are not worthy of me, or that you may possibly become less comely and thus lose my affection. Mine is no transient passion, no suddenly gotten up feeling. I have been loving you for nearly ten years with a constantly increasing affection; a love which has known no interruption or decrease. I do not love you for your outside personality; but for your individuality and personality as the best beloved of my heart. I have not lost one whit of my appreciation for you, and am persuaded will never do so. I beg you will not have such a low opinion of yourself, and do not fear to put my love to any test. If my feelings were superficial there *might*, *perhaps*, be some reason to think your bad health and decayed beauty would wean me away. On the contrary I feel it will draw me nearer to you, for honestly my love for you is all absorbing, deeply and unchangeably incorporated into my very nature and existence. Rely upon it, and be comforted by it. For my sake take care of yourself. There are elements of beauty, worth and truth in you that have not been fully developed and which can only be fully brought into play by careful cultivation. I feel that I have need for improvement to be fully worthy of you.

With you, I feel that by God's good grace, we can together raise an excellent family; and if we are both spared will do so. The responsibility is a great one, however, as children learn by example more than by precept, and we will have to keep our hearts, tempers and conduct pure. If our children are raised in an atmosphere of love, and in a home where the vanities and troubles of the outside world are barred out, they will live [to] be a comfort to us and useful members of society. I am looking far ahead, but these tempting scenes of the future, when the present is so dreary, cannot be dispensed with. My health is good just now, and I have very little apprehension of further trouble this summer. Our fare is not very good just now, tho' we generally have tolerably fair coffee and sugar; flour scarce.

Love and kisses to Ma, Evie, Kate and the Babe. Be continually comforted by the assurance of my love. If words cannot assure you, wait until I come. May God bless, comfort, protect and preserve and ever have you in his holy keeping is the prayer of

Your devoted husband
W. L. Nugent

Hd. Qrs. Brigade
Near Atlanta, Ga. Aug. 8/64

My darling Nellie:

I received two letters from you last night and a pair of saddle bags filled with clothing. The clothes were very acceptable, supplying, as they did, a want which it was utterly impossible to gratify in Georgia. We are kept so busy and confined that we cannot go out to hunt up anything of the sort; and even if we could I doubt whether a man could find a shirt in this State. Please say to Ma that I am deeply indebted to her for her kindness and affectionate remembrance. I have written her two or three letters and will write again. It is useless for me to speak of the exhilaration of feeling produced by the reception of your letters. When your letters are delayed in reaching me, I grow moody and disappointed and am only revived when some friendly hand brings a missive from the darling of my bosom. I regret very much to hear of your bad health. I would be satisfied with my present disagreeable mode of life if you could only be spared the great affliction of ill-health, because I feel that God will spare me to see you and enjoy your society for many long years after the war is over. Still it grieves me to hear that you suffer. I am too far off and too strongly bound by regulations to fly to your relief and minister to your comfort; and it is this thought which adds to the poignancy of feeling. I sometimes am inclined to kick at the laws which effect a compulsory separation between man and wife and to esteem it all wrong. Still, my own precious Nellie, what can I do? A cruel, relentless war is waged for our annihilation, and unless we present a bold front to the enemy, contesting every inch of ground, we may expect nothing but vassalage and slavery all our lives. Our rights and privileges will be totally destroyed and military governors and Yankee judges will govern us, while our lands will be parcelled out among a horde of foreign adventurers and mercenary soldiers. This is a fate to which we can never submit. The alternative of taking the oath, kissing the hand that has so severely smitten us, and bowing to the triumphant chariot of Abe Lincoln is more than freemen can endure until they have exhausted every resource which the God of Nature has placed in their power. To me it would be an ignominious fate were I compelled to rear a family forever ignored in the land of their birth, and I must still battle for freedom a little longer. My candid opinion is, that we are fast approaching the goal and that the present campaigns in Virginia and Georgia will terminate the war. We may have a desultory warfare along the border for some months thereafter; but the hard fighting will be over by the last of November. We are holding our own here at present and Atlanta is still safe. General Hood has evidenced considerable talent in handling the Army of Tennessee and is warmly supported by his troops. We have defeated the Yankees wherever they have charged our works and have so far prevented them from flanking our position. If we can prevent Sherman's flank movements we can whip them all the time when they come up directly in our front. Our losses have been severe, it is true, but then we have inflicted more than a corresponding and relative damage on the enemy. For instance in the great fight of the 22nd, we charged the flank of the Yankee Army protected by huge breastworks, drove it back for two miles, captured some 1,800 prisoners, buried about 2,000 of their dead, and wounded large numbers of them. Our loss about 3,000. In this fight we killed General McPherson, by large odds the finest officer in the Federal Army. He was worth at least a thousand men and his loss will be severely felt by Mr. Sherman. In Virginia everything is working favorably so far. The Yankees can make no impression on General Lee's lines at all. In every encounter Grant is thwarted with heavy loss. He is, however, still pegging away at Petersburg and appears to indulge the hope that he will reduce the place by gradual approaches. Meanwhile one corps of our army invades Maryland, strikes terror into the citizens of Washington and Baltimore, brings out supplies for the army, swaps its jaded horses for fresh ones, gets an astonishing number of splendid horses and beef cattle, besides large supplies of amunition, small arms etc. and quietly recrosses the Potomac with its booty. We burned Governor Bradford's Mansion in retaliation for the destruction of Governor Letcher's, laid Montgomery Blair's palace in ashes, and taught the Yankees a little of the sufferings they have brought upon us. From all indications it has had a very salutary effect upon them. I think a little more house burning will bring them to their senses. Charleston is safe. Mobile is threatened but not yet in any danger. We fear that the Yankees may invade Mississippi again and finding little opposition may strike a death blow to the planting interests in the Prairie Country from which nearly all our supplies of corn are drawn. Forrest is still in the Field, with reinforcements and will conduct the Yanks across the State. Let them try the adventure. If their Brigade (ours included) can hold two Yankee Army Corps in check for 36 hours, Forrest with his force ought to hold Smith and Washburn back until their supplies are exhausted. At any rate no one could accomplish more than he. For a week we have had rest. Scarcely a gun has been fired in front of our works. The time has been usefully employed in recruiting horses and preparing for some mounted duty whenever the order shall come. It would astonish you to go out on the battle field and see the ingenious field works erected by the Yankees to protect themselves against our fire. They are constructed in every direction and in every possible shape. Their skirmishers dig deep pits and have heavy enbankments thrown up on each side and in front with "head logs" to save their skulls from stray bullets. We have been in a good fight recently and have done well in all and splendidly in one. I will reserve a full description for another letter which I will send by mail to care Captain Henderson. All my former letters were directed to care Captain Evans at Canton and as they have failed to reach you I expect there is a box full of them at that point unless they have been delayed on the route. I wrote you two long letters and one to Ma last week, and have always written you at least once every seven days and often twice!

I think you had better come out of the Swamp and visit your Uncle Jack and Cousin Phil about ten miles due East of Carthage, Mississippi. Do this at once if you can get any conveyance. Captain Evans will certainly let Alf come out with you. I have no doubt the folks will be glad to see you and a month's stay in the hills will help you amazingly. "Uncle Jack" was very kind to me solely because of my being your husband, and would be glad to see you. At any rate try it; if he is not, I can get you a home elsewhere until your health is restored. Don't let any motive of delicacy stop you because I feel sure you will be welcome.

My health is very good now. Have taken a course of "Fowler's Solution" with considerable benefit to my self. Clarence has at last got up safely. I haven't yet seen him, however. I understand he has a fine horse. Lieut. Fowler has gone to the Swamp. If he calls on you treat him well. He is a fine fellow and a very gallant officer. The Genl. has not yet been promoted. I believe he will be soon. Tell Sis she must write to me. I will keep all her

secrets, sacredly. Kisses to Ma, Evie, Kate, Abe & the baby. Bally sends love to Agnes etc. May God bless, comfort, protect and preserve you is the
Prayer of your devoted husband
W.L. Nugent

I do not think it would be a good idea to bring the negroes back before something definite occurs. The Yankees are very busy recruiting darkies. Can't Ma get Jack's negroes back and turn off ours that have gone off? She had better wait awhile and trust to the Providence of God. Respects to all inquiring friends.

Hd.Qrs. Ferguson's Brigade
Near Atlanta, Ga. Aug. 15,64

My dear Nellie,

I have written to you several times quite recently and have forwarded the letters by hand and mail, in hope that one at least might reach you. I have directed all my letters heretofore to the care of Capt. Evans at Canton. I had been informed by Sharp Nelson that the Scouts came out to Canton regularly and hence hoped, I must confess, almost against hope that they would find and forward my letters. I presume, however, their visits do not extend so low down as Canton. I have directed my last letters to the care of Capt. Sam Henderson, as you suggested, and have written him a letter requesting that the letters be forwarded by courier to the Swamp. It is a source of great trouble and vexation to me not to hear from you; and if I did not preserve a continuous control over myself, I would become despondent and gloomy. As it is I often become "blue as indigo" for a day or so, and anxiously look ahead to the time when the exigency in our military affairs will permit me to leave on furlough. The General has now no staff officer with him but myself and hence I could not be spared. Capt. Irwin, who fills my place when I am away was wounded on the 3rd of July and is off on 60 days leave of absence to get well.

His wound was a flesh wound and though quite painful will not endanger his life. He will return to us in a few days or weeks, and my labors will be lessened. Our Aide-de-Camp is a *prisoner* at Fort Delaware. We are trying to get a few more under recent orders, but haven't yet succeeded. "Your pretty" husband—imagine him with closely cropped hair, top boots, long beard sun browned face, "home made" shirt of coarse cotton, cast off suspenders, and a soldier's jacket, has been recommended for a majority; and if successful, God willing, will return home with a star on the lapel of his coat. To appear in his *fancy* court dress would shock your nerves. The nice clothes Ma sent me are kept stored away for occasions of importance. On a grand review I would appear in uniform with a white shirt on and a neck tie. To wear these fine clothes every day would be of no service in the world. Talbott hasn't sent me the saddle bags you spoke of but when he does, I will be abundantly supplied.

Of late I have been looking out for a pair of spurs. All the prisoners our Scouts bring in are so poorly clad, so well fleeced and so miserable a looking set, that I haven't even the heart to look at their pedal extremities. For the last twenty days we have enjoyed a respite from fighting, have been lazying in a good camp, with tolerable fare and little or no work to do, and are growing fat. I find that even now the time hangs heavily on, and many a weary sigh floats, with all its unutterable and expectant anxiety, westward to the Father of Waters where dwells the idol of my heart. I do not believe I can ever be reconciled to war. The utmost relaxation of discipline and the greatest favors that could possibly be shown me, would not compensate for the burdensome separation from you and our darling child. After more than two years separation I find it just as difficult to endure the grievous burden. I often, often sympathize with your grief on this account. Your time is not so much engrossed as mine. Everything around you but seems to recall the days "Lang Syne," and the comparison between the joys of our married life then, and the unpleasant experiences of the present must be ever present with you. I live in hope that this fall will terminate the war and that we may be reunited at farthest by Christmas never to part until the natural termination of our lives shall call one or the other to the better world.

All along a line of battle extending around Atlanta and to the left of the City for miles, one hears the incessant rattle of musketry and the booming of artillery from early morn til dewy eve. Lying on my pallet at night I can distinctly hear the shells as they burst over the Gate City. The loud explosion and the whistling shell-fragments hurrying thru' the air on mission of death, is agreeable when one is camped quite out of range. But when one of these merciless missiles strikes down a fellow soldier by your side, the shock is terrible in the extreme. The sensation produced cannot well be described. You see that a man in robust health a few moments before is suddenly struck down and lies stretched out a cold and lifeless corpse. A spirit of awe and faintness almost overpowers you. I never want to see "the like" again.

I began this letter yesterday but was prevented from closing it by a reported advance of the enemy. We saddled up, moved out, drove them back and returned about midnight, tired, hungry and "wolfish." If anathemas could have destroyed the entire Yankee Army, there would not have been a single blue coat left two hours after we had left camp. When soldiers rest awhile they become very much indisposed to locomotion of all kinds; but after hurrying around a little, they become fond of the excitement and are not content unless they are on a raid. This good fortune has not yet befallen us and we are holding our train until Genl. Hood gives the order to move. We still hold Atlanta and will in all probability do so for many weeks. Genl. Hood is a fighting man and when he becomes a little more accustomed to the routine of his duties, will make an efficient officer. The people have become accustomed to the displacement of Johnston, and the soldiers are reconciled. They hated to part with old Joe. He had returned slowly from Dalton averaging when on the march about seven miles a day; had under him fought repeatedly; whipped the enemy; had been well fed; well clothed; provided with everything their necessities required; never ruthlessly pushed against the breastworks held by a superior force and led up to slaughter; almost always inflicting heavy losses on the enemy and suffering little themselves. And they were convinced that when Joe said the "set time" had come they would win a glorious victory. They had retreated nearly a hundred miles and were better disciplined, more content, more defiant and more invincible than when the first gun was fired at Dalton. For this they loved their veteran leader and would have followed him to the end of the Confederacy. Deserters were rare and the Confederate soldier with the spirit of independence was strong within him, felt as if he could solve the difficult problem of recognition unaided by foreign intervention. Everything moved like clock work; every officer knew his place; every Regiment, Brigade, Division and Corps knew when to move, where to halt, how to move when and where to form. There was no jostling, no commingling of troops, no hurrying causelessly, and no difficulty arising from the blocking up of roads. The army would have its breastworks and retire while the enemy looking on was afraid to pursue. Our communications were not interrupted, our transportation remained intact, our artillery horses were in good condition; and the whole army was always in splendid condition up to the very moment when Johnston penned his valedictory order. A great man has left us; a greater may now be over us. *Nous verrons.* The future alone can determine this matter. Meanwhile let us be hopeful and hold up the hands of our leader. My health is good just now. Kiss Ma, Evie, Abe and my darling Nell for Pa. I haven't seen Clarence yet. Brother John is well and at home thank God. With even one leg he will be a comfort to his parents. I haven't received a letter from Sis yet. May God bless, comfort, protect and preserve you is the prayer of

Your devoted husband
W. L. Nugent

Hd. Qrs. Ferguson's Brigade
Near Jonesboro, Ga. Sept. 10,64

My darling Nellie:

Many a weary day has lapsed since I heard from you last, and the present disarranged conditions of affairs induces the belief that I may not have the happiness to get a letter for sometime to come. After a great deal of hard fighting and the loss of a great many valuable men, Atlanta has been evacuated and delivered over to Sherman's tender mercies. The evacuation was the result of the loss of the battle of Jonesboro, a fight in which it is said, our troops did not behave as well as they might have done. Genl. Sherman having failed in his flank movement around our right and despairing of success by direct assault determined to make a bold and hazardous movement around our left. Swinging his whole army around on his right as a pivot, he protected his communications with one corps and with the balance of his army moved down around our left and through Fairburn to Jonesboro, some twenty miles south-east of Atlanta. General Hood was early advised of this movement but couldn't be induced to believe that Sherman would make such a movement. In consequence of this two of our corps alone engaged the entire Yankee Army. They were of necessity whipped, driven back and the Army of Tennessee was cut in two. It is fortunate for us that the enemy didn't know this else we might have [been] almost annihilated: The campaign is now virtually closed; the Yankees are reposing around Atlanta and we will have a little rest from our labors. The army is very much dissatisfied with Genl. Hood and I fear will never be the efficient arm of defense under him, that it was under the genial, gallant and able old Chieftain, who has been unceremoniously laid on the shelf and who bears with him the affection of every man and officer, I believe, in this Army. Still it is our duty to render obedience to the Constituted authorities and to "hold up" Genl. Hood's hands in the hope that something advantageous will eventually turn up. Of one thing we all feel satisfied, that the campaign has had a very unsatisfactory termination. Genl. Lee thinks we ought to have defeated the enemy at Jonesboro, others imagine differently. Our losses have been severe. I presume our army is diminished one half at least in the Infantry and Artillery. A month's rest may enable us to recruit and get in a better condition for campaigning than at present. It will be a difficult matter, however, to replace the gallant dead whose remains now hallow the soil of Georgia. They were the faithful few and stood out against all temptations to desert their colors. Their places cannot be properly supplied. The men who are caught and forced into the ranks are not to be relied upon at all. Behind breastworks they may be induced to exchange shots with the enemy; in the open field they can never be brought to close quarters. Our main hope now is the disagreement existing among the political parties North. If the Democrats are successful I look for a speedy termination of hostilities and eventually a permanent peace. If McClellan is elected our negroes will not be disturbed I think at all. The negro soldiers will be disbanded and returned to their owners, and the whole subject will be settled by arbitration and not by the sword. The Yankees are gone and the Southwest will set up a new Confederation in a year or so I have no doubt. I am encouraged by the signs of the time to be hopeful of the future. We have no news from Virginia beyond the fact that things are working along very well and that Richmond is safe.

My health is very good at present with the exception of a bad cold which makes me feel a little unpleasant. A heavy head and the continued use of a pocket handkerchief are not calculated to make a body feel agreeable.

We have been looking out for orders to go to Alabama for several weeks but "hope deferred" has made the "heart sick." I want to go home this winter and I want to be as near as possible so that all my time will not be consumed in traveling to and fro. If possible I will accomplish this thing. I think I can get the application through with the aid of a few friends and am determined to persist in it to the end. I am becoming desperately homesick every day and can hardly contain myself. It seems to me an age since I saw you, and then too, how I long to see and dandle my darling little daughter. I am glad she looks like her mother. Well, Nell, I fear I shall become bald before this war is over. I keep my head closely cropped in hopes of being able to preserve my hair. I shall never cease to be thankful for the nice clothes sent me. Love and kisses to Ma, Evie, Kate, Abe and the "Angel." Be comforted, hopeful, cheerful, prayerful and all will yet be love. May God bless, comfort, protect and preserve you is the prayer of

Your devoted husband
W. L. Nugent

Hd. Qrs. Ferguson's Brigade
Jackson's Division Cavalry
Army of Tennessee
Jonesboro, Ga. Sept. 14, 1864

My precious Nellie:

I do not believe a week has rolled its tiresome round since my connection with the Army of Tennessee that I have not written you one and frequently two letters. These letters have in the main been directed to the care of Capt. Evans at Canton, some to care of Capt. Henderson and others to care Judge Wm. Yerger at Jackson. I have often endeavored to interest people in the neighborhood of Canton in my personal matters sufficiently to gather up and convey to their destination these waifs, without any good result. I have tried to look my destiny squarely in the face and to become resigned to my fate; but feel, more and more every day the great misfortune of being so far separated from you and so circumstanced that I cannot freely and frequently communicate with you. There is so little of that human nature which makes the whole world kin, nowadays, that we cannot rely upon any one with certainty. The distress everywhere prevailing, the desolation and ruin that have prevailed to so alarming an extent all over our country, have thrown every individual upon his own resources for a support and have had the effect to isolate, it seems every human being. My charity prevents me from entertaining any bitterness of feeling on the subject and I have been sustained by an "unfaltering trust" in the justice of our cause. I have not yet received my commission as Major though I do not think there is much doubt if any, of its reaching me "in due course of mail." We are still in Jackson's Division, though we were operating with

Wheeler's Corps for sometime. The only pleasure I can feel in being promoted, aside from its enlarging my field of usefulness arises from its association with the darling object of my affections. All the honors which I can gather in this world, if dissociated from you would be of minor importance. If I can honestly gather them, throw them in your lap, and by so doing kindle a light in your eye or bring a cheering smile to your lips, I will have all the glory I desire. I can only repeat what I really feel and have often expressed, that I can have no pleasure unless associated with you. The longer I live the more I am impressed with the intrinsic truth of the Biblical doctrine of the unity of husband and wife. It is unnecessary to ask me to think of you often. It is my constant theme of reflection by day and the burden of my dreams by night. If I do not become more a lover every day I will have greatly mistaken myself. You cannot regret the separation more than I. I implore you not to indulge a moment's thought of anything producing a "distance" between us. I cannot believe and do not feel that there is any such superiority on my part. I know myself and I know you, Nellie; and if where the heart is so strongly and powerfully involved there could be any comparison of merit between us the advantage would be with you. There is, in my candid opinion, but one thing needed to make you all that the most enobled imagination could picture, and that is the pure religion of our Lord and Savior, Jesus Christ. Nature has exhausted herself in you; and if you do not by application and reflection attain a standard of excellence in mind and heart, which my rough nature would never allow me to reach, I am very much mistaken. As it is I am content for I am satisfied that you are my equal in every respect. I have no doubt, when the war is over, we will both grow wiser and better. Humility is a crowning virtue when properly exercised. A person however, may have too cramped an idea of humility. We must not think of ourselves more than we ought! but then we must think soberly. Ma and you both think too little of yourselves. She is a very superior woman and while like every mortal, she has her infirmities they are of such a kind that they lend a charm to the many excellencies of her character. I rejoice to hear of your good health, and increasing loveliness of our child. It will be a source of constant enjoyment to me, if I am spared by the mercy of God, to watch and direct the development of her mind. Teach her to recognize her father's picture so that she will know him when he returns from the war.

From all accounts Genl. Ferguson couldn't get a fight out of Jackson and the matter has now dropped of its own weight. As the General has demanded a Court of Inquiry I presume there will be some official investigation into Jackson's management of the Cavalry, when I expect rare developments. Jackson put Ferguson in arrest for not furnishing a little Inspection Report for which the General has been courtmartialed. The papers have gone on to Richmond and the General has gone to Charleston on leave of absence. It was altogether a small matter and is, I believe, generally so considered.

We have been compelled to give up Atlanta, with the loss of several hundred prisoners, and a large amount of ammunition and stores destroyed. Sherman completely out-generaled Hood, who had ample notice of the flank movement around our left. Hood wouldn't believe it and in consequence fought the whole Yankee army with one corps. Our army is reduced nearly if not quite one-half. I presume we have about 30,000 effective muskets. Our stragglers and sick are rapidly coming in and if we have a little more rest Sherman will find it troublesome to go to Savannah or Selma. I am sorry to discover a good deal of bitterness expressed against Genl. Hood by officers high in place, and am satisfied we will never do anything until Beauregard is sent here. The President acted for the best in removing Johnston but the result has been almost ruinous, to our cause. I hope everything from the Democratic party North. If they succeed there will be a fuss in the family. If the Black Republicans are decidedly opposed to McClellan and disposed to thwart his purposes he can accomplish nothing. They will withhold men and money, the sinews of war and will thus necessitate overtures for peace. At any rate I hope everything for a change in rulers. If we can hold Richmond and keep Sherman back our cause is not yet lost by any means. My health is very good just now. I hoped to get a furlough on account of an attack of dysentery but have recovered from it. The balance of the staff have gone off. I am alone, "all alone." Love & kisses to Ma, Evie, Abe, Kate and the baby. Tell Agnes Bally is well and sends love to her and the other negroes. Let me hear from you when ever you can. May God bless, comfort, protect and preserve you is the prayer of

Your devoted husband
W. L. Nugent

Direct to
    Capt. W. L. Nugent
    A.A.G. Ferguson's Brigade,
    Jackson's Division
    Army of Tenn.
    Griffin, Ga.

                  Hd. Qrs. Ferguson's Brigade
                  Jackson's Cavalry Division
                  Army of Tennessee, Sept. 17, 1864

My darling Nellie:

I forwarded a letter to you day before yesterday to the care of Capt. Sam Henderson, Canton, Miss., which I hope will reach you safely. I write again today, to care of Judge Yerger at Jackson, Miss. and will ask him to forward the letter by very first opportunity. I am induced to think one or other will come to hand and relieve you from the great anxiety under which you labor on my account. As I have often said, however, bad news travels rapidly and if anything unfortunate occurs, you will certainly hear it.

It was with the greatest avidity that I read your last letter breathing as it did such confiding affection and giving such good news from home. Your former letter gave me the blues partially. It spoke of the illness of yourself and baby. As we were unfortunate with our first child, I feared we might perchance lose Nellie, and was disposed to magnify the danger, I have no doubt. No one knows or can imagine the increasing longing to see you which has taken possession of me. It is now about eight months since I have seen you and if the absence is protracted much longer I shall begin for the first time to count the cost, and think whether or not the sacrifice will result in a corresponding good. There is so much of bad management in our affairs out west that I fear we will be driven back inch by inch as long as Lincoln chooses to drive us. Tennessee has nearly gone back into the Union now with a non-slavery constitution and Georgia is not far behind her in real sentiment. The only fear I have if McClellan is nominated is the reconstruction of the Union. If this upon a remodeled constitution is presented, with war as the alternative, and the question is submitted to the people I believe they will go back. The only two states which would not go for it are perhaps Virginia and South Carolina. The cotton states and Louisiana would go back I think beyond a doubt. I think we could live in peace with the West but fear a reunion with the East. The Yankees would kick up another row in a few years beyond a doubt, and we would again be plunged into another war.

My health is quite good at present and I do not think I will be troubled any more this winter & fall. I am heartily tired of this large army and this campaign and would not regret any change. We were all very much depressed when we read McClellan's letter of acceptance. He comes out so decidedly for War that the question is gravely discussed whether Lincoln would not be preferable. I think I would prefer McClellan and risk the consequences. I do not think there will be a great deal more of fighting.

I am not a Major yet though I do not think there can be any doubt of my receiving my commission, as the recommendation is forwarded under the order of the Adjt. and Ins. General.

I cannot conceive why you think yourself inferior to me in any respect or how my promotion would possibly create a distance between us actually or figuratively. A real man cannot love and be unkind, or unfaithful, or without protecting and defending the object of his affections. Believe me, Nellie, you occupy all my heart and possess all the wealth of my affection. I know I am unworthy of you rather than you of me. All I ask or desire is for you to remain steadfast in your devotion to me. Without the assurance of this I should have very little to live for. This War has not improved me much, I know, but it has served to increase my love for the cherished partner of my bosom. I feel that I should be supremely happy if I could see you even now. The Genl. has gone—his staff are absent sick, wounded or captured and I alone am left. Under these circumstances it is no wonder that I am lonesome enough. The blues take possession of me at times and I become quite desperate. Clarence is well and has improved greatly in personal appearance. I am afraid his morals are not as pure as they were before I left the Company. Love and kisses to Ma, Kate, Abe, Evie and the *baby*. Bally sends love to Agnes. May God Almighty bless, comfort, protect and preserve you is the prayer

Of your devoted husband
W.L. Nugent

208

Direct to
  Capt. W.L. Nugent
  A.A.G. Ferguson's Brigade
  Jackson's Cavalry Division
  Army of Tenn, and the letter will reach me.

> Hd.Qrs. Ferguson's Brigade
> Jackson's Cavalry Division
> Army of Tennessee, Sept. 26/64

My darling Nellie:

Your letter of the 26th August reached me a day or two since and gave me more than the usual amount of pleasure and gratification. I had not before its receipt heard from you for sometime and had in consequence become quite uneasy. As you express some anxiety to hear the result of General Ferguson's difficulty with Jackson, I will give you the outline. Near Dallas, Georgia, Genl. Jackson charged the Mississippi Regiments with acting disgracefully and attributed it, in an official despatch to Genl. Ferguson's not remaining with and commanding them on the field. After demanding an official investigation into the matter to prove its falsity Genl. F. wrote a note to Genl. Jackson denouncing his statements as malicious lies. Genl. Jackson at first challenged him outright and after the friends were selected, indited a second epistle explanatory of the first endeavoring to construe it into a tender of satisfaction so as to get the choice of weapons. When the seconds met to arrange the preliminaries Genl. Jackson's friend insisted that there was no challenge on his part and after some conversation there was a withdrawal of papers and an explanation on Genl. J.'s part, the matter was *honorably adjusted.* After a renewal of hostilities and some further letter writing Genl. Jackson declined to treat matters except in "an official way." This is the result of my investigations and conversations with the parties cognizant of the affair. Our Brigade has suffered in reputation by the quarreling of the Generals causelessly, having done efficient service since our connection with the Army of Tenn. and as hard fighting as any Brigade of Cavalry in the Service. I deplore the condition of things as much as anybody but am powerless to prevent it. Genl. Ferguson has been court martialed for not furnishing Inspection Reports and is now absent on leave

to await the result of his trial. His courage has been assailed by some of
Genl. Jackson's Staff, I learn; but the rumors are entirely without foundation. I have seen him too frequently tried. The Senior Colonel now commands us after a fashion.

From its position on the R. Road leading South from Atlanta our army
has "swung round" on the Atlanta and West Point road and entrenched
itself to await the approach of the enemy. The President is here now with
General Hood and doubtless we will have another move like that of
Longstreet on Knoxville terminating in the calamitous battle of Missionary
Ridge. All appearances indicate a movement towards Kingston, Rome or
Blue Mountain in Alabama Jackson County, the terminus of the Alabama
and Tenn. Rivers R. Road. From Blue Mountain the Road is pretty good to
Decatur on the Tenn. River and the distance is not great. If we contemplate any movement of the kind we have no time to spare. October will
soon be upon us and the nights are now cool. A great many persons indulge
the hope that we will soon have Sherman out of Atlanta. My own impression is that we cannot accomplish this during the coming campaign. Sherman will, I think, permit us to go to Kingston and while we are going
North will pay his respects to Selma, Alabama thence to Mobile. The route
to Charleston and Savannah may be selected with a view to isolate the
Virginia Army and recapture the prisoners moved from Andersonville. I
must confess, however, that I do not hope for any peace until after the
result of the pending Presidential election and latterly have been endeavoring to reconcile myself to the idea of another four years of war and
bloodshed. Whether our defeats have resulted from bad management or
unavoidable necessity, I do not know. The hand of God is laid heavy on us
just now, and the gloomy condition of present matters may be the prelude
to a brighter day ahead for us. I can and will hope on and work on, awaiting
the end. The spirit and unanimity still manifested by the North on the
subject of the war is an unfavorable omen.

No leaves of absence are now presented except for disability and as I am
well and healthy, there is no chance for me. As soon as the season for active
campaigning closes I will make a persistent effort to get home for a few
days at least. I am becoming almost hopelessly home sick and to so great an
extent that I fear I will be unfit for duty in the field until I can see you.
Like nearly all of our soldiers I am becoming perfectly sick of the drag of
this war, and were it not that I am restrained by higher motives, would be

willing to risk the whole thing upon the hazard of a big battle once and
forever. I feel that we can never be subjugated, because even if our armies
in the field are defeated there must be such a force kept among us "to
preserve the peace" that the Yankees' Government will fall to pieces in the
effort to keep it up. The greatest difficulty will arise after our armies are
whipped and of this no one is more aware than Abe Lincoln.

The season of the "Sere and Yellow" leaf is upon us and I often think and
dream of the cheerful fireside, the bonnie wife and caressing child, with
feelings too deep for utterance in our commonplace vocabulary. I can now
admire the prompting of the heart which inspired the well known stanza.
"There is no place like home." Before I felt its force, but now the absence
of months has more sensibly impressed its force upon me. And at this
moment as the ruddy glow of the setting sun has suffused the western
clouds and thrown a glow over the whole horizon, and the cool inspiriting
air of autumn is playing idly around me I cannot refrain from indulging a
solemn, reflective train of thought which wings its way to and nestles
around you until the emotions produced become too big for utterance and
vent themselves in the timid tear, that softly speaks its own peculiar
mission. We all have to suffer and life at best is scarcely worth the reward.

I fear this treatise has been tedious to you, but I speak as the spirit
moves me and am not in a very good mood this evening.

I have witnessed scenes of distress since we became connected with the
Army of Tennessee that would harrow the feelings of the most obdurate
hearted person on earth. Whole families ruined and thrown out upon the
world homeless and without a particle of food. Our soldiers have become
lawless to an alarming extent, steal and plunder indiscriminately regardless
of age or sex. It is this which in a great measure alienates the people and
makes them ready for reconstruction upon almost any terms. The ills we, as
a people, are called upon to endure are scarcely inferior to any we might fly
to.

The head of the family since the staff have been scattered. I am a fixture,
a part of the Brigade, and of course had to remain. I am not a part of what
is styled the personal staff of the General. The men and officers are all
anxious for Genl. Ferguson to return, and as soon as he does we will, I
hope, revive a little.

The clothes you sent me came in the nick of time. I shall always think of
you when I wear the overshirt. I am keeping the clothes to sport when I

become a *Major*. We are not fed so well of late. We have flour and a scanty supply of beef. "Only this and nothing more." To soldiers who have fed on hope so long this answers very well. The simple fact is things will have to change soon or we will have to shift our quarters further West.

My letters fail in reaching you so often that I scarcely know what I have omitted saying. Ike is still with Jno. Webb.[6] I haven't been able to see him since we came to Georgia. I understand, however, that Jno. Webb will soon be connected with Armstrong's Brigade and if this be the case I will settle this matter as Ma has requested. Have you heard from Judge Cocks? I wrote to you to go out to his place and to him that you would, in all probability come.

Bally is well, sends love to Agnes. Kiss Ma, Evie, Kate, Abe, and Nellie for me. Accept for yourself the warmest expression of love and continued devotion of one who claims no fonder title than that of your husband. May God Almighty have you ever in his most Holy keeping.

Ever yours
Will

Address

    Capt. W.L. Nugent
    A.A.G. Ferguson's Brigade
    Jackson's Cavalry Division
    Army of Tennessee

Hd. Qrs. Ferguson's Brigade
Jackson's Cavalry Division
Army of Tennessee, Sept. 30/64

My darling Nellie:

A day or two since I was tempted, having nothing else to do to take up "Ruth Hall" and reperuse it. I read it several years ago with great interest, but had no conception, adequate I mean, of its great truthfulness, peculiar tenderness and vigor of expression. And you cannot, my cherished wife, imagine how the billows of affliction seemed to roll over me afresh as I lingered over the scene in which Ruth Hall loses her little "Daisy" and retains as a memento "the little half-worn shoe." How vivid the recollec-

---

[6]Ike was apparently "adopted" by the Erin Guards. There is no evidence that Webb compensated Mrs. Smith for Ike's services.

tions that flooded my heart! How well I called to mind the time when, on my return home, you took me to the little tomb in which reposed the last remains of our precious daughter and strewed its face with flowers. How beautiful the idea "Benjamin is not," and how full of pathos! As "Ruth Hall" has it, other tiny feet may press the carpeted floor and other voices gladden the mother's heart but far beyond expression, sweeter is the voice of the babe who first rejoices the mother's heart. Do read "Ruth Hall" again—it is full of instructive lessons and prepares for the conflicts of life, in which alas! too much of sorrow ever mingles with the passing sweets. It is a source of great congratulations to me that there is always something beckoning us on ahead; some hope that springs "eternal" in our breasts. I cannot imagine why I have recalled to your mind the most eventful passage in your history. I felt moody, however, and had wept over the simple story of "Daisy's" death, assimilating the case to our own, until like all selfish husbands, I could find no consolation so great as to have a conversation with you. If I have made you weep at all don't blame me, but imagine me weeping by your side and caressing you in my most familiar way.

Our army is still moving around to the rear of Sherman and from present appearances we may soon strike the Rail Road, cut off his communication and then force him out of Atlanta. Rumors have reached us that Beauregard is ordered out here to take command and we all anticipate great activity in consequence. Our Cavalry has been kept pretty close to the enemy and on the alert all the time, prepared to strike the Road or fly at the detached bodies of Yankees who might venture out in quest of information. We haven't yet picked up any numbers of them, but live in hopes of doing so soon. The country is literally eaten out. We are living on dried beef and *unleavened* biscuits. The fare is decidedly worse than any I have had since my connection with the army. I can, after a while, become accustomed to it and get along very well. Genl. Hood will not grant a furlough except on Surgeon's Certificate of Disability. I live in great hopes, though of being able to get off about Christmas time long enough to pay you a visit. Only think it will take nearly twenty days to ride from here home.

I am dreadfully tired of Georgia and the War. President Davis made a speech in Macon, Ga. the other day, in which he states that the retreat of Sherman out of Atlanta would be more disastrous than that of Bonaparte from Moscow. *Nous verrons*. I'd rather witness it than to hear "talk" of it beforehand. The movements of our army are kept inviolably secret. We are moved about as so many chessmen on the board, without an idea as to where we are going or what we intend doing. It is a blissful state of ignorance. It may be sometime before I am able to write you again, as everything of that kind must depend upon the movements of the Cavalry. We may, at any moment be sent off to Tennessee or Kentucky and in that event we will be completely cut off from all mail communications for sometime. I wrote you a day or two since and will write weekly if there is any chance to get a letter off. I haven't yet succeeded in seeing Ike.

My health continues pretty good. Bally sends love to Agnes. Kiss Ma, Evie, Abe, Kate and the baby for me. And may God, in his infinite mercy, bless, comfort, protect and preserve you is the prayer of

Your devoted husband
W. L. Nugent

Direct to

    Capt. W. L. Nugent

    A.A.G. Ferguson's Brigade,

    Jackson's Cavalry,

    Army of Tennessee.

Hd. Qrs. Ferguson's Brigade
Jackson's Cavalry Division
Army Tennessee, Oct. 5, 1864

My Darling Nellie:

I have written to you so frequently of late that I fear, should you get the letters, you will consider my strain prosy; as, for fear of their not reaching you I have repeatedly made the same statements and "played on the harp" of a single string. At last we know the result, to a certain extent, of Genl. Hood's movements. Our Infantry has gotten completely in his rear and is destroying the Railroad completely and effectually. We have captured some prisoners, subsistence stores etc. and a train or two of cars. Our Cavalry is scattered over a wide extent of country protecting our flanks and trains, and has recently had a few slight skirmishes resulting in nothing very important. Sherman, it seems was taken entirely by surprise. At all events he hasn't yet ventured to pursue us and his intentions are altogether hidden. We may look out for some daring foolhardy campaign on his part, which will either result in victory or annihilation; some raid similar to that he

made on Meridian. Hood, I think, will be prepared for him wherever he
goes, and will fight as obstinately as it is possible for the Independence of
the South. He has informed his Army that the *headwork* is done and that
now we must go to hard knocks very soon. The soldiers are enthusiastic on
the subject and profess a willingness to undergo everything with the
prospect ahead of whipping the Yankees. A day or two since Lee's Corps
came to a creek more than waist deep and at once, stripped, and after tying
their clothes, knapsacks, haversacks etc. around their necks plunged in and
waded across, the water was up to their arm pits, singing and hallooing at
the top of their voices. Only think of 8,000 *nude* soldiers wading a creek
under these circumstances. It would scarcely have brought a blush to the
most modest cheek, the moral sublimity of the spectacle was so great. We
live in the midst of wonders and cannot be astonished at anything which
transpires. As to this latter spectacle, "honi soit qui mal y pense." It is
utterly impossible to tell where we are all going, and I can give you no
reasonable assurance that I will be able to communicate with you regularly,
I will avail myself of every opportunity, however, and will send all my
letters to the care of Judge Wm. Yerger at Jackson, Miss. I feel satisfied he
will attend to forwarding them at the earliest opportunity. Your letters
must all be addressed to me as A.A.G., Ferguson's Brigade, Jackson's
Cavalry Division, Army of Tennessee specifying no place. If your letters
are mailed at any point in "Dixie" they will reach me safely. My health is
very good just now though I cannot say much for my fare. I do not know a
single family in this country which can boast a half dozen pounds of *lard*,
and we are compelled to make camp biscuit, at best indifferent, without
any grease. Imagine one of them. If fired from a gun it would make an
excellent missile of destruction. I really would be delighted if you could
suddenly drop among us while we are at table. A long rough board, a plate
of potatoes (only occasionally); a few hard tough biscuits; a very small
quantum of jerked beef; and a cup of cold water. Inviting enough for a
hungry Confederate soldier but terrible in its consequences as to digestion.
I have always the comfort of a good chair and a fair "lay out" of blankets.
With this I am content. I can endure it for a few months, if the powers will
only grant me a leave of absence in time to kiss you "a happy new year" on
1st of January next. The news has just reached us of the progress of a
terrible battle in Virginia, near Richmond. It came over the grape vine
telegraph and lacks confirmation. We all feel confident as to the success of

General R. E. Lee and hence never give ourselves any uneasiness about the final result.

I haven't heard from the "old folks" for a long time. At last accounts the Yankees had taken all my mother's property and she was compelled in her old age to do a deal of drudgery. It won't last long I hope, and after the war is over there will be a day of reckoning. I look for peace very soon after the election if McClellan beats Lincoln. If not, we must fight it out to the bitter end and then let come what will.

Clarence is well. Tell Ma, *Mr. Butler* sends love to her and family. Bally's message of love to Agnes. Kiss all hands for me and especially our little Nellie. And now my own precious little wife, may God Almighty bless, comfort, protect, and preserve you and vouchsafe us a happy reunion is the prayer of

Your devoted husband
W. L. Nugent

Hd. Qrs. Ferguson's Brigade
Jackson's Cavalry
Army Tenn. Oct. 12, 1864

My darling wife,

I wrote to you several days since and again make the effort to communicate with you agreeable to the promise made sometime ago. Opportunities of forwarding a letter to the Rail Road are as rare and as difficult as those afforded you in the Swamp. We are now near Van West facing the Yankee Cavalry, are about sixty miles from any post-office and are kept so busy that we can't write with any satisfaction to our selves. My brother John who lost a leg near New Hope Church has recovered and made his way home. I received a letter from him today in which he says he is restless and intends going to Texas if he can get a leg. It sounds so queer to hear one talking thus and yet how many of us would be willing to compromise this controversy with the loss of a limb if we were certain no greater misfortune would befall us. It is dreadful to contemplate the many, many dangers which continually surround us, and yet I do not feel alarmed, because my trust is in the great Ruler of the Universe. In the midst of danger I feel a trust in a higher power that enables me to bear bravely up and I have a hope of getting safely through this pernicious war.

216

The Staff has all vamoosed except myself and I spend a rather gloomy time of it. As the General has been again restored to his command, I presume they will all return and relieve me from a portion of my labors. My health is very good just now and promises to continue as the cold weather is rapidly approaching. I miss the comforts of home, so genial at this particular season of the year. How intensely gratifying it would be to meet you all now and enjoy a pleasant chit-chat around a blazing fire—to dandle my little pet until she would gently fall asleep, and fondle with my little wife "till ten o'clock at night." These thoughts of home come over me at this time almost overwhelmingly and I sigh to be a freeman once more.

Our army has gone I know not where. It left Atlanta, moved to Dallas; thence to Van West & Cedar, Tenn. and when last heard from was marching across the Coosa River to the west of Rome. My impression is, Hood will make an effort to reach Dalton ahead of Sherman, blow up the tunnel & tear up the Rail Road, with a view to force the Yankees out of Georgia. If we can succeed in accomplishing this, the Yankees will never again attempt invasion on so large a scale again. The news from Virginia, not fully confirmed, is, that after three days of hard fighting Grant was badly whipped in front of Petersburg, with the loss of some 40,000 men. Beauregard is now in command of the whole South Western Department and will bring order out of chaos if the President doesn't hamper him with his ideas of military movements and strategy.

I explained in a former letter the result of Genl. Ferguson's difficulty with Jackson and I hope you will correct the mistakes so current in your neighborhood. Jackson backed squarely down and refused to fight. The President has ordered a Court of Inquiry into the matter and we will get at the truth of the matter soon. If Jackson is not made to suffer I am very much mistaken as to the facts.

Clarence is well but is very reticent whenever I speak of Evie. Gratify my curiosity and let me know what has transpired between them. Evie won't write to me, I suspect and it is no use asking her to do so any more—say to Ma that I haven't yet succeeded in seeing Ike and scarcely know when I shall be able to do so.

Cheer up, I will come home during Christmas holidays if it is within the bounds of possibility and I think my chances quite favorable. Bally is well and sends love to Agnes.

Love & kisses to Ma, Evie, Kate, Abe, & Nellie. And now my darling

May God in his infinite Mercy, protect, preserve & comfort you continually.

Your devoted husband
W. L. Nugent

Mrs. W. L. Nugent
Care Hon. Wm. Yerger
Jackson, Miss.

Hd. Qrs. Ferguson's Brigade
Jackson's Cavalry, Army Tenn.
October 14th, 1864

Dear Nellie:

A friend intends leaving for Miss. today & I hasten to write you a few lines to assure you of my continued good health and affection. We have "swung round", to use a military phrase, from Jonesboro to Cedar, Tenn., Polk County, within a few miles of Rome and are keeping the Yankee Cavalry off our trains while the Infantry and Wheeler's Cavalry are moving on to Dalton. I presume we will tear up the Rail Road and interfere seriously with Sherman's Communications; but whether the Yankees will be able to build as fast as we destroy or not is problematical. They have on hand about one month's supplies and may repair the Road within that time. Old Sherman has, it appears, provided against such a contingency so far. I hope we will so effectually destroy the Road that he will find it impossible to repair it, & will leave Georgia for a base higher up. If we can force him back to Nashville our army can be thrown rapidly to Virginia to aid in repelling Grant, who, I learn, has gained some advantage in position on the Weldon Road. I have very little fear of our success in and around Petersburg and Richmond. I am distressed, though, to see so many of our soldiers running off and going home. We have lost over a hundred men from our Brigade in this way already and I fear many more will leave. There seems to be no way of checking the evil. Our Government does not clothe, feed or pay the soldiers as it might, and we can never get a man shot for desertion. Men run off and go home with impunity & have been doing it for two years "off and on."

We are camped in Cedar Valley, have an abundance of forage, but cannot for love or money get any lard to cook with. Our biscuits are tough

& unpalatable and we can only eat them when mixed with "Sorghum" syrup, which, by the way, is an excellent substitute for syrup from the juice of the sugar cane. I would advise everyone in the Swamp to plant the Chinese Sugar Cane: not only can good molasses be made of it, but I think further experiments will develop the fact that the juice can be granulated. The cane is not injured by frost and would grow magnificently in the Swamp. The farmers here grind the corn & boil the juice as they need syrup. It is a very simple matter to make a mill you only need three rollers with cogs, set in a substantial frame, a good lever and a trough to contain the juice. A large kettle will boil enough juice for an ordinary family. The cane when ripe is very palatable indeed. I do not recollect that I have described the Georgia buggy to you. Imagine a rickety two horse wagon, a ragged urchin sitting on a "crop board", a yearling calf between the shafts, and a cotton rope for reins. This species of wagons abounds everywhere. Our army & the Yankees have taken all the horses, mules and oxen out of the country. Hogs are scarce and sell for $1.00 per lb. poor at that. I haven't seen, what I would call, a really nice looking woman in Georgia, though every cottage on every hill side abounds with them. Demoralization is so rampant that I am satisfied its influences will be felt for generations to come. I presume one great cause of the alarming amount of prostitution, is the extreme destitution among the poor women & the remarkable dispro-portion of men. While Atlanta, during the siege, could boast of scores of women, I have heard it stated as a notorious fact by those who ought to know, that there was not one single virtuous one in the crowd. The numerous factories in this portion of the state, have, however, gathered together girls from every quarter of the globe and I am free to confess, I do not believe many of them were bred in the South. I never shall forget what I witnessed when our army evacuated the Gate City. Hundreds of women congregated on the streets, and recklessly broke open and robbed store houses and private dwellings. Barefooted in the main, poorly clad, with brazen faces they would saunter along jostling against and pushing the soldiers from the sidewalks. As soon as the coveted plunder was exposed to view there was a general rush and grab. It was really a pitiful sight to see the women tumbling over one another, quarreling, calling names, etc. I hope I may never witness such a sight again.

I forwarded two letters two or three days since, which will be likely to reach you. Let me hear from you as often as possible. The messenger is waiting and I must close. Be cheerful and hopeful. Believe that I always love and think of you, and that I still cherish you as the supreme object of my best earthly affections. Love and kisses to Ma, Evie, Kate, Abe and the precious baby. May God bless, comfort, protect and preserve [you] is the fervent wish and daily prayer of

Your devoted husband
W.L. Nugent

Mrs. W. L. Nugent
Care Hon. Wm. Yerger
Jackson, Mississippi

Hd. Qrs. Brigade, Nov.14th, 1864

My darling Nellie,

I haven't heard from you for a long, long time and attribute it solely to the fact that our mail has gone limping around after the Army of Tennessee. As we will be operating around Jonesboro, near Griffin, Ga., for some time, you had better direct your letters for the next month to that point. After a trip of one hundred miles we are camped near La Grange on the West Point R. Rd. a neat town famous for the number and beauty of its daughters. I saw a bevy of them as we "went marching along," and they appeared to be in perfect good humor with themselves, tho' doubtless some of them were of the same opinion with the widow who "wished the war would stop and the men come home & get married." I don't mean this to be harsh. We all are social beings and as long as we are mortals, men & women will be fond of marrying. I attended the Methodist Church on Sunday last and listened to a fine sermon. The great scarcity of men startled me. A few old weathered seniors alone represented the civil portion of the audience. I wondered as I looked what would become of the chivalrous sons of the South if we were afflicted with four years more of this war. There are I know a great many absentees from the army, but they cannot be found in public places. I enclose herewith the most beautiful poem I have seen in a twelve-month. I know your poetic imagination and truthful nature will appreciate its surpassing excellence. The whole poem is beautiful; but how glowing the verses?

June 9, 1864–January 26, 1865

And I wondered why spirits should cling
To their clay with a struggle & sigh
When life's purple Autumn is bitter than
    Spring
And the soul flies away like a sparrow
    to sing
In a climate where leaves never die.

: : : : : : : : : : : : : :

'Twould even be pleasant to stay,
    and walk by your side to the last;
But the land breeze of Heaven's beginning
    to play
Life's shadows are meeting Eternity's day
And its tumult is hushed in the past.

: : : : : : : : : : : : : :

Leora, good-bye! Should the grief
    That is gathering now, ever be
Too dark for your faith, you will long
    for relief,
And remember the journey, tho lonesome,
    is brief,
Over lowland and river to me.

This cannot be excelled and the idea that life's shadows meet Eternity's day, when the ransomed spirit is loosed from its earthly fetters, is extremely beautiful. And what do you think of the moon's "silver hair lying uncurled down the broad breasted mountains away"? I don't know when I have been so pleased with a fleeting contribution to current literature.

We cannot hear a word from the Army of Tennessee. It is somewhere in No. Alabama or Middle Tennessee, we don't know which. Rumors reach us every day that Sherman is leaving Atlanta, but our hopes are almost as often dashed with the report that he is concentrating his forces with the view of moving against Augusta & Charleston. We will have to fight harder and oftener than ever, seeking our opportunities. We cannot afford to lose as many men as the Yankees. Richmond is still safe. Grant's last attack on our lines around Petersburg proved a miserable failure, and he is now drilling his raw recruits. The probability is that the campaign is closed in that portion of the Confederacy for the winter. As old Sherman's purposes are yet undeveloped I cannot conjecture whether or not my next orders will take me farther away from or near to you. Wheeler's Cavalry is scattered all over the country stealing horses, mules, hogs, clothes; Citizens with reason complain that their natural protectors are vandals.

My health is excellent just now; but the cold nights in Georgia have forced me to adopt our Surgeon as a bedfellow. He is a fine man; tho' somehow or other we wake early in the morning, each complaining that the other has taken all the covering. We are both perhaps right. The blankets are very narrow, it seems, and require close "spooning." So much for war & so much for whiskered bedfellows; they are both abominations.

Butler has gone home after clothes. He took a letter to you which I hope will not be delayed. I am very uneasy to know positively whether any & what arrangements you have all made about subsistence for another year. I will bring with me when I leave, enough money I hope to supply you with corn enough, and a reasonable quantity of bacon, if these articles are to be had in the country. Clarence was well when last seen. Kiss Ma, Evie, Kate, Abe, & the baby for me. Can Nellie talk or walk yet? May God bless, comfort, protect, & preserve you and grant us a speedy reunion is the prayer of

Your devoted husband
Will

Near Louisville, Ga., Dec. 1, 1864

My darling wife,

Your welcome letter of the 17th inst. reached me a few days since, and I was very much gratified to hear that a few of my letters reached you even though they were delayed a long time on the way. Especially so as it seems to have satisfied you of the fact that I have not forgotten you. It is indeed, I assure you a source of the greatest congratulation to me to know that you repose so trustfully in my constancy and rely so implicitly upon my devotion. As the main purpose of my life is to enlarge your happiness, and so to

222

mellow the lights of my own rough nature by the reflected beauty of yours that the coming years may glide cheerily and profitably away, it strengthens me in my desire to know that I have been successful. And if the Giver of all Good will but grant me the favoring smiles of his providence I anticipate a great deal of unalloyed happiness in this world. I hope and believe that our troubles will be few and resemble those incident to youth:

> The tear down childhood's cheek that flows
> Is like a dewdrop on the rose;
> Just as the summer breeze goes by
> And waves the bush, the flower is dry.

I may not quote correctly. You will find the idea beautifully expressed in "Rokeby" one of Walter Scott's Poems; which by the way would afford you much pleasure. The story is a genuine "love" romance, simple, honest, truthful, and the characters are of high degree. None of Dickens' beggars and clouts. Do you know I never could understand why you objected so strongly to *Tales* which concerned the poor, but wanted all the characters to "walk on stilts," if I may be allowed the expression. I know if you would read Dickens' novel "Great Expectations" you would like the plot. The language employed is not such as pleases me but I look beyond this to the living moving characters and admire the genuine truthfulness of "Joe's" nature. I would give you a succinct account of the book if space and time allowed it.

For a week past I have been riding after the command in an ambulance on account of a terrible "boil" in an uncanny place. I suffered severely from it and was compelled to take chloroform to have it lanced, tho' I was not put to sleep. The boil was so painful that I could not bear anything to touch it and was terribly congested with blood produced by continuous riding upon it for days. I am now nearly well and hope to be again in the saddle for duty in a day or two. I dislike when anything is going on to be a mere "looker on in Vienna." Genl. Sherman is marching through Georgia with about 35,000 men of all arms on his way I think to Hilton Head, So. Carolina. He is burning all the gins & cotton on his way; killing and taking all the stock and negroes; and tearing up the Rail roads. There being nothing but cavalry to impede his march, he is travelling four or five different roads breasting the whole country. I do not think there will be animals or negroes enough in this part of Georgia, when Sherman leaves to make one-fourth of a crop next year. The people have been, however, greatly improved in their sentiments by this raid, and welcome the little band of Confederate soldiers who are harrassing the enemy. They divide the little remnant of their supplies with us, and bid us God's speed. As we were passing a fine old mansion three beautiful ladies came out to see us pass and after blessing us, said they hoped we would *"kill* all the wretches" a very unchristian but by no means unnatural sentiment. I have no doubt that many a Yankee will bite the dust before the army takes shipping on the Atlantic Coast. Our men can scarcely be restrained from killing them even after they surrender, and I have no doubt that several have been cruelly murdered. We have had a special guard detailed to prevent this outrage and have on hand about 100 blue coats. The Yankees have been paid off and are flush. They are all robbed as soon as taken and Bounty Bonds are freely circulating among our men just now. The new issue notes are beautiful and seem to be preferred to the old Greenback. We are now near Louisville, Ga. and I presume will move on after the Yankees until they leave Georgia. This will delay my visit home until perhaps the first day of February. You may confidently expect, however, as I am satisfied the General will let me go home when the active campaign is over, which cannot be long delayed now. We will soon be on the other side of the Savannah River, and cannot go far into South Carolina on account of forage. We are constantly fighting the enemy, charging his Infantry in motion, his wagon trains & foraging parties. We keep them stirred up day and night & worry them no little. We have captured about 400 head of beef cattle from them; two or three wagons; a large number of horses & mules; 130 prisoners besides the killed & wounded, not counted. Our loss has been very inconsiderable. Eight killed & wounded. On yesterday we charged through their skirmish line and went right into the camps of the 14th Corps. The whole skirmish line threw down their guns and surrendered. We dashed on, however, after a wagon train and the Yankees escaped. The General, however, says we can't take care of the prisoners, his Brigade being too much reduced in numbers. Our men have behaved very gallantly, and go in always with a rush. I wish those who entertain contemptible opinions of our Brigade could have been present to see our men dash after the enemy. Georgia will, I think, be improved after the trial. Her loyalty having undergone the crucial test will be refined and purified, and she will be prepared to stand by our cause to the last. This is a great state, however, and is farther advanced in improvements than any other Southern State.

The news from Tennessee is encouraging. Hood is pushing Thomas who is calling vainly for reinforcements. The prospects are we will soon have Nashville and that the Yankees will be driven into Kentucky, and possibly beyond. We can hear nothing from Virginia our communication has been cut off entirely.

Sister Aphra writes me from Woodville that Mr. Boyle is growing feebler every day; that Father has been injured by a fall from his horse; that Dick's last child is a splendid boy; that Sister Amelia has her *third* child a fine son, and is now in Kentucky at her husband's Father. Thomas is in Texas married and teaching school.[7]

I am quite well now and like you are greatly buoyed up by the hope of a reunion this winter. Love and kisses to all. I haven't heard from Sis yet. I hope to see you "fat" as I think it greatly improves you. May God bless, comfort & preserve you is the prayer of

Your devoted husband
Will

Hd. Qrs. Ferguson's Brigade
Savannah, Ga. Dec. 19, 1864

My own precious Nellie,[8]

Have you thought of it? I am thirty-two years old; and yet I do not feel that old age is creeping over me. If I was only at home and permitted to enjoy the society of my pretty little wife I would again be young. New life would be infused into me and the tedious months of war, to which we must all look would not after all appear so irksome & so disappointing. You cannot imagine, my darling, how dreadfully anxious I am to be at home once more; to win the gladsome smiles back again to your beaming countenance [torn] pet you actually as in the good old days [torn] and to experience anew that fruition of happiness I felt when I for the first time had the

---

[7]Aphra married Francis Anderson Boyle. The Nugents had departed Louisiana and sought refuge in Woodville, Mississippi.

[8]The original of this letter is deposited in the Schlesinger Library, Cambridge.

privilege of calling you my own. If God spares me I am determined to go home this winter, and almost feel as if I would prefer resigning to remaining much longer away from you. After following and fighting Sherman from the North Eastern portion of Georgia to this place, we are now dismounted & occupying the position of a reserve for the militia in the trenches. On this trip our Brigade has acquired quite a character, having repeatedly charged the enemy's rear, even into his camp. We captured about 180 prisoners, killed & wounded a number, 4 or 500 head of beef cattle, several wagons. This is more than the whole of General Wheeler's Corps accomplished. The Yankees think we are the most daring Cavalry they have ever seen. So much for the Brigade.

I am well again & on duty. This is a very pleasant looking city. The streets are broad, and between each square, right in the highway, there is a circle fenced in full of live oaks, beneath whose grateful shade in midwinter the weary soldier reposes. There are a goodly number of nice looking ladies here, strange to say they all have dark eyes, not the dark lustrous grey eyes for which I have so strong a penchant, but the small bright black eye, so peculiar to extreme Southern climate. There is not much depth of soul about them, and hence my indifference. I cannot connect intellect & feeling with anything of the kind.

While I was laid up with my boil the fancy seized me and I wrote a few lines for Nellie which I inclose herewith for your gratification. Do let me know what you think about them. As little as you seem to think I am extremely fond of your good opinion and covetous of your favorable criticism. I confidently repose in your capability and believe that with me you are ever open. I hope you may always feel that every wish, every thought and every impulse of your nature may with full confidence be intrusted to my keeping. If you will always trust me, My darling, as you have ever done, in the past, and as I trust you I trust that our lives will glide smoothly over—Upon the altar of our affection I have consecrated everything of good there is in me, and if God give me grace I feel that I will always prove that I am worthy of the love you have given me and the sacrifices you have made for me. We will have need, precious, to be generous, charitable, & forbearing, as our responsibilities deepen & widen.

Do not let Nellie get the upper hand of you. Indulgence now may sow the seed of bitter regret hereafter. You can be positive without being harsh, and punishment may become necessary. If your good judgement

226

suggests it, obey its leading. I, as much as you, would regret the necessity for such a course, but would recognize & act upon it. Nellie will have need for every grace of mind, & if she grows up wilfull & disobedient, the example upon the other children we may be blessed with, it will do incalcuable harm. I do not anticipate anything of the kind though.

Has Alf tried to get corn from Bush? I believe he could if the corn has been raised.

I have no apprehensions about the fall of this place. We are prepared for the Yankees in front and unless attacked from Hilton Head or Port Royal we have nothing to fear. My health is good. Clarence is in Tennessee. By the way what did transpire between him & Evie?

Love & kisses to Ma, Evie, Abe, Kate & the baby. May God bless, comfort, protect, & preserve you is the prayer of

Your devoted husband
W.L. Nugent

[The lines enclosed were torn, only excerpts can be read].

Lines for [Nellie].
When first I heard. . . . . . .
    And saw its eyes of . . . . . .
My grateful heart . . . . . .
    That God's own promises . .
I felt that life's rough dangerous way
    Would turn for her thro beds of flowers
Mid pleasures happy sunlit bowers.

'Twas when the "sere & yellow leaf"
    Had ripened for its voiceless death
When bud & blossom; all in brief
    Had felt the blight of autumn's breath.
And the poor warbler, loath to sing
    Mid nature's drapery falling ast;
Had ceased his carol, plumed his wing,
    And fled the winters chilling blast.

I watched each fitful light & shade
    Of bright intelligence o'er her face,

Alternately & idly played,
    Her nameless innocence to pace,
The dimples beautifully flung,
    On either cheek; & deftly weeping
Heard the sigh which angel tongue
    Had whispered to the baby sleeping.

. . . .
. . . that her sister's . . in Heaven
    . . . & attend to choral numbers
. . . chase the "shades" away at even
    And let the lights illume her slumber.

. . .

Hd. Qrs. Ferguson's Brigade
Perrysburg, So. Ca.
Dec. 26, 1864

My darling Nellie,

    I wrote you several days ago from Savannah, Ga. but fear the letter has
fallen into the hands of the Yankees who took possession of the place
shortly after it was sent to the Post Office. If such is the case I have the
satisfaction to know they gathered from it lessons of devoting to the dearest
feelings of the human heart that may prove useful to them. Another one of
our seaport towns has gone and our little army has retreated towards
Charleston to defend other points. Our enemies have gained little or
nothing by the capture of this city. They will I presume leave a garrison
behind them when they resume the march and that will weaken their
grand floating army. Surely wish they would push their conquests of this
sort until it will require 200,000 men to garrison the different cities captured. In this event we can operate to a decided advantage against them
and by taking their army in detail may easily vanquish them. The war will
have to go on however for several years at least. The rumor has reached us
that Jeff Davis is dead, I hope it is without foundation. He is the only man I
know of who has the ability and nerve to carry us safely through this
revolution and if his place is supplied with Stephens I fear the consequences. Our Vice President has still a little of the old Leaven left and

might in a pinch be disposed to reconstruct on old Abe's plan. Without slavery little of our territory is worth a cent and there can be no peace as long as the alternative of abolition is presented to us. I think our army is fully as strong today as it was two years ago and equally as competent to defend our widely extended territory. We have still greater privations to undergo and must be schooled for it. We have not yet fully appreciated the difficulties of our situation and have not been made properly sensible of our duty. My greatest anxiety is on account of you and the family. If I could only be satisfied that you would be provided with food and raiment during the war, I could fight better and probably be of greater service to my country. I am very hopeful but still feel a good deal of uneasiness on your account. As the time approaches for my yearly visit I am getting restless. My trip will be delayed sometime on account of Sherman's movements, as, until it is known what he contemplates doing we will remain in South Carolina. I shall not start until we turn toward Miss. Don't let Nellie get the upper hand of you, she must possess grace of mind and heart but if she is permitted to grow up wild and wilfull we [will] have many a sad hour on her account. Now is the time to begin with her and while it would be extremely disagreeable to be harsh with her it may become absolutely necessary. I have been eating rice so long that I have become very fond of it but for the life of me I can not fancy these swamps. Near the Savannah River you see nothing but a wide marsh intersected with canals, rice mills and barns; no fences and only a few live oak trees. Savannah is a beautiful city, full of people. I have amused myself a great deal with the negroes. Their living is almost unintelligible. The ladies of this part of the world are a better class and some among them are really beautiful. Black hair and eyes predominate. We were dismounted and sent to the ditches but are now waiting for our horses.

Why don't Alf and Ma write to me? They treat me like a stranger. If I am a soldier I may be able to be of some service to them and would like to do anything in my power to assist them. I was presented with a nice coat the other day and am tolerably well fixed up for another year. Love and kisses to all and especially our darling Nellie. Teach her to know and love me as well as you do. And may God Almighty bless, comfort, protect and preserve you is the prayer of

Your devoted husband
Will

Direct your letter to
  Capt. W.L. Nugent Adj.
  Ferguson's Brigade Wheeler's Corp
  Macon, Ga. and ask P.M. to forward

Hd. Qrs. Ferguson's Brigade
Robertsville, So. Ca.
January 8th, 1865

My dear Nellie,

Ever since I read that delightful novel "A life for a life," I have thought how vain it was to use the word "dearest" in connection with my own precious wife as if there could be any comparison between her and anyone living. The thought had never before occurred to me. You are enshrined in my affections as the one indescribably dear; the repository of my love for many many years, & the source from which whatever I may expect of earthly happiness must be alone derived. The idea is somewhat singular; but when viewed in the light of truth how unique & gratifying. It has been a long time since I saw or heard from you and yet my heart beats as warmly and the glow of my affections is as steady as when for the first time I felt that I could call you mine and we were one—in every sense of the term. Days have passed since then, Nellie. Our cup of happiness filled to the brim when God gave us *Myra*, the lovely angel. We were chastened by the escape to the Spirit Land, and gladdened amid all our troubles by the appearance among us of little Nell. Sorrows have come and gone; days of trial, nights of ceaseless vigil. Are we prepared to say that we are truly thankful to God for his manifold mercies; and looking at past sufferings in the light of subsequent experiences praise the Giver of all Good that out of deep affliction he has called us to the full realization of our duty and given us an assurance that he chastened us because he loved us. To me it is an inexpressibly true demonstration that "God is not indifferent to us," and that by ways, we little dream of, he is gently leading us to fix our affections upon the things which make for our Eternal good and guide our wind-shaken, tempest-tossed barks to the Haven of Rest. The calm sunshine, the stillness of the atmosphere, the relaxation from toil and the subduing emotions, which always fill my soul when I write to you on Sunday, are very precious blessings, and if our united aspirations ascend to the throne of Grace today for the greatest of blessings; may we not hope that soon we will be reunited at home, free to do our Maker's bidding and undisturbed by war's alarms. Were I not comforted continually by a firm belief that the promises of the Bible are true, I would often feel miserable on your account. As it is, I live on, work on, think on sustained by an unfaltering trust that he who numbers the hairs of our heads will surely care for my wife & my little child. If I could see our men & officers suitably impressed with the exigency in our affairs and alive to the terrible disaster which awaits us unless there is some change for the better, I would feel more uplifted.

I regret to say that matters have been terribly mismanaged out west for a year past & there is now no prospect, that I can discover, of a change. If Mr. Davis would only call around him the honest, true hearted, patriotic & *satisfied* men of this army and listen to their pleadings, it is not now too late to remedy our losses; a few months hence it may be too late, too late. I wrote you from Savannah just before its fall, and before this letter reaches you I fear Charleston will be surrendered. Officers are flying about in handsome uniforms, wasting their time & talents, while the soldiers in the field are neither clothed nor paid. Investigation is stifled; the good & brave are sacrificed to the cabals of aspiring military men; and as our money becomes depreciated extravagances increase. Even now in Charleston 1 dollar in *Greenback* is worth 40 of our currency. It requires nearly all of our pay to feed us and how we officers in the field, without revenue are to be clothed for another year, I cannot imagine. Hood has been defeated in Tennessee and Sherman is enroute for Charleston, which he can readily take. There is no adequate force here to meet him and none which will be sent from other quarters. Genl. Beauregard is powerless for good; fettered by orders & with a merely nominal command, he can do nothing. Bragg the President's advisor, I fear from all accounts, is to be the stumbling block over which we are to fall. If during the next six months you hear of Charleston & Richmond falling, don't be unnecessarily alarmed. If we gather wisdom from this, we yet have a chance. If not, our cause is lost.

My health is excellent. I suspect I am as fat as you are. Am getting old tho' and must prepare you for a few gray hairs, and a wrinkle or two. Do you know? I am thirty-two years of age. I have succeeded in getting several yards of nice cloth to make you and baby "jackets" and will bring it home when I come. We are daily in expectation of orders to go to Mississippi and

I shall go home as soon as we start. If we do not move for a month I shall come anyhow, tho' I have to ride six or seven hundred miles. I enclose some lines which I want Nellie to learn by heart when she has learned to talk well. Love & kisses to Ma, Evie, Kate, Abe & baby. Tell Alf I would like to hear from him, & that by all means he must stay at home & *not enlist* in any company until he is compelled. I have good reasons which I will tell him when we meet. May God bless, comfort, & preserve you is the prayer of

Your devoted husband
Will

Hd. Qrs. Ferguson's Brigade
On the March January 16, 1865

My dear wife,

Your last letter reached me in camp near Robertsville, South Carolina, and relieved my mind considerably—I will endeavor to practice your philosophy and not "swim the rivers until we come to them." It is, by large odds, the safest and most satisfactory course. As concerning everything else, I have for years taken things as they come, endeavoring to look alone to the present in its moral & physical aspects, from the belief that the future is an aggregate of recurring *presents,* if I may be allowed the expression, and will hence take care of itself. There is much of moral sublimity in the feeling thus produced in the mind; by it we become the humble, persistent, busy workers of "today" and do not lose ourselves in the labyrinths of air-castles. I must confess, however, that I cannot always play the philosopher where the apple of my eye is concerned and were it not for your occasional letters, I would become dispirited enough.

As usual we are on the march for a new field of operations extending from the west bank of the Ogeechee to the mouth of the Altamaha River on the Atlantic Coast. We will pass through Augusta tomorrow and thence Louisville & Milledgeville. The Yankees have destroyed nearly all of the bridges and our route will be very much extended on that account; Since I last wrote to you, I visited Charleston and from the top of *St. Michael's steeple* had a grand view of the "broad" Atlantic, the forts guarding the harbor approaches, and the blockading fleet in the offing. The sight was inspiriting enough to one who has never enjoyed the sight. As far out as the

eye could reach there was nothing but a limitless expanse of water relieved
at intervals by the bare masts of a ship at anchor. The ingenuity of the
Yankee alone could have invented and built a *Monitor*. Through a powerful
telescope I could discover nothing but the smoke stack, the turret, and a
long dark line just above the water. The hulk, machinery, berths &
magazine are all below the water level. The Yankees were not shelling at
the time, or I might have [seen] the turrets revolving & sending their
terrible shells on the mission of destruction. The old city is pretty well
battered. I couldn't help moralizing from my *exalted* position, and as I
descended the dark and spiral stairway wondered when the carnival of
blood and the desolation of our homes would cease. We have been dreadfully scourged as a people and from present appearances are doomed to still
greater woes. We believed in the beginning that God would intervene in
our behalf and yet left undone those things essential to secure that intervention.

We hear very discouraging accounts of Hood, who with his army, is at
Tupelo on the Mobile & Ohio Railroad in No. East Miss. The result of this
movement will be to inaugurate a new campaign thro' Miss. & Alabama
and destroy the only country left from which our supplies of corn & meal
are drawn. What the effect of this will be, no one can determine. The
people in South Eastern Georgia are already beginning to hold conventions
with a view to go back into the Union and from all I hear, the disposition to
stop the war at all hazards is fast taking hold of the minds of the people. If
they take the bit, we are gone up. Our hopes are alone with our armies in
the field. That in Virginia is in excellent spirits & condition; Hood's Army
needs a new commander in the person of Beauregard or Johnston. We fear
that the President will not make the appointment because of some unhappy
prejudices he is said to entertain against these able officers. I hope for the
best.

My health is very good at present, save a little cold which keeps me from
sleeping comfortably on the ground. The climate on the Coast is quite
mild, but exceedingly damp and near Savannah, the dews are so heavy that
one's blankets become almost soaked. Your letter telling me of Clarence's
courtship and its consequences never reached me. I suspected, however,
that he had acted inadvisedly and that he got a *flat*. Silly enough for one so
young & inexperienced, and in so grave an emergency. Folks will fall in
love; and from all accounts I judge this to be no very difficult matter where

Evie is concerned. I hear she is quite handsome and the *cynosure* of all eyes. I hardly think Sissie will make her debut in society until the war is over. I believe she is now about sixteen and *mateable* beaux are *scarce*. I will make the effort to get home as soon as there is the remotest probability. My horses are now all "gone up" from hard service & I will have to get another before starting. Love & kisses to all. Tell Sis to be careful of her heart & not suffer her affections to become fixed on an unworthy object. Kiss baby often for me and tell her Pa wants to see a good child when he comes home. May God bless, comfort & preserve you is the prayer of

Your devoted husband
Will

Hd. Qrs. Ferguson's Brigade
In the Field, January 26th, 1865

My precious wife,

We are slowly moving down the Oconee River towards South Eastern Georgia and I have concluded to write you a few lines by an officer who leaves our Brigade on duty in Alabama. It is difficult to tell when my leave of absence will take the round and return. If my home was anywhere in reach I could take a flying trip occasionally. As I am now situated, however, I am compelled to apply for a sixty days furlough and have to wait until it can go to Charleston & back. I have declined making the application so long from an imperative sense of duty to my country and a desire to set an example to the many around me who are continually clamoring for furloughs. Absenteeism has well nigh ruined us, and if by my example I can encourage a higher patriotism among our men I am determined not to be outdone. You may well imagine the trial I am compelled to undergo in consequence; but I am assured you love your country too much and your husband too well to wish that he would do anything to jeopardize the safety of our cause or his own self-devotion.

The recent rains & the present very cold weather have delayed military operations and Sherman is at a stand-still. The Yankee nation is in a great flurry about peace & has already sent three Commissioners to Richmond to feel our Government. They are satisfied we can never be whipped & only hope to starve us into submission. England & France will not recognize Lincoln as President of anything but the Northern States after the 4th of

March, and a war seems almost inevitable. The Northern papers are proposing a coalition of the two armies to whip England and preserve the Monroe doctrine. Hood is at last relieved and I begin to breathe freely. The Army of Tennessee will now do some good service under Dick Taylor or Beauregard; and if it moved over here, we will thrash Sherman and save the Confederacy. The defense of Ala. and Miss. will devolve upon the Cavalry alone I think. From all accounts Lincoln is beginning to grow weak and the general crash is not far off. Let us hold on and hope. The day star of our Independence will soon dawn.

My health is very good now and the soldiers pronounce that I am improving every day. What will my Nellie say when she sees me?

I made a speech to the Brigade on Christmas and I imagine did some good. The men went away in a good humor and thoughtful. The soldiers are still bouyant and hopeful. And when we get rid of our trifling, Generals will achieve success. This good result cannot be longer delayed.

I believe I wrote to you that I had visited Charleston & seen the Yankee Fleet.

My hands are very cold and I write in the open air. Love & kisses to all—and especially our baby. I hope to see you before long and will have a chance to talk to you fully & freely. Tell Alf to write to me at Macon, Ga. May God bless, comfort, protect, & preserve you! Goodbye—

Your devoted husband
Will

Mrs. W.L. Nugent
care Capt. Henderson
Canton,
Miss.

Portrait of William Lewis Nugent
in Mississippi State Hall of
Fame. Painted by Marie Hull.

Nugent home, North State Street, Jackson. Built in 1832 and acquired by
William L. Nugent in 1871. South wing and columns added 1884.

CHAPTER VII

Epilogue

Little is known of Nugent's activities in the turbulent period between his last letter and his surrender and amnesty. In March 1865 he was assigned to proceed into western Alabama "to seek and to collect" the absent officers and men of the deteriorating Ferguson's Brigade.[1] In April he was involved in the "Battle of Selma," and in early May the surrender of and granting of paroles to the Confederate soldiers under the command of General Richard Taylor.[2] Nugent's comrade and fellow Greenvillian, J. M. Montgomery, lamented that "Disconsolate and weary, we wended our way home, took the 'damned nasty oath'.... Myself, Captain W. L. Gay, Colonel W. L. Nugent, and Captain Evans were paroled at Vicksburg."[3]

Nugent returned to an almost completely destroyed Greenville and sadly rode his horse northward to Oakwood Plantation, where he was directed to a nearby field. There, he discovered Nellie and Evie chopping weeds. Reportedly this sight moved him to sit on the ground and weep.[4] The hardships and heartaches endured by Nellie were evident in the autumn of 1865 when her health began to fail, and she died January 1, 1866. She was buried in the family cemetery on Oakwood Plantation beside her father and Myra, her first child.[5]

Notwithstanding his grief-filled personal experiences, Nugent partici-

---

[1]Special Order of General S. W. Ferguson, March 4, 1865. Confederate Archives, R.G. 109.

[2]E.B. Long, *The Civil War Day by Day: An Almanac, 1861–1865* (New York: Doubleday and Co., 1971), 664, 685–86.

[3]PWCHS, 202. Nugent signed the Amnesty Oath May 22, 1865. His pardon recorded his description as age thirty-two, dark hair and complexion, gray eyes, and five feet, ten and one-half inches in height. Pardon Papers, Confederate Archives, R.G. 109.

[4]S. Myra Smith related the story of Nugent's return to Nellie Nugent Somerville. Recollections of LSH.

[5]Smith Family Bible.

pated with other Greenvillians in rebuilding the community. The state legislature in 1865 authorized the reestablishment of Greenville at a site approximately three miles north and farther from the river than the previous town.[6] Nugent invited William Gwin Yerger to join him in the practice of law, and the firm in 1865 conducted business in a rented store. In 1866, Nugent purchased property and constructed an office, designed like a "shotgun house." [7]

S. Myra Smith experienced a series of tragedies in the Reconstruction Era. In 1866, she was saddened by the death of Nellie and by the foreclosure of a mortage on Oakwood Plantation. She accepted a lot from Mrs. Theobald and with financial assistance from her brothers, John and Philip Cocks, constructed a residence in Greenville. Her efforts to overcome the shattering loss of family and property were sadly strained in 1869 by the March death of Evie (Mrs. E. G. Comstock) from pneumonia, and the May shooting and death of Alf, as a result of a personal argument. Mrs. Smith, who was left with but the fifteen-year-old Abe and the young granddaughter, began to bake wedding cakes and developed a modest catering business. Further sorrow came to Mrs. Smith in the yellow fever death of Abe in 1878. Through all her sorrows she was sustained by a deep religious faith. She died in 1887.[8]

Although Nugent's professional career in the 1866–68 period manifested a growing legal practice, his personal life was scarred by yet another tragic event. In May 1867, he married Mary Catherine Montgomery (Kate) of Locust Plantation.[9] However, Kate died within a year. A year later Nugent was invited to deliver the commencement address at Southern University in Greensboro, Alabama, an institution from which his brother Clarence was graduating. In departing from the home of Mrs. John Webb, a widowed mother of two daughters, Nugent fell and broke a leg. The Webbs nursed

---

[6]The location selected was Blantonia Plantation, the property of Harriet Theobald. Mrs. Theobald generously donated lots for churches, public buildings, a YMCA, a library, and even individual property for the former residents whose homes had been destroyed. In recognition of her generosity Mrs. Theobald was affectionately accorded the title "Mother of Greenville." PWCHS, 48–50.

[7]Reportedly, Nugent did most of the carpentry work on the building. Recollections of LSH.

[8]Recollections of LSH; Smith Family Bible. See also, PWCHS, 135, 378. The Smiths had eight children, four of whom died in infancy, and four of whom died in their twenties.

[9]Kate, to whom Nugent had referred in his letters, was credited by her brother, J. M. Montgomery, as his inspiration for having fought in the war. He described her as "the noblist, dearest woman that God ever made." PWCHS, 201.

him during weeks of convalescence in their home, and in February 1870 he returned to Greensboro to marry Miss Aimee Webb.[10]

In spite of the thriving practice of Nugent and Yerger in Washington and Bolivar Counties, Nugent viewed Jackson, Mississippi, as affording better business opportunities. In 1872, he moved to Jackson and formed a partnership with William and J. R. Yerger. Upon the death of William Yerger in 1875, Nugent created a partnership with Yerger's brother-in-law, Thomas A. McWillie.[11] Nugent's contributions to the legal profession were more than those of a highly successful corporation lawyer. He was instrumental in the reorganization of the Mississippi Bar Association in 1885–86 and was elected president of that Association in 1887.[12] Tributes to and resolutions on Nugent's legal attributes and contributions flowed from such eminent jurists as former Chief Justice J. A. P. Campbell, Judge S. S. Calhoun, and Justice Albert Hall Whitfield, all of the state supreme court. Nugent's associates and friends consistently noted that his personal traits undergirded his legal success.[13]

In addition to his fame as a lawyer, Nugent was a staunch supporter of education, especially Methodist-connected institutions. His mother was a graduate of Elizabeth Female Academy which had a Methodist sponsor. Three brothers had followed him to the Methodist Centenary College, and still another brother attended the Methodist-affiliated Southern University. Logically, Nugent might be expected in the forefront when Bishop Charles Galloway expressed a desire in 1886 to establish a Methodist institution in Mississippi. He was selected as one of three laymen to formulate plans and to organize the institution. With the dissolution of the organizational committee, Nugent was appointed to the Board of Trustees of the newly chartered Millsaps College, a position in which he served until his death.[14]

Nugent likewise emerged as a leader in the Mississippi prohibition

---

[10]Edmonds, Nugent Family Papers. See also, Walsh Family Records in possession of Mrs. John Walsh, Jackson, Mississippi.

[11]Edmonds, Nugent Family Papers.

[12]Dunbar Rowland, *Courts, Judges, and Lawyers of Mississippi, 1798–1935* (Jackson: Hederman Brothers Press, 1935), 358. The original Mississippi Bar Association was organized prior to 1824 but had been dormant for years.

[13]Tributes to Nugent were printed in numerous state newspapers in January 1897. Undated clippings are contained in Edmonds, Nugent Family Papers. See also, Bishop Charles B. Galloway, *Colonel William L. Nugent* (n.p., n.d.). Pamphlet Collection, W. B. Roberts Library, Delta State University.

[14]William B. Murrah, "Origin and Location of Millsaps College," *Publications of the Mississippi Historical Society*, IV (1901), 228–29.

movement. In early 1881, he issued a call for a public meeting to be held at the City Hall in Jackson. Nugent addressed the gathering and was selected as a committeeman in the planning of a state prohibition convention. In that July assemblage, he was elected chairman of the State Executive Committee, a position he held for years.[15] Nugent's legal and prohibition activities did produce an agonizing conflict in 1887, when Roderick Dhu Gambrell, son of a prominent prohibitionist editor, was killed on Town Creek Bridge in Jackson. William S. Hamilton, a leader of the liquor forces, was indicted for Gambrell's murder. Notwithstanding his prohibition leadership, Nugent insisted that every man was entitled to legal counsel of his choice and that since Hamilton wanted him, he would defend Hamilton.[16]

Unquestionably, a highlight of Nugent's life was the achievements of Nellie, his "darling Babe" of whom he had so affectionately written in the 1863–65 period. Nellie was privileged to combine the tutelage of her father in Jackson and that of her grandmother in Greenville. An example of her extraordinary mental acumen was her valedictory when she graduated in 1880 from Martha Washington College in Abingdon, Virginia. Nellie's leadership in the Methodist Church and the WCTU, coupled with her role as wife of Robert Somerville and devoted mother of four children, obviously pleased Nugent. Her advocacy of women's rights was in an incipient stage at the death of her father; in time she became a state and national women's suffrage leader, and her efforts were crowned by being the first woman elected to the Mississippi legislature.[17]

Although Nugent never aspired to public office, he was keenly interested in government. In late 1874, many Mississippians opposed Republican Governor Adelbert Ames and accused his administration of imposing ruinous taxes and general misrule. Nugent was a leader in the protest and was instrumental in the formation of a Taxpayers League, which held in January 1875 a state convention in Jackson. Nugent was among five delegates designated by the League to confer with Ames and the legislators with

---

[15]T. J. Bailey, *Prohibition in Mississippi* (Jackson: Hederman Brothers Press, 1917), 54–55. Bishop Charles Galloway credited Nugent with the draft of the prohibition law subsequently enacted by the legislature. Galloway, *Colonel William L. Nugent*, 17.

[16]Bailey, *Prohibition in Mississippi*, 73; Recollections of LSH. Hamilton was found not guilty.

[17]Mary L. Merideth, "The Mississippi Woman's Rights Movement, 1889–1923: The Leadership Role of Nellie Nugent Somerville and Greenville in Suffrage Reform" (unpublished M.A. thesis, Delta State University, 1974), 26–27, *passim*.

reference to recommended reforms.[18] Nugent was further embroiled in the controversy in October 1875 through an invitation of his friend, General James Z. George, to accompany a committee to confer with Ames. Following the conference and threatened impeachment, Ames resigned.[19]

Nugent, with a thoroughly checkered life of tragedy and triumph, received a severe financial setback in 1890. J. Z. George was elected to the United States Senate in 1880 and upon departing the state requested that he be relieved and his friend Nugent assume temporary surety for the bond of State Treasurer William L. Hemingway. Reportedly, Nugent forgot his status and remained in the 1880–90 period as signatory on the bond. In 1890, the newly elected Treasurer, J. J. Evans, discovered a shortage in state funds of more than $315,000, and suit was brought against the bond sureties of Hemingway. Although some real properties in Hinds and Bolivar Counties held in joint tenancy were saved, it was necessary that most personal assets be sold in settlement of the judgment.[20]

Without exception Nugent's contemporaries referred to his Christian traits. He served for twenty-one years as church Sunday school superintendent and was described by his minister and later bishop as a devout Christian possessing "virtues and traits of character that distinguished him among all the men [he had] ever known." His religion was obviously a source of comfort in Nugent's many sorrows. He reflected this dependence upon a gracious Providence to cushion life in writing: "Were it otherwise, the golden bowl of life would always be broken, and the chords of the human heart, that are capable of so many ineffable intonations, would ever throb with pain. Trusting His goodness, we do not repine, believing that He does all things well." [21]

Following a brief illness, Nugent died of a respiratory disease in January 1897. His last conscious moment was in listening to his wife reading aloud his favorite hymns. Newspapers throughout the state memorialized the

---

[18]J. S. McNeily, "Reconstruction in Mississippi," *Publications of the Mississippi Historical Society*, XII, 305, 336.

[19]Frank Johnson, "The Conference of October 15, 1875 between General George and Governor Ames," *Publications of the Mississippi Historical Society*, VI, 70.

[20]Dunbar Rowland, *History of Mississippi, the Heart of the South* (Chicago: S. J. Clarke Co., 1925), II, 242. Family recollections were that Nugent was self-critical of his carelessness in remaining as a surety on the bond in such a casual relationship and that he was disappointed that the financial reverse destroyed his intentions to utilize his assets for benevolent purposes. Recollections of LSH. See also, Galloway, *Colonel William L. Nugent*, 18.

[21]Galloway, *Colonel William L. Nugent*, 2, 20, 23.

passing of the distinguished gentleman, and tributes and resolutions were offered by numerous groups with whom Nugent had been associated.[22]

In memory of his service to the community, Hinds County officials invited Nugent's family in 1930 to present a portrait to hang in the circuit court room of the newly constructed courthouse. Marie Atkinson Hull was commissioned to paint the portrait which was presented in February 1931. Eloquent tributes by William Watkins of the Jackson bar and Justice J. Morgan Stevens of the Supreme Court of Mississippi were followed by remarks of the United States Senator from Illinois, J. Hamilton Lewis. Lewis congratulated the people for their honoring of a man who never held high office but who was remembered as a good lawyer and a good citizen.[23]

Yet another tribute came to Nugent in 1943 when the Board of Trustees of the Mississippi Department of Archives and History invited the family to present a portrait to the state Hall of Fame. The presentation address was by Harris Dickson, an eminent jurist and well-known writer. Dickson recalled his privilege as a young man to work in Nugent's office. He stated that "Nugent was not a seeker of applause or political preferment. His post of honor was the private station, where with far-sighted wisdom, he laid many a plan that others carried out. . . . He was a man who filled each unforgiving minute with sixty seconds of distance run."[24]

---

[22]Nugent was survived by his wife, his eldest daughter, and five children of his last marriage. Grandchildren include: Robert Nugent Somerville, Abram Douglas Somerville, Eleanor Somerville Shands (Mrs. A. W.), Lucy Robinson Somerville Howorth (Mrs. J. M.), Wilbourn Sanford Gibbs, Aimee Cecile Walsh (Mrs. J. H.), William Nugent Shands, Harley Cecil Shands, and Wilbourn Coupery Shands. Edmonds, Nugent Family Papers; Walsh Family Records.

[23]Undated clippings [Jackson newspapers] and notice of the Hinds County Bar Association in possession of Lucy Somerville Howorth.

[24]Jackson *Clarion-Ledger*, May 20, 1943.

Index